John Bright

by the same author

Munich 1938
Sir Edward Grey
The Abolition of War: The Peace Movement In Britain, 1914–1919

John Bright

Keith Robbins

Professor of History
University College of North Wales, Bangor

ROUTLEDGE & KEGAN PAUL

LONDON, BOSTON AND HENLEY

First published in 1979
by Routledge & Kegan Paul Ltd
39 Store Street,
London WC1E 7DD,
Broadway House,
Newtown Road,
Henley-on-Thames,
Oxon RG9 1EN and
9 Park Street,
Boston, Mass. 02108, USA

Set in VIP Palatino by
Bishopsgate Press Ltd,
and printed in Great Britain by
Redwood Burn Ltd,
Trowbridge and Esher
Plates printed by
Headley Brothers Ltd, Ashford, Kent

British Library Cataloguing in Publication Data

Robbins, Keith
John Bright.
1. Bright, John, b.1811 2. Politicians – Great Britain – Biography
3. Reformers – Biography
941.081′092′4   DA565.B8

ISBN 0 7100 8992 9

To
A. J. P. Taylor

Contents

vii

Contents

viii

Illustrations

between pages 144 and 145

Illustrations

Sources and Acknowledgments

The manuscript material consulted for this book is widely scattered. I am particularly indebted to Professor John Vincent, Eduard H. Milligan and Martha Nash for help in locating relevant material. The extensive collection at the archive of C. & J. Clark, Street, Somerset, is largely made up of Bright's correspondence with his sister, Priscilla, his first wife, his first wife's parents and relatives, and his daughter Helen, and is only incidentally 'political' in character. I am most grateful to Stephen Clark, Bright's great-grandson, and other members of the Clark family for their great kindness in allowing me to work on the relevant section of the archive in North Wales. In the notes, this collection is simply referred to as Bright MS., Street.

Also in this collection, now, are some letters from Bright to his father and his son John Albert Bright, to C. P. Villiers, and a number of other miscellaneous items. I am most grateful to Dr Stephen Darbishire for his kind assistance in allowing me to consult them when they were kept in his home. For some reason, this collection, together with Bright's letters to his second wife, which have found their way to University College, London, would seem to have been kept back when an extensive donation was made to the British Library some forty years ago (Ad. MS., 43383-43392). The Library collection contains the letters from Bright to Cobden and Gladstone, and a number of other correspondents. Cobden's letters to Bright are also in the Library

(Ad. MS., 43649-43652). In the case of these collections, and some others in the Library, notably the Sturge and Gladstone MS., I have deliberately refrained from citing each individual letter in a note, and the references to these collections must be understood whenever a particular letter is mentioned. Indeed, once a general location reference for a particular individual with whom Bright corresponded has been made, I have not normally thought it necessary to burden the notes with additional references. My aim throughout the book has been to give sufficient information for scholars to locate my sources, while not unduly boring other readers with a mass of unnecessary information.

The location of other letters cited or quoted in the text is stated in the notes which follow. I am indebted to the following individuals and institutions for their kind assistance in giving me access to documents in their possession and for their permission to publish.

Birmingham City Library; Birmingham University Library; Bishopsgate Institute, London; Bodleian Library, Oxford; Chicago Historical Society; Cornell University Libraries; Devonshire MS., Chatsworth; Duke University Library; Durham University; Friends House Library, London; Friends Historical Library, Dublin; Glasgow University Library; Haverford College Library; The Huntington Library; India Office Library; Leeds City Library; Liverpool University Library; London School of Economics Library; Manchester Public Library; Manchester University Library; Michigan University Library; William L. Clements Library; The Pierpont Morgan Library, New York; National Liberal Club, London; National Library of Scotland, Edinburgh; Newcastle-upon-Tyne City Library; Newcastle-upon-Tyne University Library; New-York Historical Society; Nottingham University Library; Princeton University Library; Public Record Office, London; Public Record Office of Northern Ireland, Belfast; Dr M. Rogers; Sheffield University Library; The Friends Historical Library of Swarthmore College; University College, London, Library; Miscellaneous Manuscripts Collection, Yale University Library; Miscellaneous Manuscripts Collection, The University of Chicago Library.

Acknowledgments and thanks for permission to reproduce photographs are due to the Mansell Collection for Plates 1b, 5a, 7b, 11, 12b, 13, 15, 16b and 18; to Lord Aberconway for Plate 7a; to the Radio Times Hulton Picture Library for Plates 9, 19 and the jacket illustration; to C. & J. Clark Ltd for Plates 2, 4, 6, 10, 14 and 17; to Rochdale Libraries and Arts Services for Plate 8; to Paul Popper Ltd for Plate 16a; to the Royal Commission of Ancient Monuments, Scotland for Plate 12a; and to *Punch* for all the cartoons.

Introduction

The world has not forgotten John Bright. The visitor to California
will discover a fine red-wood tree named after him. In Australia
the town of Bright, Victoria, preserves his memory. The John
Bright secondary school in Llandudno commemorates his regular
visits to North Wales. In the days of his glory, corporations and
councils clamoured for portraits and busts. The portraits
continue to grace chamber and ante-room, while the busts brood
over unheeding readers in libraries on both sides of the Atlantic.
'John Bright' plates and dishes, reminders that his reassuring
domestic presence was once needed, can still be found in
northern antique shops.

John Bright has also had his full measure of literary support.
Before his death in 1889, several ample volumes had appeared,
covering his life and times. The ultimate accolade, the *John Bright
Birthday Book*, was offered to an eager public in 1883. Thorold
Rogers, economic historian and devoted admirer, produced two
volumes of Bright's speeches in 1868 and a volume of public
addresses a decade later. In 1885, H. J. Leech was responsible for
an edition of his public letters, with a second edition a decade
later. After Bright's death, one of his daughters entered the field
with a book of thoughts 'linked with memories of John Bright'.
Biographers remained busy, sometimes describing him as 'Man
of the People' and 'People's Champion'. When the *Everyman*
series was launched in the twentieth century, Bright's speeches

were an early choice, reprinting twice by the time war broke out. In 1911, the centenary of his birth, a collection of his meritorious sayings was published and generally found edifying. The official biographer, G. M. Trevelyan, published his study in 1913 and, unwittingly, brought one phase of scholarship to an end. The First World War brought a new mood and, essays and short studies apart, Bright evaded another substantial biography for over fifty years. Professor Ausubel's *John Bright, Victorian Reformer*, in 1966, virtually resumed where the old school had left off. A year later, Professor Read published *Cobden and Bright*, a study of a political partnership rather than a biography of either man; it was Cobden that excited his admiration. The conventional labels – Quaker, Radical, Free Trader, Pacifist – do not, however, disclose the full picture of a man who angered, inspired and puzzled a generation. He was never quite what he seemed to be – at once crude and profound, blunt and loving, hypocritical and courageous, self-righteous and open-minded, severe and amusing. It is only fitting that such a man should be the most successful political failure of the Victorian age.

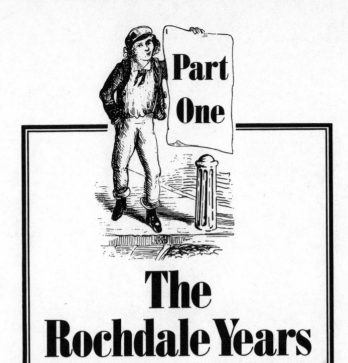

Part One

The Rochdale Years

ONE

Family and education 1811-27

The simple postal address – John Bright, Rochdale – told its own story. It was in Rochdale that he was born in 1811 and there that he died in 1889. The town of some thirty to forty thousand people in his boyhood was always his home. Rochdale was conscious of its past but even more proud of its present. Its population steadily increased with the expansion of the textile trades but although they provided the bulk of employment, the town's inner life still maintained something of its old character. Banking and legal services were largely in the hands of 'old' Rochdale families and many other small trades flourished. Though the mills might seem to dominate the landscape, their owners did not yet dominate the political life of the town. Business still took most of their time and energy. In Bright's youth, therefore, Rochdale was a turbulent and exciting place. In a confused and raw way, the new pattern of industrial life was unfolding, though many workers still retained strong links with the countryside. Just as moors and mills mingled, pre-industrial outlooks existed alongside the new modes of living. The new emerging 'class' structure challenged established habits of social thinking and concepts of community. Poverty was clearly visible and the possibility of violence was always present. Immigrants into the town, particularly if they were Irish, were not always welcome. Yet even in times of tension, new mills and fresh jobs created a sense of advance. Changes were under way which, if they could be sustained,

3

would ultimately benefit all. No one knew, however, whether industry would indeed grow inexorably or collapse in chaos.

The fortunes of the Bright family were intimately, though only recently, bound up with Rochdale. John's father, Jacob Bright, had only lived in the town for a decade when his son was born. A native of Coventry, he probably arrived in 1802. His employers were setting up a larger mill than the one in Derbyshire where he had formerly worked. As an apprentice to their father he had become skilled both in weaving and cotton-spinning but in Rochdale he often found himself sent to Manchester market delivering goods. Jacob pleased his employers and married their sister, but he wanted to start his own business. He now had a good knowledge of the technical and marketing aspects of the cotton trade, but he had no capital. His own father had been in poor health and reduced circumstances before he died.[1] In 1809, however, Jacob formed a partnership with two Manchester men who put up £6000 to begin a new business. The arrangement gave each of the three partners a third share in the profits for seven years. An unoccupied mill was found on the north side of Rochdale and operations began on Christmas Day. His son later described his Boulton and Watt steam engine as 'very primitive' but Jacob was proud of it. While similar enterprises floundered, Bright survived and prospered. Indeed, by 1816 he felt that he could conduct the business simply on his own capital, though in fact he did not do so until 1823. It is unlikely that he made a vast fortune, for the general rate of return on capital was not high and intense competition (the number of cotton factories multiplied five times between 1819 and 1839) kept profit margins down. By 1823, Jacob, who operated seven thousand spindles, began to expand his business interests in and around Rochdale.

The focus of John Bright's early life was the mill. From his bedroom window he could watch the scene of intense activity across the courtyard. The family house, Green Bank, which Jacob first rented and then owned, was solid, red-bricked and unpretentious. The master was not remote from his hands; the mill was the centre of his life. Naturally he had trade acquaintances, but otherwise, as his mill was on the edge of Rochdale, so was he on the edge of its society. His family and membership of the Society of Friends took up what leisure time he allowed himself. After the early death of his first wife, Jacob

4

married again in the year he started his business. He was thirty-four and his bride, Martha Wood from Bolton, but twenty. She bore him eleven children before she died in 1830. Since the first-born died in infancy, John was the eldest child with five brothers and four sisters. When the first children were born, Jacob could not afford much domestic help, though he could later. Not lacking in numbers, the family on the edge of Cronkey-shaw Common was self-contained; its only collective venture into the outside world was its attendance at meeting for worship.

Religion played a vital part in the life of Rochdale. The supremacy of the Church of England was challenged by a wide variety of Dissenting congregations. Even the Countess of Huntingdon's Connexion boasted a chapel with nearly a thousand sittings. The first Roman Catholic church was opened in 1829. Nevertheless, despite competition, the parish church remained the most imposing ecclesiastical edifice in the town. Unfortunately for Anglicans, however, their vicar rarely dwelt in the parish. The Reverend W. R. Hay, whose chief fame had been as a Manchester magistrate at the time of the Peterloo massacre, found that parish emoluments could be better enjoyed away from Rochdale. The Quaker meeting house, erected in 1807, could hold three hundred people, though it rarely did so, since Friends were not strong in the town. Even so, if numerically weak, they were distinctive. Jacob Bright retained the outward signs of Quaker peculiarity in dress and speech, and was proud of his long inheritance. He had been brought up by Friends, apprenticed to Friends, served Friends and married Friends; he was part of an extended family reaching across the United Kingdom and beyond.

The Quaker tradition, however, was in some disarray and the membership did not even keep pace with the increase in the national population. The sixty thousand members of 1680 had dwindled to about a third of that number. The outspoken fervour of the first generation had been lost and it seemed that the Society could either abandon its distinctive role and co-operate with other Evangelical bodies or reassert its distinctiveness at every turn, enforce its internal discipline strictly and shun compromise. Jacob Bright was not attracted to the Evangelical solution, continuing to adhere to what he regarded as the best traditions of the Society. He safeguarded his inheritance by sending his children to the schools maintained by Friends. As a boy, Jacob had himself attended Ackworth school in Yorkshire. When he was eleven, after several earlier schools, John was sent there too. 'Poor little fellow', his mother wrote, 'it was a trial to part with him then, but he seemed in good spirits and he is a child that can make himself comfortable almost anywhere . . . ' Ackworth was considered to be a model institution. Its management committee tried to provide an education satisfactory to Friends. The children, both boys and girls, had elaborate codes of conduct to master. Simplicity was stressed; parents whose children departed from the customary plain garb were reprimanded. Great stress was placed on spelling, penmanship and dictation, and the 'Ackworth grammar' became quite famous. The children were urged to 'search for jewels in the original mines of the Scriptures', rather than learn by rote from manuals. There was a carefully selected literary section in the school library and poetry came slowly into school work. By 1826, it was even felt desirable to purchase copies of Young's *Night Thoughts*, Thomson's *Seasons*, and Cowper's *Poems*. Six years earlier, happily coinciding with the replacement of leather breeches by velveteen trousers, the study of English History was introduced.

It was clearly a school from which John might have derived much benefit, but within a year he had departed. His mother's assertion that he could make himself comfortable almost anywhere reckoned without Ackworth cooking. The assistant masters (scarcely older than the senior boys) often bullied the younger ones and John took special exception to the compulsory cold bath at six in the morning. The school's punishments he considered 'harsh if not barbarous'. In particular, however, the food was insufficient in quantity and quality. As a result of John's letters home, Jacob Bright delivered a blistering attack on the management of the school at the summer general meeting in 1823. He had no wish for extravagance but he believed it clear that four out of seven dinners in a week were 'too mean and bare to supply nature'. It was lamentable that each child had only eight ounces of cooked meat per week and that expenditure per child amounted to merely three pence per day or a penny a meal. Declaring that it was impossible to support comfortably a thriving child of twelve for 2s. a week, Jacob Bright withdrew his son from Ackworth.[2]

6

John was sent instead to a new school opened under Quaker auspices at York. It was designed to supply the middle and higher classes of Friends in Yorkshire with a school which maintained Ackworth's moral and religious discipline but also provided a wider literary and linguistic curriculum. A house was taken just outside the city walls at Walmgate Bar where the master, William Simpson, professed to teach Latin, French, Greek, Hebrew and Italian. There were only some forty boys and the facilities were somewhat primitive, but John was much happier than at Ackworth. He stayed for two years – the most serious schooling in his life. The Meeting at York, which the boys regularly attended, was in a flourishing condition. John's departure from the school, however, was again for health reasons. The building was low-lying, near to swampy ground and a frequently flooding river; twenty years later, it was moved to another part of York and became well known as Bootham. John was regarded by his parents as a delicate child, without much spirit, who had to be carefully looked after. His mother frequently noted that he was six months old before he cried. Since he had been seriously ill on several occasions, it was felt essential to send him away from York and into the country.

John Bright's last school was a tiny one at Newton-in-Bowland, high in the Hodder valley on the moorland borders of Lancashire and Yorkshire. Here, play and amusement featured as prominently as school studies and tasks. The eighteen months he spent there made 'a complete change' in him. In later life, it came to have an idyllic quality, consisting of little else but fishing, swimming, walking and birdnesting. He left his mark – on the back of a bench in the small Meeting House at Newton. At fifteen, in February 1827, more strong and self-confident, he came home to Rochdale, sound in the basic skills of reading, writing and arithmetic with a little French and geography, a very little Latin and no science or mathematics.

Such an education was not unusual for one of Bright's class and background. The question of a university education never arose, for, expense apart, Dissenters could not matriculate at Oxford or take a degree at Cambridge. The University of London did not commence until 1828 and not all Dissenters approved of its sponsors. In any case, men of Jacob Bright's stamp felt little admiration either for universities or the men who attended them.

7

He had neither the wealth nor the ambition which led the Liverpool Scottish merchant, John Gladstone, to send his son to Eton and Oxford. Jacob would undoubtedly have agreed with his Quaker friend, Henry Ashworth, also a redoubtable cotton-spinner, that the universities had little connexion with the great discoveries and inventions of the age. There was little purpose in years of further education if vital practical experience could be gained at home. Their sons had enough knowledge to be able to share in running their businesses, but they were not taken out of their environment. In this way, businesses might remain family concerns without alienated intellectuals or fops complicating the situation. Throughout his life, therefore, John Bright stood outside the classically based culture of the Victorian upper middle classes. He invariably made a virtue of this detachment, stressing that such success as he may have attained in the use of English came from his reading in English. 'If all existing Greek and Latin books were destroyed,' he concluded towards the end of his life, 'is there not in our English Classics sufficient material whereon to build a future of which our posterity need not be ashamed?' Jowett's translation of Plato's *Dialogues* produced more admiration for the industry of the translator than for the wisdom of the philosopher.[3] John Bright never lost his family's belief that Rochdale had more to offer the nineteenth century than had Balliol College, Oxford.

TWO

Local life and travel 1827-37

The domestic situation at Green Bank over the next decade could not have been easy. Jacob Bright, a strong personality, remained physically robust and disinclined to pass control of his still expanding business to his eldest son. He remained firmly patriarchal both at home and in the mill – a disposition perhaps strengthened by the death of his wife in 1830. In this context, John mediated between his father and the young children. Initially, he was the only son at home and had to obey his father's commands. For the first few years he was quite content to help in the warehouse and with clerical work. He did, however, have a little room of his own over the counting-house and he often had some privacy there after he had assisted in the early morning opening of the mill. Book-shelves were installed and in the intervals between other work he started on the task of self-instruction which was to last a lifetime.

He was, however, not entirely a slave to books or the mill. Until 1833, for example, he was an active member of the Rochdale Cricket Club. In that year he achieved the modest batting average of six. He enjoyed walking and riding, and was even known to plunge into the River Roach for a swim. The urge to self-improvement, however, would not be stifled. In 1833, with a number of friends, Bright formed the Rochdale Literary and Philosophical Society. Its membership included solicitors, surgeons, spinners, printers, drapers and chemists, and meetings very often took the form of debates. John and his brother Thomas frequently took part. The members debated the propriety of dissection, the best form of government and phrenology, amongst other weighty matters. On one occasion John illuminated the audience with his views on whether Alfred or Alexander was more justly called 'The Great'. He was also able to persuade the members that the moral tendency of public amusements, such as the theatre and circus, was injurious.

The serious young men of the Literary and Philosophical Society looked to a new era. The Reform Act had just been passed and Rochdale now had its own parliamentary representation: many changes in municipal and national government were anticipated. The repeal of the Test and Corporation Acts – which barred Dissenters from most municipal and other offices – in 1828, removed the formal obstacles which prevented the entry of Quakers into public life. Many Friends, however, were still uncomfortable about the duties of mayors and magistrates and declined to serve in local government. The House of Commons, too, was looked on with disfavour. Joseph Pease of Darlington, for example, accepted nomination for the new South Durham constituency despite paternal counsel that 'as a member of the Society of Friends' he should decline.[1] Pease was duly elected to parliament and opened the way for other Friends.

Jacob Bright was described by his son as Liberal in politics. He read the *Manchester Guardian* and allowed his eyes to stray to the parliamentary reports. Joseph Hume's Radical views apparently met with particular approval. In taking an interest in politics, therefore, it is unlikely that John was deliberately defying his father. Politics was a natural outlet for his energies since his business role was inevitably, for the time being, circumscribed. He talked about political questions with his father's workers, and a certain Nicholas Nuttall aroused John's interest in the Preston election of 1830 at which the Radical politician, 'Orator' Hunt, defeated Lord Stanley. The progress of the poll, extending over many days, was eagerly followed in Rochdale. John reputedly chalked 'Hunt for ever' on the mill walls – though it is unlikely that this action affected the result.

The prevailing structure of politics made it difficult for the Brights to identify either with Whigs or Tories. An analysis of Rochdale politics has concluded that for the period between the two Reform Acts the electorate was more sharply divided within each class and trade than between different classes and trades. Political divisions were on the basis of principle, pride and religious denomination.[2] Philosophical abstractions played little part in the formulation of Bright's early political outlook. Rochdale was a single-member constituency so he had early experience of the difficulty of finding a candidate congenial to both Whigs and Radicals. The electorate in 1832 was small and there was no secret ballot. Both sides used economic and social pressure to influence the result. Initially in Rochdale the contest was between John Entwistle and John Fenton, two prosperous local bankers. Fenton was not of the 'Church party' and when Entwistle came to canvass, the Brights told him that he was so highly valued in the town that his departure to another sphere could not be supported. Nevertheless, Entwistle won. Two years later, in 1834, the Rochdale Reform Association was formed to consolidate 'Liberal' opinion before the next election. John Bright and his father were founder-members. However, it was not until Entwistle's death in 1837 that Fenton succeeded in capturing the seat.

Parliamentary elections aroused great interest in Rochdale but for sustained excitement they could not compete with the parochial struggle over the payment of Church Rates. Indeed the 'Church question' defined the general lines of political opinion more clearly and more acrimoniously than any other issue. The principle at stake, as was frequently reiterated, was the right of the Church of England to demand financial support from those outside its communion. Many Quakers had often refused to pay the Church Rate and had had their goods distrained. Over the years, Jacob Bright had been issued with some twenty-one warrants and suffered substantial financial loss. A certain William Barton, a young Rochdale cabinet-maker and leading New Connexion Methodist began to organize a campaign against the monstrous abuse of Church Rate. Leading Nonconformists, heavily committed to chapel-building projects of their own, joined the crusade. Between 1826 and 1828 ecclesiastical extravagance was attacked. Dark suspicions were raised that more wine was being purchased than was used for sacramental purposes.[3] The churchwardens were obliged to produce formal estimates and propose a rate at a vestry meeting. While

11

parishioners could challenge it, the legal situation, if the churchwardens pressed on, was unclear. The Rochdale contests became so fierce that the military were needed to protect the parish church in 1835 during the election of wardens. Both Jacob and John Bright supported this campaign, though they could not yet claim that it had been successfully concluded.

John also declared war on drink. In the early 1830s he and other young men founded the Rochdale Juvenile Temperance Band. They organized visits by well-known temperance lecturers and stumped the near-by villages themselves. Preston was an early centre of this new movement and Rochdale may well have been canvassed by temperance enthusiasts from this town. In the past, Friends had often supported anti-spirits campaigns but the teetotal movement did not meet with the entire approval of prominent Quaker brewers. Undeterred, John and his friends spoke frequently in the locality and gained a certain notoriety for their opinions. In turn, they pointed to drunkards who now lived upright lives to their own benefit and that of their families. They believed that society at large would soon appreciate the virtues of total abstinence. The key to human progress lay in personal behaviour. The young men of Rochdale believed that evils accepted as endemic could in fact be prevented. Cruelty to children, to animals, to slaves, not to mention war and capital punishment, could all be stopped. For John Bright, the temperance crusade was only a facet of this wider movement of human emancipation. The Rochdale Juvenile Temperance Band took themselves very seriously.[4]

Everything so far revealed about young Bright might suggest an inevitable career of provincial worthiness – and obscurity. However, his youthful horizons were not limited to Rochdale. He travelled a good deal in the decade after leaving school, initially within the British Isles, but then to Western Europe and the Levant. The news of the passage of the Reform Act came to him when he was travelling on a stage coach to London. He also visited Ireland in 1832, travelling with a cousin who had business there. What struck him most was the crowd of beggars that gathered round his coach at every place where they stopped to change horses. He had not seen anything like it in England. In June 1833 he travelled down from Manchester bound for the continent. In London, however, he went straight to the House of

Commons but was disappointed to find that it was not sitting. He tried again the following day but this time could not get in because the gallery was so full. Ten years later this obscure provincial visitor was a member of parliament.

When John and his companion reached Belgium they were astonished to see gentlemen kiss each other in public. John reported to his father that he saw a young man give an old gentleman *'two regular smackers* as a salute'. Undeterred, the Englishmen set off for Brussels by way of Ghent. They 'wondered at the ignorance of the Catholics' and claimed that the cathedral alone supported two thousand priests. The young temperance orator ate off 'perhaps 10 or 12 dishes, drank *vin ordinaire* (so bad that I should prefer small drink at home to it) & finished up with a bottle of Champagne!' John assured his father that they were not in want of necessities, having 'supped on veal, ham, fowl, salmon, peas and potatoes, cherries, strawberries, confects, currant cakes etc. etc. to the end of the chapter, with sherry wine of excellent quality to drink.' Brussels made an excellent impression – 'no smoke, no roads made of ashes, not many carts or carriages, being the very reverse of Manchester in all these respects . . . ' After a glass of Moselle, they went on to Waterloo where they were pleased to find a gratifying number of bones still scattered over the plain. John also derived an un-Friendly thrill from the two or three bullets he found. Later, they journeyed to Mainz and were astonished at the quantity of corn grown in the region. If the Corn Laws were off in England, the poor working men 'might live easily on less than their present earnings'. Having come back to England rather earlier than originally anticipated, John filled in time by going to the Exeter Hall where he caught his first glimpse of such notables as O'Connell, Burdett, Silk Buckingham and Hunt. When he reached Rochdale in late July 1833 he claimed that his command of French had improved.

In August 1835, he sailed from Liverpool on a voyage to the Eastern Mediterranean, accompanied by a local friend of his own age, James King. John kept a full diary of his adventures and also wrote home dutifully to his father. He was an eager observer, but one who generally found the habits of others decidedly inferior to his own. Lisbon seemed 'a very filthy city' and the head-dresses of the Portuguese ladies 'would be interesting enough' were it not that 'the faces beneath are almost universally so very *plain* to use a mild expression, that the finest head-dress would give no satisfaction.' The women were 'infinitely inferior' to the English, except for their eyes. The situation in Portugal was such as 'to render one more attached to one's own country'. The government was neither very settled nor very economical. The people had no spirit or industry. He saw them lying about in the roads asleep in the daytime. He was, however, 'decidedly pleased' with the rock of Gibraltar, though disappointed to have his view of Malta limited to that which could be gained from Valetta harbour. He then sailed for Greece.

Rather surprisingly, Bright saw the Mediterranean through a Byronic haze. Having read the poet before setting out, at every relevant point he compared his sensations with those of his adored author. It was invariably the case that his feelings were less rapturous. Cintra in Portugal, for example, seemed not to merit the admiration which the poet poured out. Approaching Greece, however, he rejoiced that dark Turkish despotism was being thrown off and that she was 'turning to the once barbarian Britain, now reaching near the zenith of her power, as her only friend. May England diligently preserve her own freedom and exert her power in the glorious task of liberating the world.' Athens itself proved a disappointment. The temples were grand but the immediate neighbourhood of the city seemed nothing but an uncultivated waste. Despite its antiquities, Athens offered 'but little allurement'.

Bright then crossed the Aegean to Smyrna, his base for excursions to Syria, Jerusalem, Alexandria and Constantinople. He browsed around the bazaars and visited a slave market. Disappointingly, the slaves proved few in number and 'with one exception all of them seemed merry and laughing'. A few days later, he was on board a small steamer bound for Jaffa. His fellow-passengers, an American total abstainer from Boston and an Armenian bishop who ate little but olives, oil and bread, discussed the principles of temperance societies as the lofty range of Mount Lebanon came into view. Bright again got out his Byron in order to feel inspired. They anchored off Beirut but found themselves condemned to seven days' quarantine. It was a frustrating time, the only light relief being provided by a resident spaniel which descended through a skylight into the soup dish at dinner 'causing a slight sensation amongst the expectant soup-eaters'. Bright was cross that the British Consul, receiving £500 a year, did not call for some days and when he did so it was to ask the captain if he had any English butter for sale. Jaffa was a wretched town which beggared description and John was glad to have an armed janissary as guide on the overland route to Jerusalem.

John found this stage of his journey most romantic. 'Imagine', he wrote back to Rochdale, 'a blazing, crackling fire under a fine palm tree whose branches spread majestically from the top of the stem, telling us we were in an Eastern country.' While the Arab servants made coffee, he was puffing away with a long Turkish chibouk (pipe) and gazing at the brilliant stars above. John reached the hills surrounding Jerusalem just in time to see the sun rising over the Holy City but confessed a slight disappointment with what he saw. In his view, the simplicity of Christianity had been abandoned and everything was 'covered with trumpery pictures' with no real veneration for the Holy Places. It would have been better to have been 'undisturbed by the mummery of an ignorant priesthood, and accompanied only by that solemn feeling of awe which seems to pervade this intensely interesting spot.' Palestine as a whole depressed him: its people were sunk into the lowest depths of ignorance 'without one ray of hope to point to happier days'. Alexandria, despite Pompey's Pillar and Cleopatra's Needle, was little better.

After a rest in Smyrna, Bright and King sailed north to Constantinople – a city of 'perfectly unrivalled' beauty. He had no doubt, however, that the Ottoman government was so bad that it stifled the wish of the people to 'march on the road of civilization'. If, as he believed, the Turkish Empire was tottering, he would not regret it if Russia became master of Constantinople. The travellers then returned to Smyrna but found difficulty in getting ships. When they did get to Athens, Bright became seriously ill. A 'Greek barber' bled his left arm, blistered his chest, administered grains of sulphate of quinine and made him drink hot water. 'Sickness', John solemnly entered in his diary, 'at all times is bad, but 3,000 miles from home, in an almost inhospitable country, in a miserable inn, without the possibility of obtaining the necessary comforts and unattended by one's friends – then its horrors are aggravated, nay increased 1,000 fold.'

15

John recovered in a few days, though he recorded that many other visitors had died of the fever owing to their eating and drinking to excess. Eventually they found ships to take them to Malta and then to Catania in Sicily, travelling via Messina, Palermo and Naples to Rome. Bright greatly enjoyed wandering through the streets of Pompeii and was impressed by St Peter's in Rome. The graves of Shelley and Keats were visited. They sailed from Leghorn to Marseilles and then journeyed overland to Paris and Calais. 'My travel has occupied more than six months,' was the final diary entry, 'and its cost was about £250'.[5]

The Mediterranean world influenced all young Englishmen who came into contact with it – Gladstone, Disraeli, Newman and Cobden had all followed part of Bright's route at about the same time – and Bright was no exception. His travel diaries disclose John the romantic, dreaming in the sun that Greece might be free, eagerly tasting the local wines, playing cards on deck, reading Pindar (though not always approving) and appreciating such female beauty as he encountered. The world of the Heywood Temperance Society seemed a long way off.[6] If most Dissenters knew Bunyan not Byron, Bright knew both. It was not easy to reconcile the sensations of the sun and the demands of business, and the Society of Friends with romantic sentiment, but he came back to Rochdale determined to try. Nevertheless, he was restless and in love. The precise facts are obscure. While he was abroad, his twenty-year-old sister, Priscilla, sent lengthy extracts from John's letters to a certain Gwen Morgan. 'The interest I feel for thee and thy family', Priscilla added, 'is not more than thou feels for us.'[7] Nearly thirty years later, in North Wales, John sought out the grave of this Gwen. 'My eyes filled with tears', he wrote to Priscilla, 'and had I been alone, I should have given way to the sorrow which oppressed me.' There was something in first love which could never exist again. Perhaps he ought not to have subjected 'the feelings' to 'the judgment' as he had done in this particular affair.[8]

THREE

Marriage and local politics 1837-41

Politics offered an outlet for the energies of a young man excited by foreign travel, yet uncertain in his personal and business future. Even in Constantinople he hoped that there would not be a general election in Britain because he had 'a sort of itching (as we elegantly term it) to be doing something . . . '. Two general statements of his views survive from this early period. The first, an appeal 'To the Radical Reformers of Rochdale' was part of the campaign, in early 1837, against the Tories who had held Rochdale since 1832.[1] He wanted to keep the opposition to them united behind Fenton who was stated to be a friend to household suffrage, the ballot, short parliaments, repeal of the Corn Laws and abolition of Church Rates. Although Fenton wanted 'to give the greatest possible degree of comfort and prosperity to the greatest number of people' the Tories should not be underestimated. They would launch again the 'engines of demoralization' which had swayed votes in the previous election. Family ties, fear and interest could yet make them formidable. This general warning was accompanied by some comments on the New Poor Law passed in 1834. It had proved troublesome in the north of England but Bright believed that in time it would be at least as satisfactory as the old system of outdoor relief. Liberals should not try to make Lancashire an exception to the legislation which applied to the rest of the kingdom. It was certain that 'were the Tories in power it would be

17

impossible to obtain from them the repeal of this Bill'. Rochdale Tories who were tempted in this direction should note that the Duke of Wellington praised ministers for tackling so difficult a matter. Rochdale Radicals should not be seduced by the speeches of John Fielden, MP for near-by Oldham, urging them not to support any candidate who did not pledge himself to the repeal of the Poor Law Amendment Act.

The Poor Law was not the only matter on which Bright disagreed with Fielden. He recollected that the MP had strongly urged operatives to form themselves into unions, but wise men in Rochdale knew that the labouring classes had never yet benefitted from such combinations. Fielden's 'The Curse of the Factory System' led Bright to write his own 'Observations' on the matter.[2] Employers, he conceded, were not free from blame, but when the 'hours of labour' were in contention, he resented the insinuation that the inspectors were cultivating the employers rather than doing their duty to the operatives. Certain inspectors, indeed, were threatened by the hands if they interfered in order to protect children. While Fielden argued that the increased speed of machinery increased the labour of adults and children, he made no allowance for the less tedious methods of spinning it made possible. Fielden talked about 'slavery' but even if all the evils of the Factory System did exist, there was still 'a wonderful difference between the Factory Operative and the West India Slave'. To talk of reducing production (and to advocate a Ten Hours Bill for this purpose) was ludicrous at a time of increasing foreign competition. The 'Curse of the Corn Laws' was much more serious for the welfare of operatives than the 'Curse of the Factory System'.

Turning to the specific issue of Ten Hours, Bright admitted that a case had been made out which called for 'the interference of the Legislature'. However, the 1833 Factory Act was unsatisfactory. It prevented children under nine from working and limited those under thirteen to an eight-hour day, forty-eight-hour week. They also had to produce a certificate stating that they attended school two hours a day, six days a week. As a result, Bright argued, most children under thirteen were not being employed at all because to restrict them to eight hours would have virtually reduced the working hours of adults to the same figure. In consequence, parents could not afford to send children to school and they scrambled about, neither working nor learning. Few working men could live comfortably without the labour of their children, therefore both employers and employed found it in their interest to evade the law and inspectors found it almost impossible to enforce. Bright's solution was to restrict the 'propelling power'. Mill-owners, who knew perfectly well that no law could be enforced which did not apply to machinery, had a responsibility which they had hitherto shirked. Hours during which children and adults might work (probably as near twelve as ten) should be fixed and then no machine or motive power should be allowed to operate for longer. The hours for children under this system would be the same as for adults and they could start work at the age of eleven. Such a scheme, he believed, would show the sincere desire of the mill-owners to improve the lot of their operatives. 'The interests of all classes,' he contended, 'are so intimately blended, that none can suffer without injury being inflicted upon the rest . . . '

Such views quickly established Bright's reputation among his peers. His willingness to take on Fielden – a man nearly thirty years his senior – was much admired. It was known locally that he stood for religious equality, opposition to the Corn Laws, hostility to 'doctrinaire' factory legislation and a vague commitment to further parliamentary reform. He was also keenly interested in popular education. The Brights had been punctilious in undertaking their responsibilities, under the Factory Act of 1802, to provide a limited education for their apprentices. John, however, wanted to go further. He wrote to Richard Cobden in December 1837 asking him to speak on education in Rochdale. Cobden accepted and spent the night with the Brights but no deep bond was then formed. Another year was to pass before the two men exchanged letters, though they may have met in Manchester. Cobden reputedly told Jacob Bright that his son had the makings of an orator. Jacob, who wanted a businessman not a rhetorician, was not impressed.

In the summer of 1838 John had other things on his mind than the possible delights of an oratorical career. At the Ackworth general meeting of that year he had met and fallen in love with Elizabeth Priestman of Newcastle. It was not, therefore, an accident that in September John chose to go to Scotland through Newcastle, with his sisters as cover. He received an invitation to the Priestman house and met Elizabeth again. On returning to Rochdale he wrote to her father explaining the strength of his feelings. Could he pay another visit to put his case? Apologizing for his eagerness, he explained that distance prevented a more leisurely approach. There were, indeed, a number of northern Friends of the 'tall, thin and long-faced variety' who found young Mr Bright decidedly too forward.[3]

Elizabeth's father, Jonathan, a prosperous tanner, and his wife Rachel, were both deeply involved in the life of the Society of Friends. He was one of the first teetotallers in Newcastle and played a prominent part in the anti-slavery movement. The home was one where 'the strongest opinions were urged in the gentlest tones'. Bright was permitted to write to Elizabeth and he explained that the promotion of her happiness could only advance his own. She replied that the will of her Heavenly Father was paramount and asked John more about his religious views. He in turn acknowledged that unity in this matter was vital. While praising the religious and moral principles of Friends, he admitted that he had not always been faithful to them in practice. Elizabeth was pleased but was disturbed by his 'interference in politics', fearing that they could never agree on this point. John conceded that violent political partisanship could destroy domestic harmony having seen politics give men 'a restless turn of mind'. However, he had taken part in election contests not from love of excitement and political strife but from a sense of duty. He had never encouraged dissipation or drunkenness. Except on one occasion, when his associates had carried the day, his election activities had been limited to what was legal and proper. He reiterated that the proper exercise of the franchise was a solemn duty which could not be shirked.[4]

It was by no means clear, therefore, that the courtship would go smoothly. John told his sister Priscilla that he could not boast of great religious experience and, if he did, it would prove he was not religious.[5] Jonathan Priestman decided to visit Rochdale to inspect the Brights. Thoughtfully enclosing a sonnet written by Garrison, the American slavery abolitionist, Bright wrote to Newcastle anxiously awaiting Jonathan's verdict. All was not well. Elizabeth replied that her papa questioned whether 'thy political engagements and the approbation which thou may have met with from thy friends may not interfere with the duties of a domestic and a quiet life.' John tried to defend himself, doubting whether the acclamation of his friends was spoiling him and claiming to know that forbearance and self-denial were sometimes required. The extent of his political activity was being exaggerated. He felt that 'any exertions of an individual in a small town attract more attention than in a large one, & possibly my name for this reason has been more prominent.' Despite the insidious temptations which attended prosperity and success, he was essentially a domestic character.

Elizabeth was reassured. She admitted in January 1839 that the political question had been exaggerated and permission to revisit Newcastle was granted. For his part, John played down the political disturbances in Lancashire. Reassured though his future wife might be, Bright was in fact being drawn into the campaign against the Corn Laws which was to make him famous.

The Act of 1815 gave protection to the farming interest by stipulating that foreign corn could only be imported, or taken out of bond, when the price of wheat reached 80s. In the ensuing decade, a sliding scale was substituted and the situation fluctuated according to the state of the harvest. In the early 1830s, after several bad years when large quantities of corn had been imported, the harvests were good and the price fell. The advocates of protection pointed out that it would be serious if the country became dependent upon foreign supplies, especially in wartime. Critics, like Colonel Perronet Thompson in his *Catechism on the Corn Laws* deplored such insularity. Economists at the time (and economic historians today), debated the advantages and disadvantages of the Laws with great skill, but while the good harvests lasted the matter was essentially academic. Only in 1838, when the first of a succession of bad harvests occurred, did the controversy widen. In that year, in Manchester, opposition to the Corn Laws was organized. Cobden and other manufacturers tried to persuade the Manchester Chamber of Commerce to campaign for the freeing of trade. Their argument, in simple terms, was that if the Laws were abolished, cheap corn would feed the population and in turn enable the exporting countries to purchase British manufactured goods, thereby stimulating production and lessening unemployment. The sole impediment, it seemed, was the obstinacy of the British agricultural interest and its political friends.

An Anti-Corn Law Association was formed in Manchester in September 1838 and speakers were sent to neighbouring industrial towns to spread the message. Bright's name, indicating that he had paid a subscription, appears on the first list of the provisional committee. However, Manchester men like J. B. Smith, George Wilson and Cobden dominated this body and only called in outsiders when they were needed. On 6 February 1839, Cobden wrote to Bright urging him to attend a special meeting of the Manchester Chamber of Commerce. Bright was not a member, but his subscription would be paid. The Association leaders were furious at a speech in the Commons by George Wood, MP for Kendal and president of the Chamber. They had been lobbying in London, claiming to speak for the whole commercial community, only to find Wood playing down the depression and criticizing manufacturers who reduced wages. At this special meeting, Wood was deposed (though he had supporters) and the Manchester Chamber was proclaimed to be solidly in favour of Free Trade.

In Manchester, Bright was merely an auxiliary vote at this stage, but in Rochdale he was the leading figure. At a big meeting on 2 February it had been Bright who moved the resolution denouncing the Corn Laws. He declared that all classes found them oppressive – except the landed proprietors. He claimed that his audience knew that flannel exports from Rochdale to America had been drastically reduced since the imposition of the American tariff. That tariff was a response to the British Corn Laws. The British government should protect the rights of industry and of the working classes. At this point, to Bright's annoyance, a body of Chartists took over the meeting. An amendment was moved which agreed that the Corn Laws were injurious but which criticized the view that the situation could be improved before the people were given their political rights. John admitted that they were 'entirely defeated by the Chartists' and he did not feel in humour for the company of two 'respectable' Friends who were coming to tea. Confident that he had done his duty but apprehensive lest the events should be misinterpreted in Newcastle, he sent off his own letter quickly. Bright had to admit that the Chartist leader who had declared that petitioning was a waste of time, was very near the truth. Changing the subject as soon as he could, he expressed disapproval of the interference of

22

ladies in the large mixed assemblies of the American abolitionists. 'I should hardly be pleased', he warned, 'to hear of thy taking so prominent & may I say so unfeminine a part . . . ' . Elizabeth was a little offended by his strong defence of manufacturers also contained in this letter but Bright replied that he had been angered by the misrepresentation to which he had been subjected.

By the spring of 1839, even a vehement defence of employers could not prevent matrimony. The correspondence with Newcastle shifted to practical questions. In March, for example, John declared that it would be unnecessary to keep spirits in their house, that is as a beverage. Wine was not so great a risk 'altho' I should certainly not approve of the practice of bringing it out after dinner on any other than *very* extraordinary occasions.' The couple were to live in a new house, higher up the moor overlooking Rochdale. He reported that the cellars were nearly finished '& which is not to be regretted & which accords well with the cellar of *teetotallers,* there is a nice spring of soft water just at the foot of the cellar step which I hope may be of use.' Both partners were agreed that they would not make a parade of any superior wealth and comforts they might possess.

It was impossible for the intricacies of house-building to engross Bright completely. Rochdale and the neighbouring towns were alive with rumour and inflammatory speeches. He gave the government some credit, felt there might be some bloodshed, but held a general convulsion to be quite impossible. This unrest and agitation made it difficult to attack the Corn Laws. The Anti-Corn Law League, formed in March 1839, had still a long way to go. C. P. Villiers introduced a motion in the House of Commons on the subject, but it fell far short of a majority. Manufacturers became more cautious about opening their purses. When the industrial and political situation seemed so precarious, it was not wise to stir up further agitation. By the end of May 1839, the League nearly ran out of money and its agitation virtually ceased, though it picked up again later in the year.

From Rochdale, Bright still felt any uprising unlikely, though it was clear to him that the middle classes would have to 'think more of the state of the working people & endeavour to improve their condition if they wish the mind of the masses to be

23

tranquil.' In the same letter, he reported that his house was advancing well. The rooms were twelve feet high – the cause of an argument with his father. Jacob Bright liked 'snug' houses, with rooms about nine feet high. John also reported that he had stopped smoking cigars and was in full agreement with his future wife on 'the bad tendency of theatrical representations'. He professed a continuing willingness to fight 'a certain drowsiness' at meetings on Sunday. For her part, Elizabeth tried hard to direct her future husband to religious rather than political matters. In the summer of 1839 it is not the Manchester of the Anti-Corn Law League which features in their correspondence but the Manchester whose Friends' meeting was in disarray following the departure from its ranks of Isaac Crewdson. The Beaconites, as they were called, introduced a form of service very similar to the main Dissenting denominations. They set up their own chapel. Bright knew many of those involved but he declared that personal feelings could not lead him to countenance wrong. The seceders could not be right because 'scarcely two of them are agreed even in what they differ from the Society . . . ' . He regretted that so many had descended 'into the bog priestcraft and a paid ministry' since he became more and more convinced that the Society of Friends was nearer than any other body to true Christianity.

Meanwhile, preparations for the new house went ahead. John reported that he had ordered a white marble fireplace for the drawing room, a dove colour for the dining room and a white-veined one for the breakfast room – the latter to be repeated in the two best bedrooms. He stressed his desire to 'keep within the bounds of Christian moderation'. John was anxious to be married and in his own house because all was not well within the family. His younger brother Thomas had married against his father's advice and Jacob did not trouble to hide the fact. Thomas described his father as 'a perfect stranger' to any feelings of Christian charity or liberality.[6] Jacob Bright was also proposing not to attend the wedding of his daughter Margaret because her husband, though a Friend, did not dress according to the manner of Friends. In addition to these difficulties, John was active in repelling a suitor for another of his sisters – the man was 'a goose and no mistake'. Shortly afterwards, she married Thomas Ashworth of Poynton. There were also business problems. His brothers Thomas and Benjamin had set up on their own account, having come to an arrangement with their father, but trade was bad. John commented that they had all 'as good be out of business as in for the present'.[7] He consoled himself by ordering a waistcoat with a light spot in the black satin to wear at his wedding. It was possible that the aristocratic lawmakers would find a terrible retribution falling upon them during the winter, but if the country did not fall apart he would be married in Newcastle in November. Priscilla, writing to her sister Margaret, thought that the bride and bridegroom looked very nice. She had never seen John 'look so interesting'. When they stood up, he 'coloured extremely'. He took great pains to complete the marriage certificate in his best style, though it had to be much blotted because of the press of people. 'We had', Priscilla added, 'jellies, blancmanges and everything in which wine etc. is generally put, and which until now has been thought impossible to make without wine . . .'[8] Fortified by a sucking-pig and soups of every description, John took his bride to the Lake District and then home to Rochdale.

The new husband seems to have abstained from local politics for three months before the excitement of the Church Rate controversy became too much for him. A new vicar, the Reverend J. E. N. Molesworth, had arrived and John Bright was determined to test the mettle of this vigorous and politically well-connected incumbent. A public meeting was held in Rochdale to congratulate Queen Victoria on her marriage. Clement Royds, a prominent local Tory, proposed that the vicar should take the chair; Bright moved that the meeting should elect its own chairman. Molesworth argued that the gentlemen who had called the meeting had the right to appoint the chairman; Bright disagreed. Eventually, after much argument, the meeting dissolved in uproar. Bright and some of his friends promptly organized their own gathering which concluded with three hearty cheers for the Queen. The Radicals believed that Her Majesty had 'shown spirit' in refusing to make some changes in her household to comply with Peel's wishes. It allegedly proved that her sympathies in this 'Bedchamber' crisis were not with the avowed enemies of popular rights. The Rochdale demonstration was, therefore, an attempt to make the Tories appear disloyal to the throne, for in private Bright saw no reason why the people of

Rochdale should express pleasure at the royal wedding, beaten down as they were by the aristocracy and the Church.

After this initial skirmish, both sides began to manoeuvre for position. In March 1840, the vicar's warden initiated prosecutions for unpaid rates, an action naturally denounced by Bright and his friends. In consequence, at the next election of churchwardens, there was a keen contest. When Molesworth declared the result, on a show of hands, the protests were so strong that a poll proved necessary. The 'Church' list proved victorious – but not for long. A legal decision in another case made it clear that even if the wardens were unanimous, the rate could not be levied if the parish refused. On 10 July, following another stormy parish meeting, the proposal to levy a half-penny rate was narrowly defeated. 'The Parish', John Bright declared, 'rejoiced that another attempt to tax them under the hypocritical pretence of supporting Religion was defeated.' At a subsequent meeting, Bright and Barton 'occupied' the pulpit, an action which caused the assembled company to seek the security of the churchyard. There, Molesworth and Bright mounted tombstones to harangue each other. The churchwarden's statement that the rate was necessary because the foundations of the church were giving way gave John a splendid opening. Mounted above the indifferent human remains of a certain R. Morrioll, he told his large audience that the days were long past when Rochdale had been a little parish supporting its church. The town's population could not now pack into twenty parish churches – even if Dissenters had wanted to enter them. The law could not compel rates from all to support the buildings of a single sect. He rehearsed the sufferings of those who had refused to pay in the past, instancing the case of a weaver on his death bed whose family bible had been seized because of his refusal to pay fourpence. The men of Rochdale, he concluded, had to choose between civil and religious liberty on the one hand and the mental thraldom of a hireling State priesthood on the other.

A fresh poll took place in the summer, with both sides accusing each other of bribery, plural voting and intimidation. During the voting days nearly all the factories and foundries in the town were closed. Drink and food could be obtained in ample measure from certain public houses free of charge. Votes were on sale to the highest bidder. The Fieldens of Todmorden laid on over thirty wagons to bring in their workmen. On reaching Rochdale, hundreds of them walked through the streets with a band at their head. Molesworth had to be given a military escort and the Riot Act was read. Bright described the move as 'wanton insult to the people' but there was no further violence. Both sides were pleased with the result of the poll. The church party won by a hundred votes but since this was in a contest at which thirteen thousand had voted, the opposition held that it would prove impossible, in practice, to collect the money.[9]

The Rochdale campaign had more than local significance. It brought Bright a wider notoriety as a Dissenters' champion. Even so, his main objective throughout had been to topple the local Tories and smooth the path of whoever would replace Fenton as the next parliamentary candidate. His views carried weight in the constituency – he could well have become a magistrate in 1839 but for the fact that he 'could not accept any office which might render it necessary for me to act with the military'.[10] He was chairman of the local branch of the Religious Freedom Society and the local Church party described him as the agent of the 'maw-worms' – the London Dissenters. Yet, despite his local fame, a Quaker could not really lead Dissenters. Bright had little interest in 'discussions over the duties, talents etc. of preachers & of the differences of opinion amongst the Dissenters . . . ' . Quakers existed uneasily on the boundary of Dissent. It was disappointing to Bright that Quakers in parliament were proving so ineffective. Joseph Pease asked questions about the coolies and British Guiana but did not vote for an enquiry into the Corn Laws. The slave trade was dark indeed, 'but our starvation laws may attempt a rivalry without being charged with excessive impudence'. If he were ever to be elected, his stand would be very different. At this juncture he was not tempted to emerge from Rochdale. As matters stood, there seemed 'no cessation of engagements' both business and public. He defended the latter to his mother-in-law on the ground that his sympathies were 'warm and strong for the poor and in opposition to the principles which oppress them' but he knew she would not welcome further activity; he was shortly to become a father.[11]

Elizabeth Bright gave birth to a daughter, Helen, in October 1840, but pleasure was mixed with anxiety about the mother's condition. After months of worry, Bright wrote optimistically in

February to Newcastle that 'our darling patient has passed over the worst part of her illness', but this did not prove to be the case. Frequent bouts of coughing left her exhausted and she was moved to Leamington Spa. There, in May 1841, John learnt that she was unlikely to recover. She lingered on through the summer but died on 10 September, reassuring her husband before her death that, fortified by faith, the prospect held no terrors for her. 'She is now arrayed', wrote John's pious yet practical father, 'in pure, yes in pure white, in angel's, yes in angel's dress, thy house is in comfortable order, and thou must look upon mine as thine for every accommodation.'[12] John himself retired to Blackpool to relax after the strain of the summer and to consider his future course.

Part Two

The Free Trade Agitator

FOUR

The campaign
in the
country
1841-3

Although preoccupied by personal problems for most of 1841, Bright could not quite forget politics. In the early months of the year, he firmly sided with that section of the Anti-Corn Law League which was prepared to contest parliamentary elections independently. He urged that a by-election at Walsall should be 'carried through with spirit', though in the event the League candidate, J. B. Smith, was not successful.[1] Placed as he was, the General Election in the summer of 1841 caused Bright considerable difficulty. He had played a large part in persuading the Rochdale Liberals to adopt the Ulsterman, Sharman Crawford, as their candidate. He had also encouraged the creation of a thorough street-by-street constituency organization. 'No mere Whig', he contended, 'will enable you to fight a Tory' and Crawford, backed by such support, could carry the day.[2] Although he told Cobden that he saw no prospect of being 'liberated' for campaigning, he did decide in June to leave his wife's side and go to Rochdale. 'We must not lose', he explained to his sister Sophia, 'or we dare not look Crawford in the face . . . . ' He immersed himself in the campaigning and was delighted when Crawford was elected with a narrow majority.[3] 'We may look forward to stirring times', wrote Bright to Cobden following this and other 'Free Trade' successes, 'and I feel certain to brighter days.'

Viewed in more sober light, the general election had produced

31

a strong Conservative government. Peel, the Prime Minister, showed no signs of repealing the Corn Laws. The League's President, J. B. Smith, was defeated at Dundee and many northern towns had failed to produce the expected victories. In addition, the League was in financial difficulties and its way forward was not clear. The Whigs had latterly committed themselves to a major change in the Corn Laws and they might emerge as the party of repeal but the relationship of their leaders with the League was cool. It was upon Cobden that the main responsibility for the direction of League policy now rested.

By chance, Cobden was in Leamington when he heard the news of Elizabeth Bright's death. The following day, he wrote to Bright expressing his sympathy and asking if he might call. Their meeting, two days later, was described after Cobden's death by Bright in dramatic terms, though that does not necessarily mean that he distorted it. Cobden urged that, once he had recovered from his immediate grief, they should together launch a campaign to take away the grief from many hungry homes by repealing the Corn Laws. They would never rest until victory had been won. It was a shrewd approach by the thirty-six-year-old newly-elected MP to the thirty-year-old widower. At this juncture, the two men were not intimate friends, though after this meeting Bright wrote 'My dear Cobden' rather than 'My dear Sir'. Their acquaintance had stretched over four years but they had neither met nor corresponded frequently. Cobden was quiet, thoughtful, energetic and precise, anxious to tackle the conversion of Westminster by reasoned argument. He knew enough of Bright's speaking capacity to discern an associate who could bring power and directness to their common platform — suitably advised. In May he had made an unsuccessful attempt to enlist Bright to speak with him in Liverpool, though he was luckier later with a meeting in Bristol. Bright, on the other hand, while admiring Cobden, did not wish to be a mere 'speaking lieutenant', echoing his master's voice. His record in the Rochdale Church Rate struggle and his good standing among Dissenters were strong assets at a time when the League was anxious to woo Dissent. Cobden, an Anglican, could not make this appeal. Bright had views of his own — for example, on the question of whether sympathetic peers might contribute to League funds — and was by no means ready invariably to defer to his more experienced partner. He pressed the suggestion that Free Trade and an extension of the suffrage could be run together. He developed contacts with Miall, vigorous editor of the new journal, the *Nonconformist* and had a keen eye for the potential of the press. It is clear, therefore, that while he wrote to Rachel Priestman that 'We are often compelled to agree to proposals not the most agreeable', the idea of involving himself in the work of the League on a scale he had never done before was not 'most disagreeable' either.

John made arrangements from November 1841 onwards for his sister Priscilla to look after his daughter and took himself off to Manchester. Cobden reported to his colleagues that there was a cry for bold measures, but little agreement on what these should be. Bright pressed for an 'agreed programme' which could mean an association with Joseph Sturge, the Birmingham Quaker Radical who was launching a Complete Suffrage Union, but no decision was reached. Bright meanwhile wrote articles for the *Nonconformist* and collected suitable data on the effects of the Corn Laws to be used in future speeches. Possibly because some members found Bright too loquacious and impetuous, the League Council decided that he was the man to send to Ireland to preach Free Trade. Bright landed just before Christmas and spoke to a large meeting in Dublin. O'Connell was in the chair and offered the use of his 'repeal' organization to get up petitions in Ireland against the Corn Laws. John returned well pleased with his reception only to find a crisis in Rochdale. Crawford seemed likely to die of a fever and Bright was invited to discuss the next step with a number of local politicians. His sister urged him to go and squash any idea that John Fenton might be a suitable candidate. Fortunately, Crawford recovered and the crisis passed.

Hunger and politics were never more closely connected in Victorian England than in 1842. 'We are inundated with beggars', wrote Bright to Rachel Priestman in early January. In and around Manchester people were living in appalling conditions, with their limbs shrunken from hunger. Trade prospects for the rest of the winter were bad. However, he disapproved of relief provided by Tories, speaking slightingly of the 'hypocrisy of the pretended friends of the poor, who would dole out a few blankets in charity, but refuse them the right to gain their own livelihood by their honest industry.' He remained convinced that only the repeal of the Corn Laws offered the answer, repeating the message frequently in and around Rochdale. 'I must begin to lead a quieter life', he confessed to his mother-in-law, 'but how to do it is difficult.'

Rachel Priestman would have been very disturbed if she had known the full range of his activities. He contributed frequently to the *Circular* of the League, emphasizing the moral case against the Corn Laws in terms which would appeal to Dissenters. It was in February 1842 that he first went up to London to lobby parliament on the eve of the new session. Bright was enthusiastic about these meetings. 'Many people here', he wrote to his sister-in-law Margaret, 'think the Tory government cannot hold out very long.' Gladstone later recalled that he was 'greatly struck' by this youthful figure dressed in Quaker costume, 'rather fierce, but very strong and very earnest.' It was the first time that the young outsider had met Gladstone or Palmerston at close quarters. While in London, Bright and Henry Ashworth tried to enlist the Quakers of the capital for the cause and were disappointed to receive 'a very foolish letter' contending that 'we were doing much mischief & wanted to reduce the comforts & wages of our workpeople!' The Prime Minister, however, remained as obdurate as some Friends. Peel had refused to receive a delegation from the League and he retained the Corn Laws, announcing in his first budget his intention to fix wheat at 56s. rather than 64s. His other measures caused Bright as much consternation. Peel proposed to reintroduce an income tax and liberalize trade in manufactured goods. If the latter was acceptable to Bright the former was not. 'No government', he wrote to Cobden in mid-March, 'can have a right to make me state the amount of my profits & it is a vile system of slavery to which Englishmen are about to be subjected.' His first reaction was to refuse to provide information and he organized a petition against income tax. He even dreamed that Manchester might set an example to the country by refusing to pay. During the budget debates, Bright observed the 'disgusting exhibition' from the gallery. The praise for Peel was odious, yet he was compelled to admit that the Prime Minister's authority and composure were striking. Repeal looked a long way off.

Bright was happier back in the atmosphere of Manchester.

Smarting under an attack on the mill-owners by the Tory Radical, W. B. Ferrand, Bright climbed onto a table inside the Manchester Exchange at the height of business and urged the assembled company to hold a protest meeting outside. According to Bright, a large number did so and they had the satisfaction of denouncing Ferrand as a vile blackguard. Those who stayed inside, however, found Bright's behaviour impertinent and were determined to remember it. Cobden, a little nervously, thanked him for this example of moral courage 'for which we shall often have need'. Bright was satisfied that Ferrand was no longer a 'problem' — his allegations about the exploitation of the truck system would not be substantiated. Even so, the prospects for the League did not seem good. By early March Bright had come to agree with Cobden that, tactically, it would be wrong to touch the suffrage question. Instead, he thought that the League should exploit the prevailing commercial gloom. Every employer in the cotton district should be persuaded to state that 'unless the govt consent to open their trade by repealing the Corn Law they will at a given time close their works.' If this was also done in the Yorkshire woollen district, Peel would be coerced into resignation or repeal. At this point, however, Cobden drew back. The simultaneous stopping of the factories would not succeed because employers would not unite. The working class, too, would be very angry. He hoped that the income tax would awaken the 'upper section of the middle class, and turn the minds of that genteel body to politics once more'. It was not a very lively hope, as Cobden privately admitted. Bright turned once more to the suffrage question, attending the 'Complete Suffrage' conference in early April. He reported favourably on the proceedings to George Wilson and saw a probability of 'real good' being done.[4] Cobden remained anxious to keep the matter confined to 'individuals' and urged Bright to stress that 'whatever political principles are in the ascendant we shall still press onward our claim for free trade in food.

This discussion has an almost academic character. Both men felt that the country was on the verge of crisis. Describing large meetings of the unemployed in his neighbourhood, Bright concluded 'we have peace, but peace the result of fear & of the application of *force*.' The country would soon become turbulent as famine smashed through social barriers. While the government did nothing, 'honest men and women and children will die of hunger & many thousands will become exiles.' He told his Newcastle relatives that he felt inclined to stay in Rochdale, gardening, planting trees and awaiting the deluge. The strain of writing, arguing and speaking was considerable and Bright announced that, in order to preserve his health, he was drinking a tumbler of cold water, rather than coffee or tea, each morning and evening. The 'quiet pleasures' of summer, however, proved elusive; by mid-June he was again in London canvassing on behalf of the League.

On this occasion, Bright tried to enlist the support of Lord Brougham, long a supporter of Free Trade in his individual way. The idea was to bring on a motion in the House of Lords to the effect that parliament should not be prorogued until some remedy for the national distress had been found.[5] Reporting to Wilson in Manchester, John stated that he formed the impression that several members of the government were 'confessedly uneasy'. At last the aristocracy seemed 'to quail before the fearful symptoms which appear on all sides'. Reports of distress from all parts of the country were creating a mood in which, if he were so minded, Peel could carry repeal legislation. The intention of Bright and his friends was to form a Committee for the Safety of the Country which would co-ordinate these reports and bring them to the attention of the government. At a time when over five thousand quarts of soup were dispensed to the Manchester poor before nine in the morning, Bright vented his wrath against the continuing splendour of the aristocracy; 'Corn Law', he concluded, 'should be the motto on the panels of their carriages.'

After this visit, which culminated in a fruitless interview with Peel, Bright returned to the north where rumours of disturbances were rife. Despite the trade depression, he saw it as his task to persuade previous large subscribers to the League that the time was ripe for further disbursement. Cobden, meanwhile, was still toying with the possibility of a passive resistance campaign. A determined fiscal rebellion, as he termed it, would terrify the government more than pikes or pistols. Bright was left to sound out opinion in Manchester. A little later, John reported to his sister that 'no payment' of income tax would soon be decided. Another project being considered was the stoppage of supplies but he wondered whether 'just now it would be wise'. Leaving

Wilson to meditate on this advice, he again left for London. At the end of July, he was a member of a group invited to discuss the political and economic situation with Graham, Gladstone and Ripon. Bright formed the impression that they were 'not very far from taking some further steps in the right direction'. In order to persuade them to do so, the League organized a series of public meetings in and around London, Bright being prominently involved. 'Poor little Helen', he mused, 'I wonder if she has forgotten me?'

Early in August, Bright was back in Rochdale. The crisis which had been simmering all summer in the north at last came to the boil. On 8 August, workers at a factory in Stalybridge came out on strike in protest against wage cuts. Their example was followed in surrounding towns, and although the initiative came from the rank and file, in particular localities Chartists were not slow to appreciate the possibilities of the movement. Within a few days, fifty thousand men were out in Manchester and the authorities told the mill-owners that if they tried to restart their mills — the plugs had been removed from the boilers, hence the 'Plug Plot' — they could not expect protection. The 'turnout' workmen marched into Rochdale on 11 August, reaching the Bright mills about eleven o'clock. They released the water from the boilers and then held a large meeting on the common opposite Bright's house. There were, he reported, from six to eight thousand people who frequently sang psalms or Chartist hymns. He stressed that the speakers were not very violent in their language, simply asking for wages at the level of 1840 and the ten-hour day. Bright's impression, after talking with the men, was that the instigators were Chartists who had other objectives than their stated demands. Even so, he was not unsympathetic, holding that 'the savage aristocracy who rule us with an iron rod are responsible for this.' The hour of retribution for the traders in famine might have arrived and Peel would learn that injustice met with its reward sooner or later.

If that hour had arrived, what was the League to do? Already, there were accusations of League involvement — the Stalybridge mill-owners were members, if not very prominent ones. Enemies saw a 'League Plot' as easily as Bright saw a 'Chartist Plot'. Bright must, indeed, have been uncomfortably aware that earlier in the year he had advocated a shut-down of the mills. In Rochdale, he was attacked at a meeting of mill-owners because he spoke against restarting any of the local mills. 'My heart aches for the poor men', he wrote to Rachel Priestman, 'honest men, worthy men, but oppressed & goaded on to measures insane & destructive.' He claimed, with an emphasis not shared by most historians, that the question was 'not one of wages but of political rights — in short the *Charter* is the object.' Nevertheless, at a special League Council meeting in Manchester Bright wanted great meetings of the middle classes to be held, attacking the aristocracy in such a manner as to force the repeal of the Corn Laws. He also wanted resolutions passed which, in all likelihood, expressed some sympathy for the strikers. Neither proposal met with general support. On 17 August, Bright published his own address 'To the Working Men of Rochdale' in which he argued that the demands for increased wages and shorter hours could not be conceded because of the state of trade. As for the Charter, that could not be gained at once since the aristocracy was too powerful and the middle classes could not yet see the safety of extending political power to the whole people. The working classes could never gain it of themselves. There was, therefore, no alternative but to return to work. Nevertheless, he continued, 'The aristocracy regard the Anti-Corn Law League as their greatest enemy. That which is the greatest enemy of the remorseless aristocracy of Britain, must almost of necessity be your firmest friend.' This statement, together with his proclaimed willingness to become poor if that would make the poor happy, resulted in the reopening of the Bright mills on 19 August. 'We worked till noon', John reported to Margaret Priestman, 'but hearing that two or three mobs were united to bear down upon Rochdale, we were fearful lest blood might be spilt, or the troops come up to our premises, & we therefore . . . resolved to shut up.'

By September it was clear that Bright's forecast that Lancashire would become a mass of burnt-out houses and mills, was not likely to happen. He was convinced, however, that the government had been frightened. 'The enemy begins to yield', he wrote to Cobden in September 1842, *'now then is the time to push . . . .'* It did indeed seem that the way was open for the League to establish itself as the chief pressure group in the country; radical yet not revolutionary. Steps had been taken earlier in 1842, chiefly by Wilson, to reorganize and expand the League's publicity machine. A complex network of agents and distributors was established throughout the country. The *Circular* was turned into a weekly journal. Tracts and pamphlets abounded and an appeal for £50,000 was launched in order to continue this work throughout 1843. Bright was not directly concerned with administration, though he was closely connected with the *Circular*. His task was to rally the faithful in different parts of the country. He fitted the part admirably, for he had an apparently insatiable capacity for believing that victory was just around the corner. He did not, however, plunge into this peripatetic existence without reflection. He recognized, he wrote to his mother-in-law on 21 November 1842, that public occupation might injure 'better feelings and higher objects' but he could not simply retire into domestic quiet. There were many men who worked harder for the League than he did but, since there seemed few speakers among them, he had to share in the burden.

The load was certainly heavy. In December 1842 and in the ensuing months, Bright was almost constantly on the move. At Covent Garden, where the League had begun its famous series of meetings, he denounced all government supporters, singling out the 'vile wretch' (probably Stanley Lees Giffard) who edited the pro-government *Standard*. Cobden then accompanied him to Liverpool before he went on to Huddersfield and Leeds, Nottingham, Leicester and Derby. 'I want a rest for a few days', he wrote to Margaret Priestman. 'This incessant meeting & speaking is somewhat hard to bear . . . . ' A week later, however, he was in Wolverhampton and, early in January, after a meeting in Birmingham, he returned north for a 'glorious meeting' in Manchester, the 'whole League almost' being there. Wilson was able to announce that £39,000 had been collected towards the target of £50,000. Rochdale had collected some £2,200 — a larger sum than Liverpool. Cobden, who had been present at the Rochdale collection, found it 'perfectly intoxicating to the Friends of the League'.[6]

After the Manchester meeting, Cobden and Bright departed for Scotland, a dark corner for the repealers. They stopped en route at Lancaster, where Bright was told that the people, having lost their assizes to Liverpool, were petitioning for a bishop instead.

'When men petition for such a calamity', he commented to Wilson, 'one need not wonder that even the Corn Laws should be somewhat valued.' When they reached Scotland, they found that petitions for bishops were not common! They travelled to Stirling via Kirkcaldy and Dundee, and then to Perth, Glasgow, Hawick and Carlisle. 'I have a cold in my head', he reported, 'which is rather unfavourable for intellectual exertions — the severe weather & the incessant labours, with short sleep often, is more than one can bear without suffering.' Bright's language on this tour had on occasion been loose. He had to write to a friend urging him to persuade the editor of a Kelso paper 'to suppress that portion of my speech at Hawick in which I declared "that if any law ever justified revolt the Corn Law was that law . . . . " '[7] But on the whole their reception in Scotland had been as enthusiastic, though not as lucrative, as they had hoped.

Bright returned to Rochdale to find his father and brother Thomas ill. Since Thomas was 'the main spoke in the wheel', John was compelled to run the business for a while. It was an annoying development because, as he confessed to the Priestmans, he was being pressed to stand for parliament. Cobden was pressing Peel hard in the House of Commons and believed, as he wrote to his brother, that the Prime Minister was 'looking twenty per cent worse since I came into the House', but he added that, 'if I had only Bright with me, we could worry him out of office before the close of the session.'[8] Bright too was coming to believe that whatever the success of his countrywide tours, it was in parliament that the issue would be decided. Whether Bright's combative style would indeed tip the balance was another matter. He was in the middle of a quarrel with Brougham concerning alleged incitements to violence and disturbance by League speakers and he was a distant adviser to the attempt in Edinburgh to make Macaulay declare himself firmly against the Corn Laws. If the House of Commons required gentle persuasion, Bright was unlikely to be successful; if it was to be frightened into submission he might fulfil the role Cobden envisaged.

Bright's constant refrain, up and down the country, was that the time for repeal was ripe. He was certain that there was nothing to be gained from soft-pedalling the campaign in order to please the Whigs. They were, he suggested to Cobden early in

March 1843, *in extremis* and would have to submit to the League. Bright became so obsessed with the repeal cause that he could not tolerate the interest of others in less serious matters. Margaret Priestman's letters to Priscilla were, he told her, too taken up with 'trifles' and 'generally I have a very great dislike of that trifling which is so common both in conversation & writing.' There was nothing trifling, however, about the League meetings at the Theatre Royal, Drury Lane, during March and April. Bright was aware that his performances there would be his biggest test so far, and he was rather worried. 'My speeches are nearly all said', he admitted to Margaret Priestman, 'and where to find anything new I know not.' In fact, there was the consolation that 'the old is mostly new to the Londoners'.

After the onslaught on the capital, Bright travelled through the west country in weather which made ' "agitating" a more pleasant and healthful occupation'. Then, after a fleeting visit to his family, he made for Nottingham to watch over the interests of the League in the by-election which was pending. A moderate Liberal, Gisborne, proved to be the choice of the non-Tories. Meanwhile, there had been developments in Durham City where the sitting member was appointed Governor of New Zealand. Lord Londonderry, 'patron' of the borough, had advance knowledge and arranged that his friend, Lord Dungannon, should stand. They hoped to avoid a contest by holding an early election. However, some local Liberals wanted a contest and wrote to Rochdale inviting Bright to stand. Not hearing from him, they then wrote to Gisborne, and Bright saw the letter in Nottingham. With his Manchester friend Rawson, Bright hurriedly caught a train north. If, he wrote to Cobden from Derby station, the wind seemed favourable when he reached Durham, he might well stand. It would be a great thing, he added, to 'turn out Dungannon (a Lord) in the Cathedral City'.

Durham, of course, was dangerously near Newcastle. A few weeks earlier, Rachel Priestman had warned that public life in London might entail membership of a club. Bright denied that it was 'needful that a man should live at a Club & for myself I have a great distaste for the mode of life often led in such great houses of assembly.' The matter had then seemed academic but now he hastily sent off a letter to Newcastle explaining his position. He was being pressed to fight, though he was most unwilling to do

41

so. If he did stand, the contest would be short and sharp. When Bright's name did go forward, the noblemen were dismayed. Dungannon claimed that, as he had previously sat for the constituency, he had little need to repeat his views publicly. Bright showed no such reticence. His speeches reiterated the basic League claims, but were spiced with slighting references to Dungannon as the lackey of the House of Londonderry. A Liberal handbill rubbed the message home by offering a reward for a 'wiry, dirty-looking Irish cur, of the lurcher kind. Has a brass collar round his neck, inscribed "Wynyard" [the Londonderry home] and answers to his name "Tin-ribs".'[9] 'Tin-ribs' Dungannon, however, came home to his kennel with a majority of about a hundred. Bright was not too displeased with the result. 'We had a capital campaign', he told Priscilla, '& if I had been three days earlier I should have been MP for Durham.' Without further delay, he left for London and the latest gossip at the League office in Fleet Street.

Bright's next speaking tour was again in the west country. His general conclusion, on this occasion, was that the farmers had been kept in ignorance of the evils of Protection, but they were responding well to knowledge. It was probably on this trip that he investigated agricultural conditions in Somerset and Dorset. He wrote up his observations in a notebook, compiling specimen domestic budgets, wage rates and expenditure per family.[10] It was no accident that this information was drawn in part from villages on the Shaftesbury estates. Noble lords who attacked mill-owners should not offer hostages. The figures might come in useful later.

Later in April he was again in the north and his speech at Wakefield on 21 April may serve as a model for his approach during this hectic period in his life. It was delivered, impeccably, in the music saloon of the Corn Exchange and an Anglican clergyman had been persuaded to take the chair. Bright began by claiming that the Corn Law was as deeply injurious to agriculture as it was to commerce. His basic contention was that

> The effect of the Corn Law is to limit and to lessen the quantity of food in the market, but it does not lessen the quantity of other commodities; and by deranging the natural quantities, it necessarily raises one in price and depresses the other.

He then gave a number of illustrations designed to support the proposition that 'If our imports are restricted by the corn law, our exports must also be restricted. If we refuse the payment which foreigners offer, then foreigners are disabled from being our customers.' All that Britain exported, he elaborated, was

> the produce of the labour of the English workman; his industry and skill provide the cargoes for our ships; the wandering Arab of the Desert, the inhabitants of the Celestial Empire, the islanders of the great Pacific, all these are supplied to some extent with the produce of our looms.

In turn, he argued, the true source of agricultural prosperity lay not in any law but in the prosperity of farmers' customers. He denied that the League was a friend to low prices.

> I am a manufacturer [he declared] and I confess I have no particular affection for low prices for my goods. All we want is, that we may have for all commodities, food included, such prices as they would fetch in the market if the law did not interfere with them.

Later in the speech he mockingly described the 'protection' of the Corn Law as the protection which the wolf vouchsafes to the lamb. His most telling passage, however, was when he described the cases of men and women in Somerset and Devon sent to prison and hard labour 'for the enormous, the unheard-of crime of stealing turnip greens, that life might be preserved! Stealing turnip greens! — and is it thus that the corn law protects the labourer?' He concluded by telling his cheering audience to forget party names and party conflicts and take care that there should be, as MP for Wakefield, a man who was for the total and immediate repeal of the Corn Law. A thousand copies of this speech, in pamphlet form, were sent to Wakefield to be distributed to farmers on market day.

It was while Bright was still on tour, delivering straightforward but strong speeches of this kind, that evidence began to emerge that during the Durham election, traditional 'head money' had been paid by Dungannon's agents. At first, Bright took little interest since he was considering other parliamentary possibilities at Sheffield and Sunderland. He even got as far as sending off an address for publication immediately the vacancy was declared. Unfortunately for Bright, Earl Grey, father of the sitting member, refused to die. Meanwhile, in secret, a row developed between Dungannon and Londonderry as a result of which Dungannon privately decided to resign, whatever the outcome of the petition against his election which was being considered by a Select Committee chaired by Lord Ashley. That Committee, in turn, did find against Dungannon and a fresh election was necessary. Bright was less than delighted at the verdict. 'I wish', he wrote, 'that I were not connected with the matter at all.' However, he recognized that he had no alternative but to stand, though he was not certain of success. 'I am no party man whatever', he told his audience. 'No man ever knew me to fight the battle of the Tories; no man ever knew me to fight the battle of the Whigs.' He was simply a Free Trader. Nevertheless, this claim did not prevent him from treating the voters to a wide-ranging address dealing with Ireland, Dissenters, and the Factory Education Bill, though everything came back eventually to the Corn Laws.

> I ask you [he implored his audience] to claim for yourselves and for your families the right to have that cheap and wholesome food which a merciful and wise God has supplied both for rich and poor, and upon which they might have been happy and comfortable if His wise laws had not been infringed by human power.

Bright was elected by 488 votes to 410. The cathedral city had fallen to a Quaker. During the campaign, Bright had declared that he prized most the votes of working men, but his triumph owed more to dissension in the Tory camp. Londonderry instructed his agents to poll his men for Bright, so vexed was he with the Durham Tories. The victor put the result differently. 'Free Trade', he claimed, 'was the only watchword, the only motto on our banners. We had no music, no flags, no delusions, but we entirely converted the constituency in a week.'[11]

FIVE

Parliament and repeal 1843-7

John Bright's arrival at Westminster was to be an important occasion.

> I want thee [he wrote to Priscilla on 25 July 1843] to make up in a parcel my new coat & best *great coat* & send them off immediately *by first train* . . . put a couple of shirts in also as my stock is not large. *Please attend to this instantly* as I must be decently attired when I enter the House . . .

He took his seat on 28 July, claiming not to be in the least overawed by the position in which he was placed. A mere party debate was on, 'clever but without honesty & without earnestness'; it was a world he would change. This new public eminence was not without its private anxieties. He had no home and no family in London. He had few intimates in the capital and, outside politics, few interests. He regularly attended meetings for worship, but showed no disposition to repeat his week-day eloquence on Sunday. 'Don't give thyself trouble about me, my dear Margaret', he wrote in mid-August. 'I have lost much — more than this world can ever restore — but I have much left to enjoy.' It was not certain whether he would really 'enjoy' the House of Commons. His position was inevitably somewhat detached; he did not have ties of kinship, school, university or religion with the majority of members, on either side of the

45

House. They in turn looked with some suspicion upon a youthful platform orator with little knowledge of the intricacies of political life at Westminster. One of Bright's first actions, Rachel Priestman notwithstanding, was to get himself elected to the Reform Club. Perhaps the bluntness of Rochdale and the arrogance of Westminster might be blended in its comfortable quarters.

Free Trade was Bright's only immediate objective. In September he wrote to McLaren, [1]

> To talk of overturning the Church is treason to my
> constituents. As I was elected to do the League's work I intend
> to steer tolerably clear of other matters at present — when that
> is done the Church must expect a trial of strength . . .

One such trial had occurred in March when Graham brought in a bill concerning the education of child workers. It provided that they should attend school for at least three hours per day on five days each week. The factory schools were to be inspected more thoroughly in order to improve standards. However, both on the management committee of the schools and as regards religious instruction, the Church of England was given a privileged position on the grounds that it was the Established Church. Dissenters, including many Wesleyans, were furious and in the end killed the proposal. Bright entirely sympathized with them, urging Cobden, despite his Anglicanism, not to support 'the new scheme of *parson* education'. Relations between Church and Dissent were strained — in Rochdale Priscilla reported that the vicar's son had hurt the author of an attack on his father first with a ruler and then kicked him — and when the moment was ripe the State Church could expect to hear more from Bright. Immediately, only issues directly related to Free Trade were taken up — even the possibility of meeting Father Matthew, the Irish temperance advocate, was avoided. [2]

The relationship between Free Trade and slavery was one obvious matter for Bright to attend to. In the summer, a world Anti-Slavery Convention had been held in London, sponsored by the British and Foreign Anti-Slavery Society. This body, wishing to protect 'free' sugar against the slave-grown product of Cuba and Brazil, urged protection for imports from the British

West Indies. Bright soon identified himself with its critics, declaring his private intention 'to overturn the Anti-Slavery Committee in the estimation of the House & the public'. His attacks were criticized by many Friends in its ranks. Its secretary, John Scoble, remonstrated with him but Bright 'did not care much about his denial of the truth of my assertions . . . '.[3] He was quite unrepentant in his advocacy of Free Trade and in consequence did not receive the welcome at some Quaker dinner tables that he had expected. 'The true policy', he suggested to Joseph Sturge, 'would be not to interfere in the matter . . . but when slave produce came in, to consume only free grown and leave others to do as they thought best.' Warming to the attack, he pronounced all legislation in this matter to be misconceived. The government should have been content to have abolished slavery within the British Empire. 'In a country where trade is so extensive as ours', he argued, 'the idea of enquiring into the moral condition of every people with whom we trade seems to me most irrational.'[4] The Anti-Slavery Society was ranging itself with the monopolists who abetted the worst crime ever perpetrated against a people. Sturge, unabashed, felt it was more important not to aid slave proprietors than provide cheap sugar for the English masses.

The League, of course, sought to exploit Bright's election success. The impression was created that the House of Commons was about to succumb to the Free Trade movement. After a meeting in Oxford, Bright reported optimistically to Francis Place, the veteran Radical organizer, that the farmers seemed to prefer the League to their old friends. Place suggested that one of Bright's recent speeches be cheaply printed for mass circulation.[5]

> Had that speech been spoken three years ago [he commented] it would not have been understood, now, the people have been educated so far to enable them to comprehend it, and to me it seems by far the most important address which has been made . . .

Bright himself considered that a Covent Garden meeting held in late September was the most enthusiastic yet. It was also good news that Earl Fitzwilliam intended to come to a League meeting at Doncaster in mid-October and had invited Cobden to visit him at Wentworth. It would be very encouraging, he thought, if the League won the impending City of London by-election — and it did.

This optimism was not altogether well founded. The League campaign in the countryside was less successful than Bright's accounts suggested. A rival, if less effective, Anti-League countered the marauding League speakers — though the eminence of Bright and Cobden ruled out robust physical methods against them. Again, Joseph Parkes, a Radical with great election experience, believed that the cry for 'Total Repeal' lost as many votes in the London election as it gained. The League's commitment to contest every by-election stretched even its resources. Colonel Thompson's suffrage enthusiasms embarrassed the Free Trade cause in certain areas.[6] Bright spent nearly a week in November canvassing in Salisbury but he was rightly pessimistic about the result. He complained that the Tories had brought down a certain Croucher, a notorious briber, and seven prize-fighters, to help sway the electorate. Not that the League itself entirely eschewed dubious electoral practices. The line between legal and illegal electioneering was not easy to draw. Increasingly, the shrewd campaigners of the League turned to registering their own voters and challenging the credentials of likely opponents. As regards propaganda, Bright was closely involved in the decision to change the name of the League's journal and bring it to London under the title of the *League*. It was a further assistance to the cause when, with League encouragement, *The Economist* was first published in September 1843.

The vehemence of the League campaign at this time may well have alienated some potential supporters, but intransigence was Bright's standard weapon. In December he wrote to Edward Baines of Leeds warning against contemplating a smaller fixed duty to replace the sliding scale. He had some fears that Lord Fitzwilliam, and those who acted with him, would counsel the League to compromise in order to secure some modification of the existing evil.[7] He shared Cobden's view that nothing less than real Free Trade would serve. 'We can now have all', he claimed, 'if we remain true to each other & to our great principle.' Meanwhile, he continued to foster close contacts with Dissenters in the wake of the education controversy. He proudly proclaimed that were Free Trade obtained, there was nothing he wished to strive more to obtain than a good education for the mass of the people. The League, in this view, had to enlist as much support as possible by promising, in return, to support other causes once it had been successful.[8] 'Could you get some leading Methodists to write to their ministers or leading men here [London] to help us', he wrote to Wilson in Manchester on 17 October. The Factory Bill of the last session and the intended paying of the Catholic clergy in the next session were the topics to speak to them upon. In the Commons, he warned the government not to suppose that the middle classes would for ever support the aristocracy against the rights of the most numerous.

> Be assured [he concluded] that we are rapidly approaching the time when the middle and working classes will be found united in one firm confederacy against the domination of a class and of principles which have inflicted such deep injuries upon this country.

Such a 'firm confederacy' could only be formed in the country. House of Commons men though they had become, Cobden and Bright still trekked tirelessly across the country. In January 1844, for example, they embarked on a further tour of a Scotland rent by ecclesiastical controversy. Bright took the precaution of contributing £25 to the funds of the Free Church. He was in good speaking form, confidently reporting that he had performed for two hours in Carlisle, 'without difficulty'. There was another 'glorious' meeting in Edinburgh. Writing to McLaren at the close of the tour, he expressed the view that the Scottish mind would now be saturated with Free Trade doctrines and he felt certain that 'the next election will help us with you'. Their only disappointment was that the Scots, even with their minds so saturated, did not open their purses. The mention of money at the close of a meeting in Scotland had the effect of dispersing the audience as quickly as if the Riot Act had been read! The incessant travelling and speaking, however, was beginning to take its toll. While in October 1843 he cheerfully reported to Cobden that he had not been in bed for two nights, in February 1844 tiredness had overcome him. He reported to Wilson that his voice was very bad and he feared that his power of doing good in the cause 'was well nigh gone'. Without undue modesty, he wrote a few days later that, as a result, there would be 'great difficulty in keeping up the meetings with "hearable" speakers'.

After a short rest, his vocal power was restored, but for a few months it was not exclusively used in the cause of repeal. On 6 February, Bright commented that he intended to say 'a few words' upon an impending Factory Bill. In fact, he appeared to be the chief protagonist for the manufacturing interest in its contest with Lord Ashley. The measure provided, amongst other things, for children between nine and thirteen to work eight hours, and between thirteen and eighteen for twelve hours. Lord Ashley, however, pressed for ten hours, arguing that child 'piecers' were called upon to walk twenty-five or thirty miles daily. Bright had stated privately that if Ashley attacked 'us', he would return the compliment. He was also concerned about the release from prison of the veteran 'Ten Hours' agitator, Richard Oastler, certain that he would mount a new campaign against the League in the north. 'I think some intelligent working men', he urged upon Wilson, 'should be got up to meet & expose him — that he should have no field unfought.' Ashley and Bright did clash in the Commons on 15 March. Moving his amendment, Ashley claimed in a long speech that the state had the right to guard the well-being of the people. He elaborated on the conditions of children and women in factories, although his language was relatively mild. The moment Bright had been waiting for had now come. His views on legislative interference had hardened since his earlier tussle with Fielden. While not disputing the arduous nature of much factory work, he argued that it was for employers and their hands to reach a mutually acceptable bargain on the matter. He criticized the hands who supported the Ten Hours proposals, pointing to the wages cotton operatives could earn. He then moved to the attack. His investigations into the conditions of agricultural labourers in Dorset had not been in vain. Why was there no agitation about the hours and wages of those who worked on the land? It was, Bright claimed, because when Ashley and his friends looked at the manufacturing districts, they looked through the right end of the telescope. When they looked at the rural districts, they reversed the telescope and everything was thrown to the greatest possible distance. Bright then complained that Ashley had employed a certain William Dodd to blacken the name of manufacturers and a bitter quarrel then ensued.[9] Ashley, 'aflame with impassioned earnestness', demanded, though he hardly received, a full explanation of Bright's insinuations.

The clash was as fierce as that between Cobden and Peel. Bright had no doubt that he had won, claiming to Margaret Priestman to have 'blown the impostor out of the water'. The Tory papers were attacking him savagely because he had possessed the courage to take 'the genius of cant by the horns or by the nose if that be a better phrase'. Ashley, who had previously thought Dodd a 'jewel' now considered him 'a fiend in the form of man' and confided to his diary the suspicion that he had been bribed by Bright and his friends. Moreover, he was aware that many of the criticisms of Dorset were true, and he was prepared to accept them when made in more temperate form by Cobden. He did not wish to quarrel with his fellow-member for Dorset, however, nor to collide with his father. He felt 'humbled, dejected and incompetent'. Bright had no such feelings. The Ten Hours men, he wrote on 23 April, 'are a sorry set in the main — some honest men, many fools and many knaves . . . . '

The fate of Ashley's amendments illustrates the complexity of the parliamentary world in which Bright had to operate. They were carried by nine and eight votes. The result was a setback for the government, but Graham would not give up. The matter came on again a week later, when he spoke in favour of twelve hours and Ashley in favour of ten. The confusing upshot was that neither figure was accepted. On this occasion, Ashley was supported by Tories like Beckett and Manners, by Whigs like Lords Palmerston and John Russell, and Radicals like Fielden and Hindley. Bright, Villiers, Roebuck, Ricardo and others voted for the government. Although some agitation developed in the north, the 'arch-hypocrite' — Bright's term for Peel — would not give way. Bright was equally unmoved by meetings in Rochdale. During the second reading, he reiterated his support for twelve hours, but complained of the powers to be given to inspectors. Eventually, in mid-May, when Peel made the bill an issue of confidence, it was passed.

The episode revealed Bright's political isolation. His strong support for the government on this issue contrasted sharply with his opposition to its Corn Law policy. His claim to speak for the manufacturing interest was only partially true, for a few employers openly supported ten hours and many more would have happily compromised at eleven. In general it is worth remarking that for all that he was a businessman, Bright took surprisingly little interest in vital contemporary measures like the Bank Charter Act. [10] The Radicals, even the 'industrial' Radicals, did not vote as a group. Bright was also very annoyed by the support given to Ashley by Russell and Palmerston. 'The Whigs', he concluded, 'are a miserable lot after all', and relations between them and the League also deteriorated. They were increasingly annoyed by League tactics at by-elections and the continuing pressure on sitting members to favour total repeal. Not that the League was making much headway in this respect. It was also finding it increasingly difficult to select suitable parliamentary candidates and the commitment to fight every election was quietly dropped. A new focus of activity was urgently needed. It was decided to step up the registration scheme and to create as many Free Trade voters as possible by acquiring a stock of property qualifications. Something like this was necessary, Bright wrote in July 1844, for the Whigs were very active in the constituencies and their hatred knew no bounds. This hatred was effortlessly reciprocated. The mood in League circles was one of frustration, for Villiers's annual motion in favour of repeal on 25 June brought little fresh support. Bright, who had become the prime target of backbench Tory hostility following the Factory Bill struggle, was given such a stormy reception that he was forced to sit down. Cobden, who had abstained on the Factory Bill, was listened to. The number who had voted for Villiers was down on the 1843 figure and Bright tried to put the best gloss he could by including members who were paired or absent to reach a total of 166 repealers in the Commons. 'So we are progressing', he claimed, 'and when a bad harvest comes if not before our work will be done.'

To be politically dependent upon a bad harvest was unsatisfactory, and Bright actively explored other sources of support. The continuous reiteration that every reform had to wait for the repeal of the Corn Laws was becoming less effective. The support of Dissent was of considerable importance, but it proved difficult to muster. The Dissenters' Chapels Bill, which substantially confirmed Unitarian ownership of chapels originally Presbyterian, showed again the division among Dissenters and the difficulty Bright was in as in any sense a leader among them. He supported the measure, claiming, after its passage, that 'the intolerance of the Wesleyans & other Dissenters has received a check.' What really alarmed him, however, as it did Miall the founder of the Anti-State Church Association a few months earlier, in April 1844, was that some leading Dissenters showed such enthusiasm for the doctrine of the Trinity that they were even co-operating with bishops in its defence. The strident tones of Miall's new association, though congenial to Bright, did not please more sober Dissenters.

If Dissent as a whole was divided, Bright could not even claim to speak on behalf of the Society of Friends. His supposed elevation of Free Trade above slavery's evils upset many Friends but Bright was not inclined to change his attitude to the Anti-Slavery Committee. It was 'a shabby and dishonest body' that persuaded the veteran, though nearly senile, abolitionist, Thomas Clarkson, to sign a memorial to Peel against foreign slave-grown sugar. He also saw sharp practice in the failure to report, in the account of the proceedings, his charge that a recent meeting had been unrepresentative of the whole society. Those Quakers who were prominent in its ranks were displeased, while John reported his conviction that he was 'more convinced than ever that the education and habits of the *very rich* "friends" are not such as to make them very useful in rough times . . . . '

Bright's readiness to find hypocrisy and dishonesty in the behaviour of all who differed from him is understandable, for it was not absent. Equally comprehensible is his own belief that he was free from reproach, for at thirty-three, still uncertain in an alien world, the language of elevated earnestness was his solace and armour. He was, in fact, a lonely man. 'In London', he wrote to Priscilla in August 1844, 'notwithstanding its tumult & excitement I often feel very lonely & especially when I return at or after midnight to my lodgings . . . . ' He had recently seen a fine brougham for £168, a high price, but unsurpassable in beauty and usefulness. If only Elizabeth had still been alive 'how much she would have enjoyed some things which I might now have afforded her . . . . ' He rarely saw his baby daughter. The only remedy for loneliness was a further bout of campaigning.

'I have been deeply pondering Game Law matters', he told

Margaret Priestman in January 1845, 'and am astonished at the iniquity of the Game Legislation & the multiplied evils it has produced.' Here was a possible way of distinguishing between the 'agricultural' and the 'landed' interest to the advantage of the League. Bright began to work up the issue into a considerable agitation. For months, articles in the *League* seized on any incidents involving poachers and painted them as the victims of landlord oppression. It was not clear whether the League was opposed to field sports but its argument was that since landowners insisted that the British people should eat British food it was right to know how much of that food was consumed by game. Farmers were circularized asking for details of damage caused by game together with information on the compensation they received. Armed with ample replies which formed the details of his case, Bright took to the country on 3 February, the day before parliament opened. He launched a strong attack against those who kept game, 'a kind of vermin', which consumed produce which should have been eaten by the people. He urged the farmers not to be afraid of landlords and their agents. They should unite, he told an audience at Aylesbury, to obtain deliverance from evils which only their own divisions perpetuated.

In a lengthy speech in the Commons on 27 February 1845, Bright moved for the appointment of a Select Committee to examine the Game Laws. While admitting that he was not a farmer, he claimed to have a good deal of information about agricultural conditions. He painted such a dire picture of the ravages of game that it would have been difficult to resist his call. In fact, Peel and Graham had already agreed to take the issue calmly and assented to the Committee, though holding out no promise of legislation. This result was a victory for Bright at a time when the League leadership needed a success. For the first time, when speaking in the Commons, he had refrained from attacking individuals and expounded a factual case. This restraint was not accidental. He confessed to Wilson that he intended 'to make a very calm dispassionate speech — to come out in a "respectable" character.' Cobden was delighted with the result. The character of the speech took the squires aback and had 'put Bright in a right position, shown that he has power, and it will draw the sympathy of the farmers to the League.' Bright's desire to cut a 'respectable' figure did not extend to accepting an invitation from the Speaker to an official dinner. The members of parliament, he told Rachel Priestman, attended in court dress and this custom would prevent his accepting the invitation. 'I will not make myself look like a mountebank', he roundly declared, though he qualified this statement by adding 'for any ordinary purpose.'

Bright did not let the Game Law question rest within the walls of Westminster. On 26 March, he went up to St Albans to attend a public dinner and to present a piece of plate to a farmer who was reputed to have exposed his landlord's game system and to have been turned from his farm in consequence. Again, his speech was quite mild. He told his audience that he knew a tenant who had spent £1,000 annually for years on artificial manure — without benefit, because his farm was ravaged by game. He revealed that he had been overwhelmed by letters on the subject and had himself written between thirty and fifty letters a day for weeks in reply. It would, he concluded, 'be a fine thing for this country when farmers lose a little bit of that overweening confidence they have in the farmers' friends.' That, of course, was the object of the exercise.

It was not until mid-April 1845 that the Committee started work. Many farmers came to testify to the damage they had sustained and the inadequate compensation they had been offered. In the many hearings that followed, Bright tried to fix attention on the landlord/tenant relationship. When heated argument developed about the damage caused by winged game, as compared with their help in consuming noxious insects, Bright was in danger of getting lost. Feelings, as well as feathers, were distinctly ruffled during the exchanges. The Committee, to Bright's regret, decided not to report during the summer but to request reappointment in the next session. Even so, some landlords became more careful about their game and the issue had served its purpose of increasing the League's popularity among farmers. [11] Bright enjoyed the Committee's work and was neither intimidated nor impressed by the dukes and lords who came before him.

Although Bright liked to believe that the whole country was obsessed by the Game question, he confessed in April 1845 that it was being overtaken by 'Maynooth'. Indeed, ultimately Ireland was to play a much bigger part in Bright's own life than pheasants and worms. His two brief visits to that country had left a deep impression and he was in close touch with his own MP, Sharman Crawford, on issues of Irish land reform, education and government. During his Durham election campaign, Bright had attacked an Arms Bill then being discussed which would have given the police very wide powers. He was fond of declaring that Ireland was a magnificent island with a soil more fertile than England and with a generous, warm-hearted and intelligent people. Yet, there were two million paupers and government depended on force rather than consent. The people had to endure an Established Church to which only one in ten belonged.

The arrest of O'Connell in October 1843 and the conspiracy charge brought against him, had deepened Bright's concern. The Irish leader had declared himself a Free Trader, although relations with his Repeal Association (for the repeal of the Union with England) were not close. Indeed, within a couple of years, Cobden was speaking of his 'complete antagonism and repulsion' towards the Irish party and its leader — he would as soon have an alliance with an Ashantee chief. Bright did not take the same view, regretting the sentence of a year's imprisonment and fine imposed on O'Connell after a taxing trial. The situation in Ireland was very fragile and Lord John Russell launched a strong attack on the government's actions. On 15 February 1844, released pending sentence, O'Connell appeared in the House of Commons to cheers from Opposition benches. Bright could not be present — a disappointment because he had hoped to give the Irishman a cheer on his entry. A few days later, to Bright's delight, O'Connell appeared at a League meeting in Covent Garden, where he was given a most enthusiastic reception. In the Commons, however, Russell's motion for a committee of inquiry was defeated. 'So much', Bright concluded, 'for Ireland & yet Ireland has gained in the debate & her old bloody church must go before long.'

Peel was well aware that repression would not solve the social evils of Ireland. Consequently, the Devon Commission was set up in November 1843 to examine the Irish land system. The following year, Peel and Graham set about fashioning a more conciliatory Irish policy. Maynooth College, the Catholic seminary, already received a government grant and Peel proposed to treble it. The idea caused a storm of protest, chiefly from Anglican Tories. Even though the principle of a grant had already been established, to increase it seemed to be a deliberate blow at the Anglican ascendancy. The Prime Minister deemed it expedient to make a goodwill gesture to the Irish clergy. Like many other Dissenters, though not all, Bright did not see the proposal in the same light. He was firmly Protestant in his convictions but was equally strong in his opposition to the establishment of religion. But, while he had no wish to strengthen Catholicism, he also disliked political 'No Popery'. He passionately wished to see the Anglican Church in Ireland disestablished, but he also wished to see all churches so treated. The Maynooth grant, therefore, appeared to him a significant move in the direction of establishing Catholicism. He was not in sympathy with Peel's political motives either; whereas Peel hoped that the increased grant would mollify the Catholic clergy, Bright hoped that they would remain intransigent. The government was trying to offer them 'hush-money' and they should not consent to be silenced. In the division, the Tories split almost equally — 148 for the measure and 149 against. Bright and 35 Liberals voted against, but Lord John Russell, who had spoken strongly in support of the measure, led 169 supporters into the government lobby, saving the Prime Minister from defeat. The rift between Bright and Cobden on matters touching education and establishment was complete; they voted in different lobbies.

From a League standpoint, both the Game Committee and the Maynooth affair offered some encouragement. Bright had hoped through the former to 'give the Corn Law a blow of a serious nature' and had some reason to be satisfied. The Maynooth vote had highlighted the uncertain relations between Peel and many of his followers. His budget in 1845 embodied further moves in a Free Trade direction and his inactivity over the Corn Laws began to seem anomalous. Russell started to worry that Peel might repeal the Corn Laws and outflank him. Many Whigs still sat on the fence but, for the first time, Lord John voted for Villiers's motion in June. There remained the interesting possibility that both Whigs and Tories would split and destroy the existing party system. Both Bright and Cobden were intensely interested in the implications of such an event. The role of the League — and it was beginning to show itself 'an awkward customer' — might be crucial. In early February, Bright had noted that the Whigs were restless and the Tories 'moody and sullen' behind Peel. Was it, then, simply a matter of waiting for the Whigs to declare themselves and falling in obediently behind them? Bright and Cobden seemed rather divided in their attitudes. Conscious that the agitation had been transferred to the floor of the Commons, Bright wrote to McLaren that he was anxious to prosecute it with his customary uninhibited vigour. It was a sign of the times, however, that Cobden was invited to dinner by Charles Buller, Russell's go-between, to meet Lord Howick (shortly to be Earl Grey) 'to discuss Free Trade tactics a little'. Cobden reported that Howick was in very good temper with the League and quite disposed to throw the fixed duty overboard. Bright was in no mood to play up to whiggery by moderating the tone of his attacks on the aristocracy. To be drawn too deeply into the Whig camp might be to forfeit some interesting possibilities.

The relationship between Bright and Cobden may have been rather strained on just this issue. Bright, for example, told his sister that Cobden had found a speech he had made in the Commons on 6 February powerful and excellent. To his wife, Cobden commented that while powerful, it was 'rasping', adding that the milk-and-water people would be critical of it. Such unpopularity did not worry Bright, indeed he courted it. He wanted victory, when it came, to be victory for the League. Cobden showed sad signs of enjoying the Commons for its own sake. It is indeed true that in these months Cobden kept telling friends that the most unlikely people, Lord Ashley, for example, told him that he was the most popular man in the chamber. It is also true that he avoided actions which could upset the Whigs and also moved for a committee of inquiry into railway gauges with the intention of improving his standing as a 'man of business'. Bright felt that there was little in gauges to benefit the League. He may also not have relished the label 'fanatic' applied by Cobden to all who voted against Maynooth; certainly other Dissenters did not. In any case, there was already some anxiety about Cobden's business affairs which might cause his withdrawal from public life.

In this uncertain situation, Bright felt a considerable responsibility for upholding the position of the League in the country. He went up to Sunderland, dining with Quakers there 'in the hope of strengthening their faith', during the by-election contest between Colonel Thompson, the veteran opponent of the Corn Laws and George Hudson, the Tory railway 'King'. [12] It was galling that Hudson gained a comfortable victory since he had boasted of his support for the Corn Laws. The defeat put Bright in a bad temper. He confessed to the Priestmans that he had hardly been civil to anyone, his short temper being due to 'hard work — knocking about from "pillar to post", the result of the Sunderland election and the baseness of some of the electors'. The League's registration campaign had some success — but not enough. He again turned his mind to ways of manufacturing more League voters. Cobden reported to Wilson in October 1845 that he and Bright had been talking over the idea of Leaguers buying a landed estate in Buckinghamshire 'with a view to creating 1000 county votes'. The scheme would be announced 'not as a scheme for creating votes, but strictly with a view to establish a model farm with a model lease . . . . '

In September, Bright took a holiday in Scotland and it was while there that he received a letter from Cobden confirming his financial difficulties and stating his intention to give up public affairs. In reply, Bright excused himself from hurrying to Manchester on the grounds that his sisters were with him, but urged Cobden to delay.

> Your retirement [he argued] would be tantamount to a
> dissolution of the League — its mainspring would be gone. I
> can in no degree take your place — as a second, I can fight, but
> there are incapacities about me of which I am fully conscious
> and which prevent my being more than a second in such a
> work as we have laboured in.

It was an honest statement, and a few days later he did come to Manchester to help mount what was to prove a successful rescue operation for his friend.

Meanwhile, the situation in Ireland was deteriorating. By the middle of October 1845, Peel and Graham agreed that if reports from Ireland were correct, then it would be necessary to suspend the Corn Laws — and it would be impossible to reimpose them. 'The Corn Laws are on their last legs', wrote Bright to Margaret Priestman on 26 October, 'if legs they have remaining.' The deficient harvest and the failure of the potato crop would do the

League's work for it. Parliament was not sitting, but there was confident expectation of repeal in the next session. He had some faith that 'Peel will do the thing completely when he next touches it.' The League did not leave everything simply to the sad course of events in Ireland. It prepared for a final monster campaign. In mid-October, one of the League's celebrated bazaars was held in Manchester. For £30, Bright engaged a train in which to convey about 750 workpeople from his mills to see the spectacle. Bazaars met with his approval, but balls did not. In March, he had declined to permit his name to appear at all in connexion with a ball on behalf of the Baths and Washhouse scheme in Manchester.[13] Similarly, in October, he was glad to hear that Priscilla had not been at Cobden's 'because I don't think you are in your right place at dancing parties.'

While Bright concerned himself with the morality of balls, the Cabinet wrestled unsuccessfully and inconclusively with Ireland and the Corn Laws. To try to accelerate a conclusion, Bright and Cobden decided to embark on a further round of meetings. After Manchester, Sheffield, Leeds, Bradford and Wakefield, Bright returned to Rochdale. In a letter of 29 November, he outlined his forthcoming itinerary — Gloucester, Stroud, Bath, Bristol, Nottingham, Derby and Stockport, almost on successive days. The meetings, he claimed, were better attended than ever before and 'all the working classes are fairly uniting with us'.

The previous day, Lord John Russell's letter to his Edinburgh constituents was published in which, to the dismay of some of his colleagues, he declared that it was no longer worth while to contend for a fixed duty. Bright recognized the importance of this letter. The entire Whig press and *The Times* now favoured repeal and the monster would be run down. When the House reassembled, he forecast that Peel's government would break and a general election follow. On 4 December, *The Times* announced that parliament would meet in January and be asked by the government to repeal the Corn Laws. Bright could scarcely contain himself. 'I believe it is true', he wrote on reading the report, 'and the reading of the article has almost made me ill — what a glorious prospect is now before us.' The report was premature. On 6 December, Peel resigned, being unable to persuade Lord Stanley and others to accept his proposals.

The Queen sent for Lord John Russell. He set out from

Edinburgh on 9 December and had the good fortune to espy Bright on the platform as his train stopped at Normanton. Bright was in high spirits at the overthrow of 'monopolist government' and climbed on board to congratulate Lord John on his letter. Lord John was in turn very cordial and inquired after the League. This euphoria was again premature. Russell ran into serious trouble trying to form his government, and in the end gave up the attempt. He had made a preliminary approach to Cobden, offering him the Vice-Presidency of the Board of Trade, if he should be able to form an administration. Cobden declined. In the 'chaos of parties', Bright was afraid that some compromise might emerge which fell short of total repeal. The League directed all its efforts towards making that impossible. It inaugurated a new appeal for funds, and Bright reported on 23 December that a Manchester meeting had raised over £60,000, of which his own firm had contributed £1,000; it was the most extraordinary occasion in the kingdom. While a Friend wrote to complain of the severity of his public language, Bright was unrepentant. At this critical juncture it was necessary to speak harshly, since public men were moved by public opinion and not by principle; oaks were not cut down with straws.[14]

Peel withdrew his resignation and resumed office, introducing proposals for the repeal of the Corn Laws in the Commons on 27 January 1846. He did not, in fact, propose the immediate suspension of the Corn Laws, urging instead the gradual reduction of the duties over a three-year period, when they would be entirely abolished. Bright was not pleased. The following day, he attended a meeting at Ricardo's with Villiers, Gibson, Cobden, Earl Grey and James Wilson. They were all, he reported, of the opinion that immediate repeal was vital. Bright suspected that 'everybody' seemed 'desperately anxious' to get rid of the League, Tories and Whigs alike, and in order to do this might concede immediate repeal. 'Don't appear to reject the measure as an insult or a wretched compromise', he advised Wilson, 'but treat it firmly and uphold your own principle.' The feeling in the clubs, he added a couple of days later, was that Peel would get his proposal through pretty easily. However, it remained a proposal for phased repeal and as such it was carried on second reading by the votes of 112 Peelites and 227 Whigs and Liberals against 231 Tories and 11 Whigs.

At long last, Bright approved of the Prime Minister. Peel's speech on 16 February he considered the best he had ever heard and he crawled into bed at three in the morning well-satisfied. The following day he rose in the Commons to pay tribute to Peel who had come back into office as the true minister of his sovereign and of the people; the 'arch-hypocrite' had come a long way. The next few months were not without anxiety since the possibility of a revolt by the Whig peers was a real one. However, on 25 June, the Corn Law Bill passed all its stages in the Lords. 'I wish you had been here', he wrote to Wilson, 'we have not seen the last of the Barons, but we have taught them which way the world is turning.'

The League leadership was jubilant. Triumphant meetings took place in many towns throughout the ensuing weeks. In Rochdale, the Free Traders got into the church tower and rang a victory peal, inevitably provoking a further confrontation with the vicar. A huge procession marched through the town on 8 July 1846 carrying, amongst other things, a monster loaf with the names of Cobden and Bright inscribed on its sides. The workpeople from the Bright mills carried twenty-five celebratory silk flags. John Bright, with other manufacturers, brought up the rear of the parade. The workers were treated to dinner by the owners, at the close of which, by popular request, John Bright was persuaded to say a few words. He acknowledged that they were celebrating a day of deliverance. The years ahead would see steadier trade, steadier profits and steadier wages. Employers and workpeople should cultivate feelings of justice and respect for each other. He trusted that if 'before long' there were political institutions against which they would struggle, they would struggle together. A sum of over £5,000 was raised for Bright by public subscription, with which he purchased a library of over twelve hundred volumes. They were housed in a large oak bookcase on which motifs symbolizing Free Trade in corn were prominently carved. In Rochdale, the victory was presented as one for the commercial and industrial classes against the great proprietors of the soil and, in part, for the north over the south. Amidst all the rejoicing, however, it was time for Bright to take stock, both in his private life and in his political career. The great cause which had taken up so much of his time and energy had been successful; what next?

Part Three

Manchester and the 'Middle-Class Spirit'

SIX

War on the Whigs 1847-52

John Bright's immediate objective, after the repeal of the Corn Laws, was to find another wife. He had wanted to marry again for some time, but his public life had left little leisure for courtship. All was not well in the domestic world at Rochdale and remarriage might enable him to escape some of its tensions. There had been occasions, over the previous few years, when he described himself as miserable. Priscilla reassured him that domestic happiness could yet be in store for him. In helping to obtain good for others, she wrote in April 1844, his own would follow, 'provided thou dost not neglect thy own best interests, and here lies the difficulty in political life.' Little Helen remained a consolation, but he did not see much of her, though he sent affectionate paternal *billets-doux*. He had a cook at his London lodgings and a boy who opened the door, cleaned his boots and ran errands, but the atmosphere was not very 'cosy'. To complicate matters, Jacob Bright senior showed an unwelcome disposition to take as a housekeeper a woman his elder children disapproved of. Even worse, he had presented them with an ultimatum: either they raised no objections or he would spite them and marry her. This crisis, in early 1845, was followed by the death of his brother Benjamin, who was only twenty-eight. 'Perhaps some escape may offer', John wrote gloomily, 'but I doubt it. As a family we must love each other & try to avoid the rocks on which others make

65

shipwrecks.' On top of this, Priscilla, who was his confidante in family matters, confessed that she had a suitor. John was taken aback. 'I thought it was I who was to leave thee', he wrote, '& not thou who would leave me, but perhaps I was premature.' He went to inspect the suitor's property and was not displeased with it, but in the end there was no wedding. But if Priscilla and John did not marry, their father pushed ahead. 'I hope he will not marry at Rochdale', wrote John. 'Better to go to world's end for such a disgusting scene.'

The question of his own remarriage had been on Bright's mind throughout 1845. He reported to Priscilla that a friend had 'some fair ones on his list' — adding, on reflexion, 'don't mention this again'. Female beauty was not without its attraction to him. He described the wife of Mr Dennistoun, MP for Glasgow, as 'magnificent! perhaps the finest woman as *animal* I ever saw'. It was unfortunate that the ladies he met at dinner tended to be fond of gaiety, though Bright's own dining-out was already not strictly utilitarian. The phrase 'I must give up going out to dinner', first appears in his correspondence in February 1845, to be repeated frequently as the years passed, though always without effect. His London lodgings improved in standard nearly every parliamentary session. In February 1846, for example, he had rooms in Lowndes Street, between Lowndes Square and Eaton Square. 'I could', he admitted, 'have saved something by going into a more retired street, but I thought dear Priscilla and Helen would like a cheerful look from the windows.' He had to pay correspondingly, and not merely for the room with the view. About the same time, he expressed the opinion that the nurse who helped to look after Helen was not 'nice enough'. A second wife, suitably assisted, would make a better nurse.

Bright's choice fell upon the daughter of a Yorkshire Quaker family. In November 1845, when in Wakefield, he called, not for the first time, on W. H. Leatham at his bank. Leatham, he regretted, had not been fully converted to repeal. His mother had been, though for good measure Bright sent her a copy of the *League* containing one of his recent speeches, just to make sure. Mrs Leatham was a widow with four sons and an unmarried daughter, Margaret Elizabeth. On this occasion, Bright took dinner with the ladies and called on W. H. Leatham's wife, Priscilla, daughter of the London banker, Samuel Gurney. Afterwards, his mind frequently went back to that domestic scene at Heath, near Wakefield. Within a fortnight of the passing of the repeal legislation, he was pondering his next step. It would be an exaggeration to say that he was lost in love. He reported to Priscilla that on closer acquaintance with Miss Leatham — he had contrived a further visit to Yorkshire — he could find no fault with her 'except that to which I have often alluded with some levity'. Her opinions and good sense were admirable and the fearlessness of her character was 'not without charm, tho' very different from that which is of the gentler kind'. His existing mode of life was unsatisfactory and he claimed that he was 'more in need of what is good than of what is merely striking to the eye', yet the inference that a more striking woman than the 24-year-old Miss Leatham would have been desirable is inescapable. He could not decide whether to write to Mrs Leatham 'with full explanations' or to hold back. The following day, 10 July, he wrote to Priscilla to say that the die had been cast. Letters were about to be posted to the ladies at Wakefield. 'I think I have well considered it', he added uncertainly, '& cannot do better. I must trust the best judgment I have been able to exercise.'

In his letter to Mrs Leatham, Bright admitted that his admiration for her daughter had extended over a period of years but could not be acknowledged when he was engaged in a great and absorbing political movement. He did not know how Elizabeth herself felt, since they had met so rarely, but if he should be successful in his suit, he could guarantee that he would continue to give her the comforts and luxuries to which she was accustomed. 'I am not rich,' he added, 'but I have a prosperous business, from which I derive an income much beyond my present expenditure & affording a prospect of such a competency as I may with propriety desire.' In his letter to Elizabeth, Bright admitted that parliamentary life interfered with the quiet routine of the family circle, but he believed that his period of intense activity was over. Public life, however, had been a duty. Turning to another point, he considered that his previous marriage and his daughter did not constitute an obstacle. As for religious questions, he remained attached to the customs and opinions of Friends, but confessed that over the past four years he had been thrown into the company of others and the rough usage of the world tended to embitter the spirit. In conclusion, he stated his belief that 'all our blessings are sweeter when shared with those we love.'

The female Leatham reaction was somewhat guarded. Consulted by his mother, W. H. Leatham strongly urged that Bright should be given the fullest opportunity of seeing his sister. He hoped that she would 'treat him with the full respect that is due to him & for which I feared . . . she seemed hardly careful enough about.' If Bright should gain her affections, she should not 'fetter his liberty by extorting any promise from him to lay down *for ever* all connexion with public life.' It was possible that he would be ready to retire for a season, but he should be free to return. It seemed likely that parliament was his real calling. The points that Elizabeth would have to concede were 'of no great consequence to *her* sex but of much to *his*'. He admitted that many Friends disliked Bright 'on account of his political struggles' but reported that the Gurneys considered him to have 'advanced much in all good things the last year or two'. Mrs Leatham therefore replied that John could visit her home to pursue his suit.[1]

'Perhaps satisfactory, but not without difficulties', was Bright's assessment of the position after two long walks with Elizabeth. The chief snag was his public career, and time alone would show whether his suit would succeed and 'if to succeed is best'. By the end of July, Bright was more convinced that he had made the right choice, but the future was uncertain. He reported to Priscilla that he had some 'curious information' about previous suitors, but then pulled himself up with the comment that such things should not be talked about. He felt sufficiently confident to inform Cobden on 29 July of his marital intentions, but shortly afterwards doubt again intervened. A note from Wakefield was 'very short & hardly more than acknowledging the receipt of mine.'

Elizabeth seemed 'undecided & *very cautious*'. John became vexed and irritable as Elizabeth kept him waiting for months. By mid-September, things were 'no worse — perhaps better'. They went riding near Harrogate, but on his return to Rochdale she kept him waiting many days for a letter. 'We grow older', he commented wryly, 'but not much wiser in some things'. There were financial complications and Elizabeth was not satisfied with One Ash in its existing form. She wanted nine bedrooms and a bathroom, or ten bedrooms without it, together with three servants' rooms in the upper part of the house. A good deal of time was spent in discussing the most judicious positioning of the 'closets'. At the end of September, John hoped that these matters were settled, but even so remained uncertain. During a fortnight with the Leathams in October, he reported an increased confidence in him and more freedom of communication. Afterwards, he departed to Ben Rhydding, near Ilkley, for a 'cure' and from there urged Elizabeth not to think that many waters could quench his love for her. By mid-November, he was writing to Priscilla asking her to draw up a list of plate and linen already at One Ash so that wedding presents would not be unnecessarily duplicated. On his thirty-fifth birthday, he was delighted with a beautiful watch guard from Elizabeth, 'made entirely from her own hair, fitted up with elegant gold studs & fastenings.'

Thereafter, wedding preparations went steadily ahead, though there were still some complications. 'It is a misfortune', John lamented to Priscilla in March 1847, 'for me that M.E.L. is considered to be rich', for all sorts of people were now coming to him for money, though he could ill spare it. His new circumstances made him acutely conscious about money and status. His sister Esther currently had a suitor and John was anxious to know his financial position. It was, he wrote, just as foolish to ignore this question as it was wicked to care for nothing else. In this case, his only objection was that the suitor 'speaks broad "Yorkshire" almost & seems so wanting in refinement of manner.' The suit failed. Priscilla was in an awkward mood too. She was now thirty-one and for years had been surrounded by marriages without herself marrying. When one possibility did present itself, John was firmly against it, declaring that her reasons would justify her in marrying anyone — which was no recipe for marital happiness. Simultaneously, she was reprimanded for failing to report on the progress made by the workmen improving One Ash for the new bride. Elizabeth was apparently making difficulties about the date of the wedding and the state of her future house.

Nevertheless, in mid-June 1847, the wedding took place and

the couple set off on their honeymoon, travelling all round the coast of Wales. Unfortunately, the house was still not ready. From Swansea, after a month, he wrote anxiously for news of One Ash. The journey, he complained, was being prolonged beyond what he intended and 'it is more expensive to live thus than at home in quiet'. The news was disappointing and they had to stay for a while at Wakefield. He found that both Elizabeth and her mother feared that 'the paint will be very offensive' and he hoped that something could be done. Eventually they moved in, but the notion that John would be long 'at home in quiet' proved somewhat premature.

The anxieties which preceded and accompanied his second marriage were in part a reflection, on Bright's side, of his own uncertainty about his future. He had always claimed that it was for the work of repeal that he had entered the Commons and subordinated his business and domestic life. It was in this cause that he had made a reputation for himself in and out of parliament. The rallies, the propaganda and publicity of the League gave it a fair claim to being the most sophisticated political machine of the century. Its leading members, Bright included, liked to believe that it was the League which had forced repeal: the reality was more complex. Peel had not simply bowed before agitation in the country. In conversation with Bright in July 1846 he remarked that he had had no conception of the depth of public feeling on the Corn Laws. Bright entered this remark in his diary, not appreciating that Peel was discounting the League's significance. The weakness of the League had also been seen when the demand for immediate rather than phased repeal had been unsuccessful. Nevertheless, the League had become a remarkable body and Bright's first thoughts, in the spring of 1846, were to keep it in being. However, the last number of the *League* appeared on 4 July 1846 with a report of the final meeting of the League Council in Manchester two days earlier. Seconding Cobden's motion that the League suspend its active operations, Bright drew the lesson that 'there is in public opinion a power much greater than that residing in any particular form of government.'

If the League had disbanded, ostensibly successful, Bright was not satisfied that it had adequately dented the existing social and political structure. The depth of his animosity against the aristocracy had not diminished. It had given his oratory its bite and vigour. Cobden had expressed the hope that their agitation might not become 'a strife of classes' but, speaking at Covent Garden on 19 December 1845, Bright stated that he was 'not sure that it has not already become such, and I doubt whether it can have any other character'. The struggle was that of the many against the few, between 'the numbers, wealth, comforts, the all in fact, of the middle and industrious classes, and the wealth, the union, and sordidness of a large section of the aristocracy of this empire.' He lambasted 'a fat and sleek dean, a dignitary of the church and a great philosopher' who recommended Swede turnips and mangel-wurzel for the consumption of the people. He mocked the hereditary Earl Marshal of England who, 'as if to out-herod Herod himself, recommends hot water and a pinch of curry-powder.' He implored his audience to remember that even if repeal should come and the League disperse, they had discovered in registration, especially of the 40s. freeholders, a strong and irresistible weapon 'before which the domination of this hereditary peerage must at length be laid in the dust'. The question for Bright, in the next phase of his career, was how far this sentiment was in fact shared by the average League supporter. His greatest strength as a politician, his oratorical capacity before large audiences, might no longer be so effective if the task was to carry his own class with him rather than attack another. It was appropriate that the struggle for the evolution of a vigorous, non-deferential, middle-class movement should take place in Manchester itself, home of the League and self-styled leader of provincial cities.

Mark Philips, who shared Manchester's parliamentary representation with Milner Gibson, had announced his decision to step down at the next general election. Whatever he may have whispered at Wakefield, John Bright had set his sights on succeeding him. It was a more congenial and prestigious constituency than Durham. The difficulty was that Cobden's name was also being mentioned. In a private letter to his Stockport constituents on 17 July 1846, Cobden declared that he would not desert them, adding that Bright was a suitable candidate for Manchester. It was a declaration, however, which he declined to make publicly. There was opposition to Bright from

71

some of the leading families in the city, even from the Potters who had paid his election expenses in Durham in 1843. Cobden admitted that Bright took no pains to conciliate people of his own rank and therefore, mistakenly, many supposed him arrogant and supercilious — and this indeed may be part of the explanation. In an attempt to clarify his prospects, Bright wrote to Cobden on 29 July. He conceded that if Cobden wanted to stand for Manchester he would not press his own candidature. He would never think of himself on the same level as his friend, but, if Cobden did not intend to stand, he would press his case. He had received approaches from other constituencies and would have to say something definite soon. Cobden, who was about to go abroad, suggested that they should meet to talk over the matter. After they did so, Cobden did write that Bright's obvious ambition to sit for Manchester should be gratified, but he still declined to give a definite negative to approaches he received, particularly since they were from men who had helped rescue him from financial disaster. He left for the continent leaving the position unclear.

A certain amount of rivalry now entered their relationship. If Cobden felt that Bright pressed too hard, Bright felt that Cobden was being unreasonably dilatory. John identified his opponents as the '*Guardian* party' because that newspaper was their mouthpiece and they were also to be found in the newly-formed Commercial Association. His friends were grouped around the recently started *Examiner*, a paper in which Bright had a financial interest and for which he wrote. On 20 August, Bright wrote to Villiers that the selection meeting in Manchester had been very stormy. Of the thirty-five people present, sixteen were for him and seventeen against, and a decision was postponed for a fortnight. By the end of the month, Bright claimed that he had a majority, telling Villiers that he had written Cobden a letter 'from which I think he cannot escape'. If no reply came, he would either await the decision of the next meeting 'or write a letter in the Manchester papers stating my opinion of the course Cobden has taken with respect to the representation & withdrawing from the affair altogether.' He did not admit to Villiers that his chances of marriage would improve if he did withdraw. If Cobden did not have 'the fairness & magnanimity to leave the field for me after all he has said on the subject, I shall not envy him the course he has taken or the fruits it may yield him.'[2] The end of September found him sitting gloomily at home, pessimistic about his chances and consoling himself with the thought that he had not 'deceived or played an ungenerous part towards anyone'. Then came news. He added a postscript to Priscilla to say that he had just heard that Cobden would stay at Stockport. He later defended Cobden against her strictures. It was not the case that Stockport forced his hand, rather that he had solicited the renewed pressure from his constituents in order to ward off Manchester. 'With some weaknesses', Bright continued, in lordly fashion, 'he has great gifts & virtues & I will not desert him, as long as I can think well of him.' The way was now clear for Bright to be selected, though he wrote privately that if he thought that the Manchester constituency as a whole was like the '*Guardian* clique' he would 'wipe off the dust of my feet against them'. Bright at last relaxed with a visit to Ben Rhydding, where there was a capital billiard table.

Fond of the cue though he was, John could not rest for long. There was renewed opposition in Manchester and, larynx reinvigorated, he returned to the fray. There was an attempt to find a candidate acceptable both to Whigs and Free Trade Conservatives. The atmosphere was bitter. 'I can't quite understand the conduct of the Potters,' he wrote to Wilson on 5 November. 'It must arise from envy or jealousy', for they would surely have no objections to 'extreme opinions'. He was contemptuous of his critics. 'Lord Lincoln or Lord Ashley or Lord anybody else would suit them', he wrote to Rachel Priestman. 'They are very angry about me, & the more so that they feel hardly able to see their way to an effective opposition.' Various possible opponents were being canvassed, including Gladstone and Lord Lincoln, Peelite son of the Duke of Newcastle. Bright dismissed Lincoln as 'just a nobody', nevertheless, he was sufficiently apprehensive to hope that Cobden could be persuaded to write a letter in his support. 'Would it not shame', Bright explained to Wilson, 'the poor sneaks who prefer a Tory Lord to a man of their own rank, whose chief fault with them is that he is wanting in "social position". . . .' So strongly did Bright attack the idea of an aristocratic candidate that Villiers, son of a peer himself, felt bound to protest. Bright graciously admitted that the son or relative of a peer might be as good as any other, but the great fault was to be swayed by rank. Manchester would do much better not to choose someone like Lincoln because, if the father was in one House, there was little need for the son to be in the other. 'And perhaps', he continued, 'it is sometimes almost needful to fight one prejudice with another — if they run me down for want of "social position" it is a great temptation to us to try to rouse a middle-class spirit against my aristocratic opponent.' In fact, Lincoln did not proceed, but Bright had secured his position without assistance from Cobden. On 26 December Bright told Villiers that he believed Cobden's family was withholding a letter of support and admitted that there had been 'much unpleasantness between some of Cobden's friends and mine'. It was monstrous that he should be accused of want of sincerity to Cobden. As for Cobden himself, it was not until 18 January that he wrote a cool letter to Bright stating that he was bored by the whole affair of the Manchester candidature. John in turn drew Villiers's attention to the fact in none of Cobden's speeches abroad 'has he ever mentioned your name or mine as of those who have done anything for Free Trade — possibly he has not been well reported.' However, recognizing that his success would depend more on constituency organization than a letter from Cobden, Bright turned energetically to registration and other matters. 'We need no patronage from any man in Manchester,' he proudly proclaimed. 'We have *sloughed* off a number of those who wished to patronize & rely now upon the mass of the tenpounders only.' Confident that he had done as much as he could to secure the seat, Bright returned to the politics of Westminster.

Peel's government had been defeated on an Irish Coercion Bill by a combination of Whigs and Protectionist Tories and the Prime Minister resigned. Since then, Lord John Russell's government had continued in office without an election. The Tories were in disarray. Bright, however, certainly did not feel that the Whigs were 'his' government. He was not impressed by the way in which ministers tried to tackle the terrible problems of famine in Ireland. They dared not 'grapple with the real malady, which is the existence of the laws of primogeniture & entail & the consequent possession of the whole of Ireland by a proud & idle & pauper proprietary.' He did not, however, at this juncture seek to portray himself as Ireland's champion. He spent his time trying to fend off another Factory Bill and standing up for the interests of Dissenters. The candidates for Manchester were all canvassed for their views by Ten Hours advocates and Bright was declared unworthy of the support of those concerned for the welfare of factory children. Certainly, Bright had not changed his opposition to legislation and he presented a memorial to the Home Office in favour of the status quo, but he was not optimistic. While the government did not have a view, Lord John spoke in favour of further limitations of hours. After the second reading, Bright wrote to Smith on 26 February warning him to expect the worst. He doubted whether the government could now avoid ten hours, although he continued to attack the proposals in committee. 'Great interests & great principles' he wrote to Wilson in March 1847 'are trifled with by a combination of fools & knaves, & where the mischief will end I know not.' Not surprisingly, in their victory, the Ten Hours reformers singled out Bright as the principal villain, describing him as 'a horrid brute', a 'heartless Quaker' and a man full of 'bile and bad feeling'.

Bright was unmoved. He relieved his feelings by launching an assault on the proposal to create a new diocese of Manchester. He had heard rumours, he told Villiers, that the priestly lord was to be paid for out of the Consolidated Fund. Such a proposal 'would lose every spark of confidence among the real liberals & dissenters.' He also identified himself with continuing Dissenting objections to state aid for church education. 'Thou wilt be surprised to hear', he wrote to Priscilla in April, 'I am to take the chair at the Education meeting tonight in Exeter Hall.' Baines and Sturge had persuaded him. In the Commons on 20 April he defended the 'braying of Exeter Hall' against the strictures of Macaulay. Nonconformists did not object to grants because the Church of England received money from them but 'because Nonconformists themselves, in accordance with the principles by which they are so, cannot receive public money for the teaching of religion in their schools; and, therefore, they object to the State giving money as an advantage to the Church schools. . . .'

Bright also had the pressing commercial anxieties of his

future constituents to worry about, not to mention his own. The rise in the price of raw cotton had led many to become gloomy about trade prospects at the end of 1846. The obvious solution, he believed, was to find an additional source of supply. He began to urge the possible merits of Indian cotton, which, besides being cheaper, would also be more moral in that it reduced dependence on American slave-grown cotton. He wrote round to various Manchester businessmen with such success that by February he was rather alarmed at the amount of work he had carved out for himself. He had an interview with the President of the Board of Trade to press his case. 'I have very bad accounts still from Lancashire', he wrote to Wilson on 25 February 1847, 'we are stopping our mills after this week.' It was unfortunate for the workpeople, but there was no help for it. 'Self-preservation', he told Priscilla, 'is the first law of nature', and it would not be a kindness to waste capital in order to keep them in employment. The strain told on his brother Thomas in whose hands the direction of the business now lay, and he had to go to Leamington Spa to rest. It is not surprising that John confessed that he was not spending much time in the House of Commons; there seemed more important things to do in the north.

Quite apart from business, Bright did not find the Commons very congenial. The 'League party' was broken up, with Cobden away, and Gibson in minor office. The effort had to come in the country and Bright wanted to hit the aristocracy by capturing the county seat of South Lancashire. A 'liberal' candidate was mentioned, but Bright commented sceptically that 'what is now or will be the liberal party I know not'. He had the idea of getting Villiers, who sat for Wolverhampton, to contest South Lancashire, hoping that he would transfer if elected. If the Wolverhampton people objected, they would be 'excommunicated'. 'I am annoyed at having to be away for a month owing to the *event* in prospect', he wrote to Villiers shortly before his wedding, 'but if it be needful to forward your election I shall be much tempted to curtail the time of my absence.' Bright's case was that South Lancashire would set an example to all other counties. He and Wilson were working on a scheme for 'bringing the whole north of England into a complete system of registration & preparation for election contest'.

It is an illustration of his enthusiasm at this time for the details of campaigning.

Finding it increasingly difficult to hold his majority together, Lord John Russell decided to call a general election for July 1847. Bright hurried over to Manchester, leaving his new bride with her mother. In the event, he and Gibson were returned without opposition. There was a large assembly, he reported to her on 29 July, amongst them a knot of Chartists and Ten Hours men who unsuccessfully tried to shout him down. He now watched eagerly for signs that men of his stamp had improved their position at the expense of Whigs or Tories. 'I don't see that the Whigs gain much so far by the returns', he wrote to Villiers on 2 August, 'nobody believes in their good intentions or their power & the maker of new Bishops in these days deserves whatever ill may befall him.' Villiers was returned for South Lancashire, though in the end he did not leave Wolverhampton. The defeats of Macaulay at Edinburgh and Hobhouse at Nottingham were gratifying because they warned the Whigs of the penalties incurred for trifling with the popular party.

Throughout the election, Cobden remained on the continent, preaching Free Trade to princes, prelates and professors. In his absence, a move developed to put him up, with Lord Morpeth, for the West Riding in an attempt to defeat a protectionist, Beckett Dennison. A row had developed in this constituency between Earl Fitzwilliam and many of the town Liberals. Fitzwilliam, though opposed to protectionism, had resented the League registration campaign and, rather than see his personal influence further eroded, supported Dennison. The news of his election reached Cobden in St Petersburg! 'It is amusing', Bright wrote to Villiers concerning this and other contests, 'how great a Boro' monger I am because . . . The League after all was rather formidable — its dying kicks have scattered a few of its old enemies!'

The general election result gave Lord John Russell a normally reliable majority, but the parliamentary situation was still far from stable. The governing majority consisted of Whigs, Liberals and, often, Peelites — though the possibility of a Tory reunion remained. Friction between Whigs and Liberals could produce some odd voting patterns. The group associated with Bright was not very numerous. As a gesture, Russell had given Gibson a minor post in the government, but that was hardly a concession to the vulgar masses. Bright was furious at Whig superiority. The suggestion that the defeated Macaulay might find a seat at Stockport left him almost speechless. Bright might find it helpful to believe that 'the popular party is making great progress & the revolution is not yet stayed', but the truth was that his 'popular party' was still only a dream. It was incoherent even in an age of incoherent politics. It had no leader and no national organization. Cobden returned to England in October 1847, but his pre-eminence was far from being universally acknowledged. Bright and Wilson tried to create a 'party' feeling, but their efforts met with suspicion, if not hostility. 'I think you are the most suspicious person I ever knew', wrote Bright bluntly to Villiers in November. 'You can't put a fair construction on what your friends do, so that even you believe I am trying to dupe you, or am a dupe myself.'

Bright was handicapped by the fact that money was tight in Manchester during these months of commercial crisis. There was little enthusiasm for new political crusades. Bright's own family business was in difficulties. Thomas Bright explained to an American cousin in January 1848 that their concern had not managed more than 2½ days per week in the year October 1846 to October 1847. They had lost £10,000 in that period and could not contemplate another such loss — fortunately prospects were improving.

The John Bright who came up to London at the end of November as the proud new member for Manchester was therefore less buoyant than he appeared. In town, he settled into a daily routine. In the morning, he wrote letters in the coffee room of his hotel, then went to his club, then to the House, back again to the club and then finally to his hotel. It did not take more than a few weeks for him to be 'deadly tired' of this London solitude. 'Thy being here would give a new colour to everything', he wrote to his wife, '& I hope next session to find a residence in town.' Looking at parliament he formed the impression that at last men of business were taking hold of public affairs. In a debate on 13 December he even claimed, amidst laughter, that 'the present Government is essentially of the middle class.' He argued further that no government could survive 'which does not sympathise with the great middle class of this country'. Nevertheless, he was anxious 'to give a little impetus to the *liberal* liberals in the House' and he valued his independence. If the government did wrong, he would attack it and not be shackled, like his colleague Milner Gibson, by minor office.

However, 1848 was the year of revolution. In February, the monarchy of Louis Philippe in France fell. Bright's attacks on the aristocracy seemed in tune with the times. Liberty, he told Jonathan Priestman, was on the march, although the British government seemed only to think of parliamentary majorities rather than opinion out-of-doors. The conclusion he drew from these developments was that another League, for different purposes, was imperative. Writing to Wilson in early March, he considered that the government was in bad shape, with Lord John out of health and out of humour with his colleagues. It seemed very likely that conditions would cause the working people to make an attempt at disturbance. He was becoming strongly impressed by the idea 'that we must have another Reform Bill before long & the sooner the better for we are still in the hands of the Philistines & they make us grind at their mill.' As the weeks passed, he grew more passionate. 'Surely Manchester may yet lead again the crusade against the wretches who learn nothing from revolutions abroad', he wrote, '& who are blindly intent on their own destruction. We are the slaves of a privileged class. . . .' Since retribution might strike that class, it was time to draw the lines very sharply between reformers and the government. Gibson, for example, gained nothing from his membership of the ministry: it was 'not worth his while to be a martyr to Whig imbecility'.

As conditions worsened, Chartism did indeed revive. Bright was alarmed. He deplored revolutionary violence and repeatedly told working men that industry, frugality and temperance were the only sources of their regeneration. Nevertheless, unless the aristocratic order was overthrown, there was some danger that the fate of the manufacturing class would be precarious. It was necessary to save the Whigs from themselves. Certainly, the Chartist demonstrations seemed threatening, reaching their height at the famous Kennington

Common meeting on 10 April, but then the alarm passed. Writing on 23 April, Bright continued to feel that the political agitation was not likely to be soon lulled. 'We shall have', he continued, 'or ought to have, a powerful agitation in favor of a real parly reform, & to gain this would be worth some time longer of commercial depression.' The British had allowed themselves to be deluded into believing that they were a free people, with a representative system of government, but it was, for the most part, a sham. The government had recently insisted on keeping the income tax, and its programme of expenditure was almost reckless. He was convinced that the middle and working classes were beginning to see that only if united could they defeat their 'insatiable enemies'.

Cobden was much more cautious. About the same time as these comments, he was calming his wife's fears that he was about to start a new League. He suggested instead that agitation should be directed at the redistribution of seats and the introduction of equal electoral districts. Wilson, too, did not want to plunge into a campaign for parliamentary reform. Bright admitted that there could be 'no greater folly than starting a coach by which the middle classes will not travel', but he did not give up easily. While the Chartist riots might frighten some into inactivity, they should prompt more to deal with the dangerous uneasiness which prevailed among the people. 'We shall again have to fight with "beasts at Ephesus"', he declared, 'the men who opposed Free Trade will I fear oppose any rational attempt at reform.' The reformers, however, as the West Riding by-election of December 1848 illustrated, did not have a common platform. After the result was declared, Cobden wrote to Edward Baines (whose 'ultra line upon dissent, education, etc.' he had been trying, through Bright, to modify) that with three or four great rents in the Liberal party, 'it was wonderful that the defeat was not more signal'. To Bright he complained that Baines was a great obstacle to future progress. 'If he were not there', he added, 'I could undertake to rally the party tomorrow and in two years beat both the Tory and Whig aristocracy.' Bright himself, though he confessed that he was 'pretty well tired of mixing up religion in any way with a scheme of school education', was more optimistic in his interpretation of the poll.[3] He was convinced that in the future *'our friends*, without the Whigs, can win'. The voters would be attracted by

> Free Trade in sugar, ships and corn, for a real retrenchment of expenditure, for municipal or household suffrage, ballot, three year parliaments, no property qualification, repeal of law of primogeniture, abolition of church rates, no capital punishments & for no more public money or taxes of any kind to any sect or body of religionists under any pretext whatever

— in fact, for Bright's programme! Cobden, however, gloomily remarked that it was useless 'trying to get hold of the country, whilst the West Riding is passing out our hands'.

These differing reactions to the West Riding result broadened into a more general difference of opinion on the best strategy to follow. Cobden wished to give the Liverpool-based 'financial reform' campaign enthusiastic backing. 'We can't conceal from ourselves', he wrote, 'that there is less warmth now for organic change amongst the upper section of the middle class.' If government expenditure was cut down, the spare money could be given to the consumers, thereby enlarging the means of the industrious classes by extending the commerce of the country. By the same token, 'our own order' would be strengthened for a future assault upon the oligarchy. Bright replied that he also favoured one thing at a time, if it was well-defined, but 'financial reform' was not. The question of representation could not be shirked. Still enthusiastic, he told Villiers that there was 'a basis for a growing party & that you & we & many others should go on together if possible.' They could have 'a party out of doors more formidable than we had in the League & can work the constitution so as to reform it through itself.' Bright's zeal was not very infectious. Cobden made it clear that he would not wear himself out again in a cause which, however admirable, would be futile. He had most old Leaguers on his side. Henry Ashworth, for example, warned George Wilson that unless the financial reform movement was clearly put first, many would say that the leaders of the League, smarting under the West Riding defeat, were driven to Chartism to replenish their following. That, he warned, would be more than 'some of our friends' would like. Bright admitted that there was 'something like a split apparent' between the financial and the parliamentary reformers. The national Parliamentary and Financial Reform Association, which tried to heal the breach, proved still-born. Bright began to look for new causes and issues which might offer a way forward.

'I often feel quite distressed about the miserable Irish', wrote Bright to Rachel Priestman in March 1849, 'they are dying of hunger & fever & cholera & nobody seems to have a notion of what is to be done to help them.' Grants of money seemed only to postpone their ruin and 'an amalgamation of the Scottish & Irish, or English & Irish blood' though desirable, was impracticable.[4] He had expressed his interest in Irish questions on several previous occasions in a manner which flattered neither the Irish nor the London government. In the Commons in April he urged parliament to retrace its steps in Ireland. Once land was freed, then remunerative industry, the only sure foundation of union and peace, could develop.[5] The government did introduce a new Encumbered Estates Bill with the objective of speeding up the transfer of land to owners who were in a position to inject fresh capital. For once, Bright was pleased, describing the measure as 'excellent' — perhaps because he took a little credit for it himself. As soon as the parliamentary session ended, after a brief visit to Rochdale, he set out for Ireland determined, unlike most British politicians, to see for himself.

Accompanied first by a Dublin Quaker, James Perry, and then by one of the Commissioners of the Board of Works, Bright spent a month during August and September travelling about the country.[6] He journeyed from Dublin to Wexford, Cork, Kerry, Limerick, Tipperary, Connaught and back to the capital. In his diary and letters he painted a picture of almost unrelieved gloom and despondency.[7]

> The proprietors [he wrote to his wife] are nearly all
> bankrupt, great numbers of farmers are gone away —
> thousands of the peasantry are in the workhouse or in their
> graves. I believe we can form no fair idea of what has passed

in these districts within the last 4 years & I see no great
prospect of solid improvement. Here we have in perfection
the fruits of aristocratic & territorial usurpation & privilege &
unless these restrictions are removed, industry will be as
hitherto, impossible.

Bright was agreeably surprised to find that on a number of
occasions 'demonstrations' welcomed him. It was pleasant and
unusual to be appreciated.

Cobden was never slow to see the political potential in any
situation. No sooner had Bright landed than he wanted to know
whether there was 'any prospect of the Liberal men in the
House being able to join with the Irish party upon some
rational principle of co-operation.' Bright was hopeful, reporting his favourable reception and the fact that his speeches on
Ireland were well known. There was some talk of a 'practical
party' in Ireland and they could expect more steady and cordial
support from Irish members than in the past. There was
indeed a 'great field of usefulness in these Irish questions —
the whole population are with us on the franchise & the Tenant question & except the Orangemen, on the Church too.'
Even the tenants of the north might support his proposed
'Tenant Security Bill' since, while they had custom on their
side, they did not have legal security. He had formed a small
committee in Dublin to help him frame the bill. Writing to one
of them, a Quaker, Jonathan Pim, he made a point of claiming
that 'English members are often as well acquainted with Irish
questions as Irishmen themselves.' He had, indeed, been
claiming for years that Irish members neglected their opportunities in the House of Commons and had failed to lay on the
table of the House 'any one measure which they believe to be
necessary to the prosperity of their country'. In dismissing the
charge that Englishmen could not understand Ireland he
staked a claim for the leadership of that country,[8]

The more I see and read of Ireland [he concluded] the more I
am astonished at the incapable and imbecile character of our
statesmen and the more thoroughly am I convinced that our
aristocratic institutions are the great barriers which time and

ignorance and selfishness have opposed to the welfare and
progress of the nation.

He could do better.

'I am reading about Ireland & thinking about her almost continually', he wrote to Rachel Priestman in mid-October 1849. If
England had no connexion with Ireland, its problems would
soon be settled in the blood of its proprietary classes — a
development which he sometimes thought preferable. The
basic trouble, as always, was aristocratic government, which
would see people perish by thousands rather than yield anything. In November, he addressed a long letter to the Prime
Minister declaring that parliament should enact against entail
or any kind of settlement which tied up property beyond the
lives of persons actually mentioned in the will or deed. Similarly, parliament should insist that estates be divided among all
the heirs of a deceased person. The existing practice prevented
the best use of land by frequently burdening it with charges
which often thwarted development. Further, in order to facilitate transfer of land, the stamps on deeds of sale should be
abolished or minimized. Tenants should have 'a claim upon
the owner for compensation equal to a certain number of years'
purchase of the increased net annual letting value which has
accrued to the farm.' He was thinking of investment in building, draining, fencing and reclamation of bog. The enormous
pauperism of Ireland made this question 'infinitely important'.[9]
He also spoke in public on Ireland, urging the Irish to work out
their own salvation; in doing so, they could count on the support of the 'great Free Trade party'.[10]

He continued to discuss the land question with Irishmen,
particularly with Jonathan Pim, throughout 1850. He willingly
relayed petitions on tenant right, replying to the senders that
he was anxious for a just bill on the subject. In June 1850, he
reported to Pim that he had his own bill in draft, commenting
that it was marvellous that landlords and government could
contemplate leaving the question unsettled for another year.
Nothing much happened partly because, to his dismay, Bright
was outflanked by the formation, in the summer of 1850, of the
Tenant League. Frederick Lucas, John Gray and Gavan Duffy,
the leaders, called for the three 'f's' — fair rent, free sale and

84

fixity of tenure. Bright wrote to Cobden in October expressing annoyance that the League was complicating a question already difficult enough. It was disgusting to see men like Lucas — his brother-in-law Samuel Lucas's brother and a convert to Catholicism — lending themselves to such impostures. In the same month, he told Villiers that the Irish were again being hoodwinked and cheated. They were seeking what they could not get, and what, even if they could get it, would do them no good. On another occasion, however, he suppressed his irritation at the perversity of the Irish in ignoring his advice and conceded that the Tenant League was good in so far as it brought Catholic and Protestant together in one cause. If the Tenant Leaguers failed in their attempt to interfere with free competition in land, they would be compensated 'if they learn to know & to respect each other'. It was a pious hope. A year later, he had to confess to Cobden that the distrust which existed in Ireland was extreme and each party seemed to believe no good of the rest. There was a possibility, however, that if the Tenant League did fail, Bright could take the initiative on Irish matters.

The other issue on which Bright concentrated in these years was India. His committee of inquiry into cotton production in 1848 had been unproductive. Its report had stated that Indian cotton had a high potential which was not being realized, in part because of transport difficulties. Bright took up the matter again in 1850 when, acting as spokesman for the Manchester Chamber of Commerce, he pressed for a Royal Commission on the subject, explaining that although his committee had examined many witnesses, more information was needed. In a lengthy speech on 18 June, he stressed how precarious the supplies of cotton were. Anticipating that his plan might be seen as an attack on the East India Company, whose charter was to expire in 1854, he denied any such intention, stating simply that the investigation would benefit both Britain and India. The request was refused. Sir John Hobhouse undermined Bright's position by revealing that the Manchester Commercial Association did not support the Manchester Chamber of Commerce in this matter.[11] Bright was undaunted. He told Cobden in October that he was reading Indian history,

although the subject was so vast and the chance of doing anything so small that he feared he was wasting his time. However, Bazley, the President of the Manchester Chamber, with
his support, was establishing a fund to pay for a private investigation in India. Alexander Mackay, a barrister, was chosen
for the mission and Bright briefed him before his departure. He
repeated that Mackay's task was neither political nor philan-
thropical, but purely commercial. Naturally, politics could not
be ignored, but he had to concentrate on the cotton question.
Travelling widely, he should immerse himself in the problems
of land tenure, labour supply, and communications. 'You are
not', he stressed, 'departed to India as the enemy of the *Indian*
Govt, but as the *friend* of Indian industry and the Indian people.' His final request was that Mackay should discover 'how
far Bishops and Clergymen sent from England are converting
the natives & how far their labours are worth the effort in time
and money.'[12] Unfortunately, Mackay died in India towards
the end of his tour. His report was subsequently published,
but the 'Manchester Commission' was a disappointment.
When Bright did return to the subject of India, he tackled
political as well as commercial matters.

Bright's concern for Ireland and India, while genuine, was
quite natural for a Lancashire MP. His stance on these questions, however, was also part of his war on the Whigs. 'Bright
must come out with another great Irish speech', as Cobden put
it to Wilson in January 1850, so that they might go to parliament 'in a position to be able to claim the great body of the
Irish people as partisans of the Manchester school.' The orator
obliged, though he also used his Irish experience to reopen the
argument for a parliamentary reform campaign. The case, he
repeated, was more glaring and undeniable, if possible, than
the Free Trade cause ever was. 'With the Whigs in office', he
continued, 'we suffer greatly & our only chance is to have
something well-defined which will draw a line between them
& us & this can only be had on the question of Reform.' Cobden remained convinced that the country, and the higher middle class especially, was unsympathetic.

The general political situation depressed Bright, particularly
since he had a number of family anxieties on his mind. In 1848,

Priscilla had married Duncan McLaren, the Edinburgh Radical, and John had not approved of the match. His objection to McLaren was not political but because Priscilla was his third wife, he was fifteen years older than his bride and he had children enough already. In 1849, his sister Esther married James Vaughan, a barrister, but she died a year later at the age of thirty. In March 1851, old Jacob Bright had a stroke and died shortly afterwards. Two years later, again at the age of thirty, his brother Gratton died in Italy. His own family, on the other hand, grew steadily. John Albert was born in 1848, Mary Harriet in 1849 and William Leatham in 1851. As for Helen, it was delightful, he wrote to his wife in February 1851, to know that they passed pleasant evenings reading together. If Helen read without leaning forward, he suggested, 'that is, occasionally standing up, & having her chest expanded, it may do her lungs great good, but not too much of it.' Besides Helen's lungs, there was also the poultry yard for the MP for Manchester to worry about. 'When I come down', he promised, 'if not before, we must try to get rid of the rats.' However, in the same letter, which extolled the merits of the Great Exhibition — 'a wonderful sight' — Bright announced that he wanted, if his wife did not mind, to go to Paris in August. Leaving the rats in Rochdale, therefore, he attended a fête for English visitors and was introduced to Louis Napoleon. French people, he reported, lived out of doors during the summer, but there was 'no grossness, no drunkenness and no vice visible — which is precisely opposite to what is seen everywhere in London'.

Bright had departed from Paris convinced by the parliamentary session that if Russell was overthrown and a Tory government formed, 'it would give a tremendous impetus to the advancing & really Liberal party.' Peel was now considered a model statesman and his death, in July 1850, was described by Bright as a tragedy. It was Russell's behaviour over the restoration of the Roman Catholic hierarchy that particularly disgusted Bright. 'Our real danger', he wrote to his sister-in-law Margaret, 'is in the Church Established and not in any Church not established. Nonconformists are the only bulwark against the growth of Popery & in proportion as they take sides with the Establishment they are less useful & safe as bulwarks.' Wiseman's vindication of the creation of a Catholic hierarchy he described as 'masterly and unanswerable'. He could conceive nothing more contemptible than the spectacle of a Nonconformist minister lending himself to a cry which was intended 'not so much to discredit Popery because it is Popery, as because it threatens the ascendancy of the English & Irish Establishments.'[13] In the Commons, he mocked both the Prime Minister and the Church of England with delightful humour. Honourable members knew that he was no friend to the bishops of any Church, but if the Anglican Church found them necessary why should not the Roman? — 'To talk of this nation, its Crown and independence, being menaced by a petty sovereign or prince at Rome, is really too ludicrous.' He poured scorn on a Church of England 'having 15,000 learned clergymen for its guidance and control, thrown into a paroxysm of terror, and all that by a Church which, in these realms, has not the thousandth part of the advantages possessed by its opponents.' On the evidence of this particular episode, he thought privately that Lord John was sinking into a state of 'hopeless imbecility', nevertheless, the government continued in existence and the parliamentary session had been 'a truly disgusting waste of time to all of us'.

Even so, Bright continued to urge upon Cobden that 'a *leading* is only wanted to produce a great *following*' and that they were equipped to provide it. Cobden remained discouraging, failing to observe any breeze in the direction of Reform. In a letter to Sturge on 26 November 1851, Bright was compelled to admit that it was quite impracticable to talk in terms of manhood suffrage. He had never adopted the term himself. What he favoured was 'the widest extension of the franchise which will meet with any fair amount of acceptance from the public.' If he were a minister, he would propose a rating suffrage with a twelve months residential qualification together with payment of poor rate six months prior to the compilation of the list. His restrictions, he claimed, were not directed against any class, and his proposal was designed 'to bring up the middle & richer classes . . . to as great a measure as possible'.

Meanwhile, the government at last seemed to be getting into difficulties. Palmerston, the Foreign Secretary, was behaving with even more than his customary jauntiness. Towards the end of December 1851, Lord John succeeded in forcing his resignation. The Foreign Secretary had once more offended the Court by expressing his approval of Louis Napoleon's *coup d'état* in France. Bright was delighted that the supposed friend of constitutional government all over Europe had come out badly. *'Perhaps'*, he concluded, 'we who were hooted & bullied last year were not wrong?' He was referring to the famous Don Pacifico debate of the previous summer when Palmerston had carried the day against speeches from Gladstone, Peel and Cobden. The Foreign Secretary had espoused the claims of a rather disreputable Iberian Jew against the Greek government. Don Pacifico had been born in Gibraltar and Palmerston declared that a British subject, wherever he was, ought to feel that the watchful eye and strong arm of England would protect him. His opponents accused Palmerston of bullying and indifference to the rights of small nations. It was inevitable that Bright should vote against the government. Not to have done so, he noted in his journal, would have been inconsistent with his past and destroy whatever influence he might have in the future. What was most disturbing, however, was the support Palmerston had received on this occasion from 'our friends in the Radical ranks'. It was a warning that the 'popular' party might founder on foreign policy. Bright and Cobden both saw Free Trade as a prelude to a completely commercial foreign policy — John never specifically based his attitude on the peace tenets of the Society of Friends. Indeed, he steered clear of the Peace Society and in the summer of 1850 said that he was too busy to attend the international Peace Conference at Frankfurt.[14] He realized how unpopular his vote against the government on Don Pacifico had been in certain Manchester quarters but he was quite determined, as he wrote in his journal, that he would not be 'a mere joint of a Whig tail'.

Such defiance was good for his morale, but did he have any alternative? In the competition for middle-class support, Palmerston appeared to be winning. Even in Manchester, more and more businessmen were coming to feel that a firm foreign policy in the Near and Far East greatly benefited cotton exports. Bright and Cobden could not compete with the popularity Palmerston had gained from his clever handling of the visit to London by the Hungarian rebel leader, Kossuth. His surprising resignation, therefore, put some fresh heart into

A *BRIGHT* IDEA!

The Peace Recruiting Sergeant Trying to Enlist the Duke.

Bright, though Cobden was as gloomy as ever, stating that
even if they were in power they could not carry the country if
they tried to put their policies into action. The rift between
Russell and Palmerston, however, suggested to Bright that the
Whigs would be broken up 'out of which great good would

come'. It was also encouraging that Lord John was attempting to demonstrate to his colleagues that a little Reform Bill would not do great harm. He did not think much would come of this attempt since the Whigs were 'a decayed party, a tradition merely & I think the sooner they are "abolished" the better for progress in liberal government.'

Bright's judgment that the government would not long survive proved correct. On 20 February 1852, Palmerston's amendment to a Militia Bill was carried and the following day the government resigned. 'Happily this time', he wrote to his wife, 'there is no hope of the Whigs coming back to office & we shall take care they never come back in their present shape.' The six years since the repeal of the Corn Laws had not seen the effective moulding of the 'middle-class spirit' into a coherent political movement. Nevertheless, with the political situation once again excitingly uncertain, Bright turned to the game of politics with renewed zest.

SEVEN

Isolation and defeat 1852-7

Derby and Disraeli formed a Conservative government in place of Russell, but, lacking a parliamentary majority, it only existed on sufferance. Lord John tried unsuccessfully to repair his relations with Palmerston on the one hand and Graham on the other. Bright now found himself in a stronger position at Westminster than he had ever been before. For the first time in his career, he found himself being courted by the leading politicians. Disraeli never ruled out any alliance if it suited his purposes and suspected that Bright might not be as averse to some kind of deal as his rhetorical righteousness might suggest. The two men had dined out together as early as 1850, when Disraeli hinted that he accepted Free Trade as a permanent solution. Bright described him as a 'strange fellow' and waited. Lord John, for his part, purported to believe that Free Trade would not be safe if the Tories were in power as well as in office. He also talked timidly of Reform. Bright, of course, did not want the result of an election to jeopardize Free Trade, but that did not make him obsequious. He met the 'little man' in mid-March 1852 and told Wilson that he 'seemed much disposed to fraternise with the Manchester men', though he added sceptically 'but in more prosperous times his old complaint will probably return.' It was therefore essential, he wrote to Baines in mid-April, to make the ballot a condition of their future support. Bright was in an unusually cheerful mood, writing to his wife that both in politics and business everything seemed going on pretty favourably. There was even a chance that businessmen rather than untrustworthy lawyers might increase their representation in the House.

The Tories dissolved in the summer. Bright and Gibson defeated their Tory opponents in Manchester, but the ease of their victory was deceptive. In his five years as member, Bright had done little to ingratiate himself with the city's social élite. He was not a Manchester man and did not care for such expressions of civic pride as the purchase of robes for the corporation. John Potter, newly knighted and fresh from a third year as mayor, might well have stood in 1852 had he not been deterred by the possible threat to Free Trade which a Derby government might pose.[1] An arrangement with the Tories was also unlikely while they dabbled with 'no popery'. Ignoring these considerations, however, Bright pointed to the results as another triumph for the 'popular' party.

In the country as a whole, Derby and Disraeli strengthened their position considerably and the Peelites lost ground. The obvious solution for the Opposition seemed for the Whigs and Peelites to fuse, but the person of Lord John seemed a stumbling block. Since Palmerston would not serve under Russell, Irish votes would be crucial. Parliament would assemble in December, and in the interval the various factions tried to strengthen their position. Bright believed that a Russell government could not survive if it were 'merely Whig'. Having stated this opinion, he went off to Scotland for a holiday. Passing the lodge at Lord John Russell's house near Callander, late in August, he left his card to remind the little man that Radical pressure could not be ignored. Later, he had the pleasure of encountering Lord John jogging gently along on his pony and they talked politics for a while. Russell said that it was clear that Derby would not be able to go on. Bright said that the same would be true of his successor. The impasse would not be removed until a better system of representation was obtained. Cobden, convinced that they could only expect obstruction from Russell, was not impressed by this encounter. Parliamentary reform apart, he argued, they had more to gain from the Tories or Peelites than from the Whigs. In reply, Bright stated that he would not keep Derby in, merely to keep

Russell out. The next government, whatever its label, would have to be more forceful than the last 'and in its foundation certainly some negotiation with us will be needful & I think the radicals will be strong enough to gain something considerable.'

It was partly in order to consolidate this strength that Bright consented to attend a banquet in Belfast in September. Such a dinner was a nuisance, but it was advisable not to throw away any chance of uniting Irish and English Liberal politics. In February, he had supported Sharman Crawford's Tenant Right Bill, earning praise from the Tenant League for his speech. At the same time, he had issued an invitation to Irish members to co-operate with him. What would be ideal would be for the Tenant League and Crawford's followers in the north to reach an accommodation, with Bright as broker and spokesman. In Dublin, therefore, on his way north, he closeted himself with Frederick Lucas, now MP for Meath, to promote the idea. He spent ten days in the south, reading *Uncle Tom's Cabin* in his spare time. His travels reinforced his conviction that nothing less than an overhaul of the system of land tenure would improve the country's position. The Belfast dinner, well attended by leading Liberals, including Crawford, was a success. He was able to reassure Rachel Priestman that 'nobody seemed to take more wine than very *temperate* wine drinkers would sanction.' Belfast was refreshingly vigorous and made him optimistic. On the issue of tenant-right, he made a general appeal for co-operation between individuals even if they differed on points of detail. Not everybody was satisfied. It was conceded in the north that Bright was in advance of most English politicians, but issues like retrospective compensation and allowance for soil improvement could not be dismissed as of secondary importance. The *Northern Whig*, however, took the view that differences were slight and could be overcome. Bright was surprised to find that the Irish, whether as individuals or collected in a meeting, were just about as reasonable as the English. Nevertheless, he reported to J. B. Smith, relations between sects and parties in Ireland were more bitter than at any time since 1829.

At the end of October, Bright kept up his bid for Irish support with a long letter to the *Freeman's Journal* which had attacked him for not endorsing the proposal to compensate tenants retrospectively. He switched the subject of debate from the land to the church question. Equality, he contended, was essential between Roman Catholic, Protestant Episcopalian and Presbyterian. That could be achieved by endowing the Catholic and Presbyterian churches, but the better principle was that there should be no church in Ireland connected with the State. The financial problems could be resolved by setting up a 'Church Property Commission' which would have the tithes and other property of the Established Church in trust and make disbursements to the various ecclesiastical bodies. They would then have to depend on their own resources. The bulk of the fund would thus be made available for the educational and moral improvement of the people of Ireland. Since he did not belong to the churches involved, Bright hoped that his plan would be accepted as a dispassionate solution.[2]

It was not only Ireland that Bright had in mind in making this proposal; the principle could be applied in England too. 'That overgrown & monstrous abuse', the Church of England, might yet be undermined. The religious census of 1851 revealed the numerical strength of Dissent and, with Miall in parliament, an effective campaign might be waged. The doctrinal controversies within the church caused him amusement. 'The old political machine', he commented, 'which has made a pretence of being a Christian Church, is now being daily more exposed to the sight of its true character.'[3]

When parliament reassembled, the government's future was obviously precarious. Disraeli's budget was under heavy assault from Gladstone and others and he looked for support from any quarter. At ten o'clock on the evening of 15 December, he discussed the situation with John Bright, pointing out that if the Tory government survived this challenge, a vigorous reforming programme would be undertaken. He hinted that there could be room for Bright, Cobden and Gibson in the cabinet. Bright laughed. Putting aside the 'immorality' of such a scheme, Manchester would not allow it.[4] Disraeli retorted that a man of genius and power could do anything with a large constituency. Bright would not be drawn, noting in his diary that Disraeli seemed unable to understand that radicals were motivated by morality. In fact, the suggestion was not as 'immoral' as Bright pretended. His feelings about the

Whigs need no repetition, even if Russell was temporarily being friendly. The Peelites, he told Wilson on 26 November, were a shabby 'undecided' lot. That only left the Tories. Disraeli's approach, however, was too obviously that of a desperate minister in a dying administration.

The difficulty of forming a new government, Bright reported to Wilson, was so great as to be 'positively ludicrous'. A combination of Whigs and Peelites 'would be most advantageous if we were ambitious & ultimately for the country it might do no permanent harm.' It did, indeed, occur. Lord Aberdeen was Prime Minister, Gladstone at the Exchequer, Russell at the Foreign Office and Palmerston at the Home Office. Sir William Molesworth, a Radical, was made First Commissioner of Works but, while appreciating the gesture, Bright thought Molesworth would be ineffective on his own. He could understand why neither Cobden nor himself had been included, but he thought Villiers should have been asked. 'The man whom Sir Robert Peel followed', he wrote to Russell, 'is somewhat better I think than a man who merely followed Sir Robert Peel.'[5] Villiers did subsequently achieve minor office. Bright took heart from the fact that, in his opinion, Molesworth's entry into the cabinet was an indication that the Radicals could not be disregarded. While Cobden found the situation so depressing that he contemplated withdrawing from public life, Bright argued that they had to maintain 'a distinct policy — steady, right, not factious, but quite independent' and they would soon find themselves able to make progress. One of the things he had in mind was the secret ballot, but he found Russell and Graham spoke strongly against it. If Lord John so disliked secrecy, he remarked sarcastically, he would surely invite a reporter from *The Times* to attend the next cabinet.

Cobden had written that he was 'sick of this everlasting attempt *out of doors* to give the semblance of an agitation which does not exist' and Bright sympathized. He had been in parliament for nearly a decade but while he might make speeches on Ireland or the Ecclesiastical Titles Bill he was little nearer influencing the decisions of government than when he first entered the Commons. Britain remained a country 'where accident of birth is supreme over almost every description & degree of merit.' Revived commercial prosperity fed social ambition rather than reforming zeal amongst his own acquaintances — and he felt the pressures himself. His brother-in-law, W. H. Leatham, already an Anglican, had become a Deputy Lieutenant in Yorkshire — an 'absurd appointment' in Bright's view. John himself, however, rented a good house for the 1853 session and when his wife and three children came down to join him they were naturally accompanied by two nursemaids. He met the new Prime Minister and others in the cabinet at a 'rather distingué' party given by Molesworth and tried to reassure his wife that he was not being acted upon by 'the Grandees'.

It was in these circumstances, when the domestic mood seemed so flat, that Bright again turned to India in 1853. On this occasion, he began to consider the whole future of the sub-continent. The East India Company's charter expired in 1854 and a fresh India Act was required to renew or amend it. In his diary on 11 March 1853 he noted that he had spoken an hour and asked a question on the government's intentions for India. The Foreign Secretary thought Bright had taken a long time to raise his query! During the rest of March, Bright both pressed ministers and tried to arouse interest in the country. His object, he told Baines, was to prevent the further existence of the East India Company. The government seemed to be wavering and one more push might succeed. He argued that American slavery was involved, for a supply of cotton from India would give the first great blow to that evil institution. While British rule in India had been characterized by war and plunder, together with titles and pensions for the marauders, it could be redeemed by giving freedom to the industry of the Indian population. For good measure, he added that 'peace, civilization & the success of missions are all deeply involved in this question.' He wrote in similar terms to Sturge in Birmingham, urging him to arrange meetings and speeches. Instead of the existing arrangements, there should be a Secretary of State for India with a permanent council of five able men to advise him. They would be responsible to parliament as other branches of government were. Bright became a leading member of the India Reform Society, formed in mid-March, but he was not very satisfied with the agitation. 'I wish some new speakers would come out', he wrote in mid-April, 'I never recollected a great question more entirely let down by those most deeply interested in it.'[6]

The Cabinet committee which considered the fate of India presented its report towards the end of May. It urged the retention of the Court of Directors, with certain changes in membership, but the Cabinet as a whole was uncertain. On 3 June, however, Sir Charles Wood, the President of the Board of Control, in a lengthy speech, defended both the British position in India and the system of dual government. He proposed minor changes in the composition of the Court and the establishment of a separate governorship of Bengal. Aware of the opposition he was likely to meet, Wood had written to Lord Dalhousie, the Governor-General, asking him for information on railways. Cotton, he wrote, was all that the Manchester people cared for, and if he could satisfy them on this subject, they would be kept 'in good humour'. When Bright rose to speak, he had not been appeased. He condemned the government for failing to seize an opportunity to undertake a fundamental reformation of Indian government. 'I never spoke', he noted complacently, 'with more ease and satisfaction.' He received so many compliments when he sat down that he was forced to ask himself whether he was more pleased with his success than with his likely impact on Indian policy.[7] He did not answer his question. 'Just up to the standard of Whig imbecility' was his general verdict in a letter to Baines. The new court was scarcely, if at all, an improvement and any administrative change ought to have been in the direction of responsible government. However, although Cobden joined in the attack on the East India Company, 'that nest of jobbers', only 140 members were found to oppose the bill. Bright consoled himself with the reflection that the passage of twenty years would prove who was right; few guessed that a day of reckoning was much nearer.

Important though the Indian question was, to some extent it was already overshadowed, in the late spring of 1853, by general concern about the 'Eastern Question'. For months, the Russians had been pressing for Ottoman recognition of their claim to protect the rights of Orthodox Christians in the Empire, but it had been refused. In the wider international context, relations between Napoleon III and the Tsar were bad, and the Austrians were uneasy. Lord Aberdeen was cautious and pacific, but Palmerston and Russell were less restrained. The result was a vacillating and uncertain foreign policy. It is, indeed, arguable that had Palmerston been in charge, he might both have avoided war, and maintained the integrity of Turkey, by a firm yet conciliatory attitude.

At the end of May 1853, claiming to be against British intervention, Molesworth had a private word with Bright about the 'Turkish difficulties'. Bright declared that if war broke out, Constantinople would inevitably fall to the Russians. Having made his position clear, he does not seem to have taken a very lively interest in the problem. The Russians, however, kept up their pressure and invaded the principalities of Moldavia and Wallachia, taking themselves in July to the mouth of the Danube. Encouraged by certain newspapers, popular anti-Russian feeling in Britain was growing, but Aberdeen had opposed Palmerston's suggestion, made before the invasion, that Britain should immediately send a fleet into the Black Sea if the Russians did launch an attack. Aware of rumours of Cabinet dissension, Bright commented privately that it was difficult to see how Aberdeen and Palmerston could co-operate. He was, however, complacent about the situation, writing both in his diary and in letters that war was most unlikely. Lord Clarendon had written a note, which Bright found reassuring, stating that war between Britain and Russia, arising out of the Eastern Question, was not to be contemplated. Cobden was much more agitated, entering into debate with Palmerston and Russell on the issues at stake. Bright congratulated him on these speeches, but continued to exude confidence. There was no case for fighting Russia, and that was that. He was eager to get back to Rochdale at the close of the parliamentary session for he had bought a barouche and a magnificent chestnut to pull it; he simply needed an opportunity to show it off.

Duncan and Priscilla McLaren visited Rochdale in August (and no doubt admired the barouche), but McLaren chiefly tried to interest Bright in a big Peace Conference he planned to hold in Edinburgh in October. He found his brother-in-law curiously non-committal. In fact, despite his Quaker principles, Bright was not very enthusiastic about either the Peace Society or Peace Conferences. It is true that he addressed a meeting at

99

the Corn Exchange in Manchester in January on the subject of International Arbitration. Bright himself, however, described this speech as 'without preparation, but so as to please the friends of peace present'. He had contented himself with a general exposition of the obvious merits of settling disputes by arbitration rather than by war. The following month, he told his wife that Cobden was taking him to talk about 'peace' with Samuel Gurney, but he did not see 'much use in it'. In April, he grumpily declined to send Sturge a subscription to be used by the Peace Society, stating that he already gave his time and £500 a year to the public and would give no more. It was Cobden again, in a letter on 10 September, who told Bright that he ought to attend the Edinburgh Conference, not only in the interest of peace, but in fairness to McLaren. A week later, however, having taken Helen back to school in Brighton, he departed for a jaunt round northern France. The ostensible purpose of the trip was to discover evidence of Napoleon III's peaceful intentions towards Britain. In fact, for three weeks, he gave himself a pleasant holiday in Brittany and the Loire, without his family, though he dutifully reported his progress to Rochdale. Even so, his obsessions did not leave him. From Cherbourg, he felt compelled to write to Wilson informing him, by no means for the first time, that ignorance, poverty, pauperism and crime were the price that England paid for a territorial House of Lords. He found the French people content and not under the impression that they were living under what some English papers called an 'insupportable tyranny'. On this occasion, however, Paris did not please him since there were so many idle people on its boulevards and so much drinking at the doors of cafés. There was so much 'unintelligible "jabber" of conversation' — presumably French — that he felt almost stifled by it. The truth was, of course, that he was enjoying a little idleness himself.

When he returned to Britain he could not avoid going up to Edinburgh, much as he would have liked to. His speech there, in October 1853, was not in any way an analysis of the Eastern Question, being for the most part concerned with generalities about the expense and unpleasantness of war. He denounced a standing army as completely unnecessary and unchristian. Instead of splitting hairs about burning candles on the altar, or about the amount of labour a man might do on the Sabbath, the churches ought to attack the war machine. He was almost ashamed to belong to a country which conducted itself like a tribe of Red Indians. As far as the immediate situation was concerned, he did not believe the government wanted war, but they nevertheless allowed themselves to be the promoters of a false opinion and servants of the powerful military interest.[8] Afterwards, Bright was pleased with his speech and even enjoyed the occasion — it had, indeed, been something of a family party, with Mrs McLaren entertaining about forty people in her house for the duration.

Bright's Edinburgh speech, delivered with such reluctance before an audience which included nine MP's, was not the prelude to a personal campaign on the danger of war. For the next six months, he was most concerned about parliamentary reform. A number of ministers were now prepared to take up the question and in late November 1853 a Cabinet committee considered the possibilities. Through Molesworth, Bright put his case. He urged that Russell's proposal to reduce the borough franchise to £6 and the county to £10 or £20, together with some redistribution of seats, was 'the least they could do'. The scheme to preserve the £10 borough franchise, advocated by *The Times*, was 'purposely adopted to exclude the *whole working classes* & so directed, it was partial, unjust & might, if continued, be dangerous.'[9] Bright admitted that a great number of people were not fit to have votes, or would not benefit the country if they did, but there were also well-qualified people who were excluded. He argued against *The Times* even though the paper gave as one of its arguments that 'turnout workmen' were not to be trusted with votes. On the other hand, he firmly supported the employers in the major strike at Preston to which the paper was referring. 'The battle', he wrote to Cobden on 5 November, 'must be fought out, when combinations are entered into. When once the natural adjustment of wages is departed from, then there remains only to learn who is the strongest.' In trying to raise a movement in support of parliamentary reform, Bright as usual had no encouragement from Cobden, who believed that the Turkish question would become so important that the public mind would not think about anything else. It was particularly sad for

101

him to have to admit that the 'so-called Radicals of the old school' seemed to be more keen on intervention than either the aristocracy or the government.

The development of the Turkish crisis seemed to confirm Cobden's judgment. Turkey had already declared war on Russia and moved its fleet into the Black Sea. The Russians, who were supposed to have undertaken not to take the offensive during the winter, nevertheless attacked, destroying the Turks at Sinope on 30 November. News of this 'Sinope massacre' reached London on 11 December. Four days later, Palmerston's resignation from the Cabinet was announced. His opposition to the reform proposals and intention to withdraw had been known to the Prime Minister before the news from Sinope. The public, however, supposed that Palmerston disagreed with the Cabinet's foreign policy — an impression he did nothing to eradicate. Calculating that it would make the government more responsive to Liberal views, Bright was 'heartily glad' about the resignation. He considered Palmerston to be a clever and unscrupulous impostor, bent on forming a combination of Tories and country gentlemen to bring the government down. Bright hoped that the 'democratic dupes', who had followed Palmerston in the past, would now see him in his true light. But, if that was Palmerston's stratagem, it was clear by the end of the month that it had failed. Bright feared that he would attempt to slip back into the government, and that parliamentary reform would be modified to receive him. In a short time, indeed, Palmerston did return. In this fluid situation, Bright kept trying to persuade Cobden that they had a duty to keep public opinion 'onward' if they could. He was in fact successfully induced to address a Reform banquet at Sheffield — 'not so well as usual, the subject of Reform not being so familiar to him as economical questions', was Bright's comment in his diary. When Bright, Cobden and Gibson spoke in Manchester early in the new year, they made it clear that, national emergency or not, they expected a Reform Bill. They were perhaps surprised to find that Lord John Russell agreed with them.

These confident public speeches masked internal forebodings. At the end of December 1853, Bright conceded to Cobden that war seemed to be more likely. The government had committed itself to Turkey and there was little prospect of Russia turning tail. If the worst should happen, he had no doubt that their own position would become one of acute isolation. He expected to be hooted down in the House. 'Losing a Reform Bill & gaining a war', he commented sadly, 'I don't see how we could be worse placed.' In the end, of course, they would be vindicated, but that was a long way off. Remote in Rochdale, he raged to Villiers against Palmerston and the insult contained in the fact that he sat on their side of the house. Depressed both by the international situation and by the sudden death of his brother Gratton, it was an apprehensive Bright who came up for the new session of parliament at the end of January 1854.

He dined at Lord Granville's on 8 February in a small party which included the Prime Minister and the Bishop of Oxford, recording afterwards that both Aberdeen and Granville were strong for peace but they thought the country violent for war. The Prime Minister, he was pleased to learn, believed that the much-used phrase 'the independence and integrity of Turkey' had little meaning. His hopes of peace momentarily rose. On 18 February, however, he wrote to his wife that he was so disgusted at the immorality of government and people that he contemplated retiring from public life. 'I feel I must either allow myself to grow into indifference', he wrote prophetically, 'or else sustain an injury to my temper from the disgust with which I am filled.' He accosted Lord Granville in the street and reproached the government for its course. If the Greeks rose in rebellion, what a position the country would be in, fighting for the Turk to maintain his despotism over the European Christian subjects! The absurdity of the situation, as he saw it, threatened to overwhelm him. 'We have helped to set up the Pope', he lamented to Rachel Priestman, '& now we are to set up Mahomet!' All of this by ministers from whom much was expected! He almost despaired of his country — even the birth of another daughter on 1 March, his fourth child by his second wife, scarcely cheered him up.

The dinner at the Reform Club for Sir Charles Napier, commander of the Baltic Fleet, which took place on 7 March, was an indication of what lay ahead for Bright. The ultimatum to Russia had been sent (though it had not expired), and it was still conceivable that the Tsar would withdraw from the principalities. Palmerston, who presided at the dinner, and Graham, the First Lord of the Admiralty, who spoke, took it for granted that war would occur. Their language about Russia was boastful and swaggering. The Queen was upset by the tone of this occasion. So was Bright, even more so because Molesworth had been present. He was so agitated that he could not sleep and he resolved to raise the matter in the House. He denounced the reckless levity manifested by ministers of a civilized and Christian nation. Calling Bright 'the honourable and reverend gentleman', and brushing aside Cobden's protest, Palmerston bluntly told Bright that his opinion on his conduct was a matter 'of the most perfect indifference'. It was a foretaste of what was to come, but Bright still had not given up all hope. He stayed up until the small hours on 16 March, writing a last appeal to Lord Aberdeen to keep the country out of war. He suggested that Turkey might make concessions concerning the Christian populations to all the Christian Powers, rather than to Russia alone. He rejected the notion that the English people had made up their minds to go to war. A portion of the London press was strongly for it, but what he described as the quiet and more intelligent sections of the population had their doubts. He dreaded the collision with the United States which threatened, the probability of disputes with France when the two armies had to fight together, and the likelihood that Austria or Prussia, or both, would take sides with Russia. Finally, appealing directly to Aberdeen, he begged him to consider what the reputation of his ministry in history would be, if he went to war.[10]

The appeal, which was kept private, was to no avail. Aberdeen had an emotional conversation with Bright for half an hour, but offered no hope of avoiding war. After so much uncertainty, it came almost as a relief when war was officially declared on 27 March 1854. Bright buried himself in Blue Books on Near Eastern Affairs in preparation for a speech in the House of Commons. Four days later, he delivered the first of his four major speeches there against British involvement. He stated at the outset that he would not adopt the approach of a 'peace at any price' advocate. His opposition was based on grounds which were generally accepted in the House. It was plain to him that Turkey was in decline and the fatal mistake had been to encourage her in resisting Russian requests. He held no brief for Russia, but she had reason to complain because she did have rights and duties in the matter. Criticizing the role of the British Minister at the Porte, Lord Stratford de Redcliffe, he declared that it was tragic that Turkey had been allowed to reject the Vienna Note, drawn up by the four Ambassadors. At the Olmütz conference, the Tsar was quite sincere in his conduct. Russia had never intended to march on Constantinople, and he could hardly believe that members opposed the improvement in the status of the Christians who might at some stage establish their own state in Constantinople. More generally, he claimed that the whole notion of the 'balance of power' was a mischievous delusion, inherited from the past. The intervention of Britain in European wars was not only unnecessary but calamitous, with grave consequences for commerce and the economy. He was told that the war was popular, but for himself he did not trouble whether his conduct in parliament was popular or not. 'I care only', he concluded, 'that it shall be wise and just as regards the permanent interests of my country, and I despise from the bottom of my heart the man who speaks a word in favour of this war . . . merely because the press and a portion of the people urge the Government to enter into it.'[11]

Bright had little expectation that his words would change the government's mind; he wished primarily to 'clear himself from any participation' in a course which he believed to be evil. His fundamental proposition was that British interests were not involved and it was not his duty 'to make this country the knight-errant of the human race'. In this peroration, he painted a glowing picture of the benefits which might have been gained if the principle of non-intervention had been adopted. Britain would have been saved from much pauperism and become a garden, 'every dwelling might have been of marble, and every person who treads its soil might have been sufficiently educated.' In the circumstances of the spring of 1854, of course, there was little means of judging the accuracy of Bright's forecasts. His account of pre-war diplomacy seemed, to most of his contemporaries, far too uncritical of Russian actions. He seemed much more confident and trusting than

they were prepared to be. His estimate of the commercial consequences of the war, while serious if it proved correct, seemed
to put trade before all other considerations. Tennyson had
Bright in mind when he wrote of

> The Broad-brimmed hawker of holy things,
> Whose ear is cramm'd with his cotton, and rings
> Even in dreams to the chink of his pence.

Bright's isolation was almost complete; no anti-war group of
any significance existed in the Commons. Molesworth, who
continued to support the government, was described by Cobden as 'the most shameless political traitor I have yet met
with'. Many Radicals were attracted by the idea of a crusade
against Russia — Bright had to declare that he had 'sympathy
for the serfs of Russia' — and, initially at least, they were prepared to give encouragement to the ministers. In this situation,
therefore, Bright had three possible courses before him. He
could launch a speaking crusade in the country, he could
withdraw from public life or he could 'wait and see', intervening occasionally as events unfolded.

What most shocked Bright, in private, during the first summer of the war was how little common justice and humanity,
not to say Christianity, seemed to influence public opinion.
He wrote to Cobden and others reiterating that only the most
flagrant dishonesty or imbecility could have produced the war
— a comprehensive but not altogether illuminating explanation. The spectacle of the National Day of Prayer nauseated
him. 'Prayer for success', he noted, 'seems much like a gang
of burglars seeking the Divine blessing upon their guilty enterprises.'[12] Nevertheless, despite the attacks on him by cartoon-
ists and columnists, he still led a busy life. He dined with Cobden and Gibson, but also with Lord John Russell, Monckton
Milnes, the Duke of Newcastle and the Bishop of Oxford,
amongst others. He made no attempt to disguise his feelings,
but they in turn did not ostracize him socially. His chief occupation was to speculate upon the likely length of the conflict
with Delane of *The Times*, Disraeli, or anybody else he met at
dinner. He believed that the parties would be forced to reach a
settlement before six years. The likely solution would be for

Constantinople to become a free city, with the provinces forming an independent state under the protection of the Powers. It
is worth recalling that, nearly twenty years earlier, when Bright
visited the city he had not then been averse to it coming under
Russian influence — there is no need for this to be 'a lesson
learnt from Cobden'.[13] Indeed, the general disposition to
accept that Bright did not have a mind of his own, does not
rest on strong evidence. It is true that in November 1856 Cobden wrote that over 'the last two or three years I have made
him (Bright) my mouthpiece on many important questions,
and have given him budgets of facts and arguments upon the
war', but this statement does not come from the pen of a
detached observer. Cobden did indeed supply facts and figures, but Bright could, and did, read and select for himself; he
was not a mere 'mouthpiece'. Cobden's mind was more subtle
and reflective but the implied assumption that any acute
observation made by Bright was 'probably inspired by Cobden'
is only, at best, conjecture.[14] In his 31 March speech, for example, when he spoke about the growing strength of the United
States, Bright certainly expressed views which Cobden would
have shared, but he had his own family and commercial
sources of information about developments across the Atlantic.
Cobden, incurably didactic, liked to believe, until the end, that
he retained captive the 'speaking lieutenant' of 1841 but it was
a role which Bright had ceased to play since the time he had
become MP for Manchester.

It was his position in Manchester which was now in
jeopardy. While Bright resisted pleas from Sturge of Birmingham that a conference in favour of peace should be organized
— 'it may be best to rest quiet at present — when the war is
over, people will see its cost in lives and money' — he could
not endorse the Patriotic Fund set up to support the war. One
of his erstwhile supporters, Absalom Watkin, invited him to
Manchester to be present at a meeting in aid of the fund. Privately describing Watkin's invitation as 'a queer notion',
Bright's reply took the form of an open letter, dated 29
October, which had a wide circulation. Bright dismissed the
eighteenth-century Swiss jurist, Vattel, to whom Watkin
appealed for support, and addressed himself to asking why the
British government should have intervened in a dispute, three

thousand miles away, between two independent countries. It was obvious from the start that he could not think of any reason, but he made a detailed examination of the diplomatic Blue Books before saying so. The government's policy was marked with an imbecility 'perhaps without example'. It was wholly false to maintain the most immoral and filthy of all despotisms over one of the fairest portions of the earth.

> My doctrine [he stated] would have been non-intervention in this case. The danger of the Russian power was a phantom; the necessity of permanently upholding the Mahometan rule in Europe is an absurdity. Our love for civilization is a sham; and our sacrifices for freedom, when working out the behests of the Emperor of the French and coaxing Austria to help us, is a pitiful imposture.

The letter caused a storm in Manchester, but he claimed to be calm. 'Parliament is not a necessity for me', he wrote to a relative, '& I would gladly resign my seat rather than shut my mouth at such a time & on such a subject.' By early December 1854, he professed to have received over a hundred letters expressing approval of this letter; he did not reveal how many hostile ones arrived.

There was little in the letter which had not been spoken in the Commons in March. In the intervening months, however, the war had taken shape and the initial elation at the victories of Balaclava and Inkerman gave way to more sober reflection. Russell of *The Times* sent back graphic reports of the military incompetence in the Crimea. The ill-fated charge of the Light Brigade had a deep impact at home. Sebastopol was not taken. However, the disappointment did not lead to a movement for peace; quite the contrary. Bright found himself faced with the prospect of a hostile public meeting in Manchester. Initially, he was not going to attend, writing to Wilson that the best plan would be to arrange for someone well-disposed to speak and defend his consistency. If he did attend the meeting (which was supposed to denounce the letter to Watkin) his presence would not prevent a resolution being passed and a speech on the war 'would perhaps not be listened to with much patience'. Cobden, however, advised Bright to go and urged Wilson to try to pack the meeting, to be held on 18 December, with his supporters. Accordingly, Bright did change his mind, though with no enthusiasm. As predicted, the scene in the Town Hall was so crowded and noisy that no one could be heard and no vote was taken. Afterwards, Bright spoke to his supporters in the League Rooms, claiming that the scheme to damage him had totally failed. In fact, however, he deceived himself about the strength of his position in Manchester. His old enemies in the city were determined to unseat him and his old associates were wavering. Mark Philips, for example, declined to be present at a soirée planned for Bright and Gibson in the new year. The writing was on the wall.

Nevertheless, he returned to Westminster and, four days later, speaking as 'a plain and simple citizen, sent here by one of the foremost constituencies of the Empire' he defended Cobden from attacks made on him by Lord John Russell. At the close, nevertheless, he returned to a personal statement.

Let it not be said [he declared, despite his recent unhappy experiences] that I am alone in my condemnation of this war, and of this incapable and guilty Administration. And even if I were alone, if mine were a solitary voice, raised amid the din of arms and the clamours of a venal press, I should have the consolation I have to-night — and which I trust will be mine to the last moment of my existence — the priceless consolation that no word of mine has tended to promote the squandering of my country's treasure or the spilling of one single drop of my country's blood.

In other parts of the speech, he was both amusing and grave. He particularly singled out the 'signs of improvement' detected in the Turk by ministers and by Palmerston in particular. They had indeed got up an army 'which the Government, so far as I can hear, has since permitted to be almost destroyed.' He conceded that another sign of improvement, perhaps, was 'that they have begun to wear trowsers; but as to their commerce, their industry, or their revenue, nothing can be in a worse condition.' Then, gravely, he turned to the sad fate of an MP who had gone out to the Crimea leaving a large young family behind: 'The stormy Euxine is his grave; his wife is a widow, his children fatherless.' Bright's skill as a speaker lay in his capacity to produce such a simple yet eloquent statement soon after a passage when he had been mocking the government. It drove home the point that lives were at stake, and what followed showed his political skill. Sir Robert Peel, when he had addressed the House on an occasion when a dispute might have led to hostilities with the United States, had shown great gravity of countenance and solemnity of tone, 'his whole demeanour showing that he felt in his soul the responsibility that rested with him.' It was up to the Peelites in the government, he implied without saying, to separate themselves from the egregious flippancy of some of their colleagues.

However impressive the speech, 'You and I and Gibson', he wrote to Cobden, 'are but three men'. They could give some trouble but if only some more of their parliamentary colleagues who were there 'chiefly through our labors' would help they could cause a lot more. Cobden found consolation in the military and administrative incompetence displayed in the Crimea. It might even have the outcome of inducing the middle class to throw off aristocratic rule and govern themselves. 'The Whigs', wrote Bright in a survey of the political scene on 18 January 1855, 'are very much averse to Gladstone and the Peelites & yet without them & us, they cannot make a Govt of any strength. . . .' It was clear that the government was in difficulty but he thought it would survive. However, when parliament reassembled, the Radical member for Sheffield, Roebuck, moved for a Select Committee of Inquiry into the condition of the army before Sebastopol. This motion brought disagreements in the Cabinet to a pitch. Russell resigned, Newcastle renewed his offer to resign and Palmerston repeated that he was prepared to try administering the War Department. In the end, the Prime Minister decided that the entire Cabinet would have to resign. The Queen asked Aberdeen to stay his hand, but when Roebuck's motion was passed by a substantial majority on 29 January 1855, he did resign. Bright did not vote, his feelings being very mixed. Lord John, he thought, had behaved very badly in deserting his colleagues in the hour of their peril. At one point, he had been tempted to vote with Aberdeen as 'most likely to make peace' — Roebuck's motion, after all, was 'in the sense of more war'. 'It is pleasant', he wrote to his wife with satisfaction, 'to see the quagmire into which the war has landed everybody except our small band. . . .'

'Palmerston Prime Minister! What a hoax!' wrote Bright in his diary. The aged 'charlatan' had indeed achieved his ambition, but Bright could not understand how a septagenarian was expected to redeem the situation. The only encouraging aspect was that the new Prime Minister would be utterly discredited unless he achieved an armistice and made peace very soon. He admitted, however, that even Palmerston could not carry all the burden of guilt. The people, too, seemed to think nothing of their destruction of Britain's 'ancient ally'. Cobden agreed. The appointment of the 'exploded sham' was the proof that the nation was in a state of senility. Comment on foreign affairs either took the old aristocratic line of 'balance of power', or the equally unsound line 'adopted by our so-called "democrats" on behalf of Mazzini and the "nationalities"'.

Palmerston got off to a bad start. His first speeches created such a poor impression that Bright believed the country would soon share his opinion that the Prime Minister was 'a bubble and a sham'. 'Everything is again in confusion', he wrote home on 22 February, 'Gladstone, Graham, Herbert and Canning are out.' He had even heard that Palmerston had resigned. Gladstone entered into a solemn correspondence with Bright about where he should sit in the Commons now that he had left the government. 'I think we could do something if we could go together', Bright commented to Wilson.

At this juncture, Bright formed the impression that the chances of peace were considerable. In December 1854, the Austrian government had agreed with Britain and France to summon a conference at Vienna to seek peace on the basis of 'Four Points' — the Tsar would be required to give up his protectorate over Moldavia and Wallachia, allow freedom of navigation on the Danube, agree to the Ottoman Christians being put under a general European guarantee, and accept a revision of the 1841 Straits Convention to give Turkey greater security in the Black Sea. If Russia did not agree to such a peace, Austria would join the Allies. Lord John Russell would represent the British government at the negotiations which would take place in Vienna during March and April. Bright's third speech, delivered on 23 February was therefore almost conciliatory in tone. He almost regretted the resignations on the grounds that the government was weakened. Perhaps the only man in the country who could really bring peace was the Prime Minister and he should have the courage to take his opportunity.

> The Angel of Death [he concluded] has been abroad throughout the land; you may almost hear the beating of his wings. There is no one, as when the first-born were slain of old, to sprinkle with blood the lintel and the two side-posts of our doors, that he may spare and pass on; he takes his victims from the castle of the noble, the mansion of the wealthy, and the cottage of the poor and lowly, and it is on behalf of all these classes that I make this solemn appeal.

It was perhaps the most celebrated passage in any of Bright's speeches. The biblical reference was readily grasped by his audience. The members were again caught by his simple, well-balanced phrasing. Its tone, too, impressed opponents as being more 'statesmanlike' than his previous wartime speeches. A stage had been reached in which, whatever the justice of the war, all parties were ready to accept the consequences of death — even from Bright. The speaker was not the least of those who were pleased with the performance. He hoped also that some of the 'late animosities' in Manchester might be appeased.

Bright returned to his constituency and gave speeches in early March and early April. He dwelt upon the demoralizing aspect of the war and attacked the doctrine of 'constant intervention' as a hindrance to the country's prosperity. On the whole, he was pleased with his reception, believing too that the difficulties of the Allies would compel peace. By the end of April, however, he was not optimistic, telling Sturge that war looked likely to continue. When it became quite clear that the Vienna talks had failed, Bright made his final war speech in the Commons on 7 June. This time, his approach was less 'statesmanlike'. He spoke banteringly of the ministerial statements and narrowed down the ostensible object of the war to the safeguarding of Turkish security. He deplored the government's tendency to speak of Russia as a Power which could be taken to Bow Street and be bound over before some stipendiary magistrate to keep the peace for six months. Showing an unusual concern for national *amour-propre*, he contended that

> if any diplomatist from this country, under the same circumstances as Russia was placed in, had consented to terms such as the noble Lord had endeavoured to force upon Russia . . . he would be met by one universal shout of execration, and, as a public man, would be ruined for ever.

Bright's own solution was a curious one. He wanted the Straits to be open to all, with British fleets visiting the Black Sea in the course of the season and Russian fleets visiting the Mediterranean. As a result, there would be no wrangling about the Straits 'and the balance of power — if I may use the term — between the fleets of Russia, France and England, would be probably the best guarantee that could be offered for the security of Constantinople and Turkey. . . .' This argument was, of course, pure *real-politik*, and, as has been noted, if Palmerston had said this, Bright would have made a great outcry.[15] The Prime Minister, however, showed no interest in the proposal and, as things stood, it was of no interest to Russia either.

Roebuck's Select Committee, the ostensible reason for the resignations of the Peelites in the spring, conducted itself in open session and ample discreditable information was becoming public knowledge. Although no lover of the army, Bright could not resist associating with critics of the aristocratic stranglehold over it. Anything which discredited the government was important. When he read the report of the Sebastopol Committee he concluded that the Aberdeen Cabinet stood convicted of 'ambition, duplicity, lies, recklessness — all may now come to some serious reckoning'. When Roebuck's motion of censure was debated in mid-July, however, it failed; most members neither wanted to pursue Lord Aberdeen further nor change the government again. Bright saw an opportunity to attack Palmerston and was gratified to find that the press gave him considerable space. 'I think', he told his wife, 'it is because I put more earnestness and originality into what I say than the old Party talkers.' Although Palmerston survived, Russell at last dropped out. His equivocal position at Vienna had been exposed and he had no alternative but to go. Bright had no regrets for Lord John, but continued to believe that Palmerston had been made to refuse peace at Vienna. One day, even the so-called Liberals who supported the government would wake up.[16]

> John continues to be very unpopular [wrote Thomas Bright to America at this time] owing to his opposition to the war, and, if we had an election just now, I almost think he would have to retire into private life, such is the strong feeling at present in favor of bloodshed . . . I am ashamed of my country.

Bright was increasingly convinced that the only way to reach the public was through the press. For years, he had attacked the 'tax on knowledge', the newspaper stamp. Gladstone had removed the advertisement duty in 1853 and his successor removed the newspaper stamp in the summer of 1855. *The Times* retained its great influence, but within months a rash of new daily penny newspapers appeared, though still for a readership which was basically middle class. Bright and Cobden already had the *Manchester Examiner* but they felt that Free Trade and peace needed a voice in the capital, if it could remain 'permanently honest'. 'The temptation to trim', he wrote to Wilson, 'is so great, when profit is opposed to principle & especially in London, where all sorts of attempts are made on the virtue of public writers & generally with complete success.' In appealing for money, Bright wrote to Sturge that there was 'no use in building on a bad foundation — a *new paper* is far better in our case.' That would take time, meanwhile, even Wilson and the *Examiner* were reprimanded for their treatment of the fall of Sebastopol early in September 1855. 'You have written against the war for two years past', Bright wrote, 'if your opposition was sound, then this war is a huge crime & these victories are not proper subjects for "delirious" rejoicing. Yet turn to your paper. . . .' Bright was despondent that the newly-formed *Daily Telegraph*, which was picking up circulation rapidly, had gone to the 'war-party'; so much for the benefits of a cheap press. On the other hand, he argued against Sturge's suggestion that their new editor should be someone who held 'the abstract peace principle'. Only in 'non-intervention' could reformers find unity. In the autumn, he was depressed by the thought that victory would only prolong Palmerston in power.

Meanwhile, in *The Times*, and elsewhere, rumours began to appear of a coalition between Disraeli, Gladstone and Bright to oppose the government. It was true that Bright saw a good deal of Disraeli socially, and had come to admire Gladstone, commenting in July that he was 'far ahead of every other man in the House as a speaker', but the combination was quite fanciful. It was, Bright explained to Villiers, a trick 'to detach some of Disraeli's men from him & to persuade the war-public that a factious opposition to the Prime Minister was being concocted & thus to bring new supporters to the Govt or to pave the way for a dissolution.' There was, he believed, a conspiracy between Palmerston and *The Times* which could not go on much longer — nor could the war. However, he detected another alarming possibility. Palmerston's evil genius would crown its career by involving Britain in a war with the USA, arising from attempts to enlist Americans to serve in the Crimea. In December 1855, he wrote to Villiers of rumours that the Bedford Whigs (Russell's associates) were 'opening their eyes a little, & think peace is wise now, then home politics — a real reform, & more show of sympathy with *us* & a broader basis for their political action for the future.' — parliamentary reform had been dropped from consideration with the outbreak of war. Bright wrote to Cobden that if Russell were to be helped up again, there would have to be greater precision in the contract than previously. Other correspondence with Cobden in December was less equable. They quarrelled temporarily about the management of the projected newspaper. The ill-tempered exchanges with Cobden, even though the rift was repaired, are perhaps an indication of strain. His countrymen may well have been stupid, but the degree to which Bright harps on this theme in letters seems to show a man under stress.

About the middle of January 1856, Bright found himself suffering from an attack of giddiness in the head which, in his own words, 'deprived me almost entirely of the power of mental labour'. This giddiness could not be attributed to loss of sleep following the arrival of his sixth child. He consulted his homeopathic doctor, who prescribed a suitable medicine and saw no reason why he should not speak in Manchester, as planned, on 2 January. The prospects of peace seemed better and Cobden urged Bright not to disparage possible terms before they were agreed upon. Bright, however, was in uncompromising mood when he talked about the balance of power, lords and cathedral clergy. He brought his remarks to a close in military style:[17]

> We must borrow our metaphors from events which pass before us. If I am a political soldier, I strive to maintain the ranks and to confront unflinched all the batteries that ridicule or malice may point against us. I wish to pass on uninfluenced by the baits that seduce or by the temptations that feed ambition. I wish to make a lodestar of my political career; and if I felt what I hold to be just and true, above and beyond the dignity of representing this great city in the Imperial Parliament, I trust that I shall not on that account be less worthy of that dignity to which your favour and confidence have raised me.

When the cheers had died down at the close of the speech, which had lasted for two hours, his friends noticed that he was flushed in the face and unusually excited. He was taken home to Rochdale; it was to be many months before he spoke in public again.

John Bright was only forty-four when his breakdown occurred. Explanations of his illness were confidently advanced at the time and historians since have been scarcely less reticent. Some contemporaries believed that in his busy life as platform orator and parliamentarian he had driven himself on relentlessly until his system could take no more. Rest and quiet, therefore, would restore him. Cobden was prepared to be more specific, both as to diagnosis and remedy. His friend had 'sprained his brain' and should go abroad to recuperate. He also, apparently, consumed too much meat — twice as much as Cobden — and fish and vegetables should be substituted. Then again, Bright did not sleep enough. A little later, he came to the conclusion that John ought to be cupped. There was, indeed, a prejudice against bloodletting, but he thought that the swing against the practice had gone too far. 'Cupping', he suggested, 'will relieve your brain from the pressure from which it had been suffering.' Others, noting the attacks on Bright in *Punch*, *The Times* and other newspapers during the war, believed that he had finally wilted under their sustained onslaught. During the war, however, Bright did not conduct a physically taxing campaign, either in parliament or in the country. Therefore, if he was physically exhausted after the few speeches he made, it was from the accumulated burden of years rather than from months of intense activity. He did not relish the attacks on him during the war, but his own political style was intensely combative. It has been noted that he continued to dine out during the war with people who opposed his views.

The trouble went deeper. If the immediate attacks did not unduly disturb him, his general situation did. He had become driven in on himself without sufficient intellectual or emotional discipline. He felt the waste of war intensely and was unable to comprehend why men, even men he respected, could take a different viewpoint. Why did he make so little impression on them? Was his own judgment at fault? Was the voice crying in the wilderness an absurdity? Was he doomed to endless opposition, and all to no purpose? The answers did not come easily, if at all, yet he needed to have them. He was not content to be a mere prophet apostrophizing a heedless generation. He could not claim for himself the confidence of the absolutist and the assurance of the martyr. Although labelled 'peace at any price', he had gone into the parliamentary market place and haggled about the war in utilitarian fashion. Although he pretended to believe the 'balance of power' to be mere mystification, his own solution to the Straits crisis had depended upon it. He had bandied Blue Books about with the best, and pitted his diplomatic judgment against the Prime Minister's. There would be no consolation for him in the fact that the Russians were about to accept terms which he had declared they could never be expected to accept. His judgment of the economic consequences of the war was not altogether accurate either.

The Society of Friends could not offer complete comfort at this critical juncture either. The Quaker ties in his family had already loosened. In November 1851, for example, Gratton Bright wrote to Margaret reporting that the local Monthly Meeting committee had paid Jacob and himself a visit and asked them 'once more *nominally* at least to join them . . . We gave them no hope. . . .'[18] Priscilla Bright had been automatically excluded from the Society on her marriage outside its ranks — a rule which John strongly opposed. John did not follow his brothers in this parting of Friends, but he was dissatisfied with the Society and disconsolate about its future. 'There seems nothing but decay in our monthly meetings', he reported to Rachel Priestman in 1852, 'we are too few to afford any warmth, nobody comes in & the children born in do not remain in.' To John Pease he had expressed the view in December 1851 that there were 'grievous errors, not in the *principles*, that is the *religious* principles of our own Sect, but rather in its polity & in its organization.' At very considerable length, he recounted the faults, stating that he saw no future unless changes were made. 'It may be', he admitted sadly, 'that we are destined to extinction, but if it be so, let it not be said that we refused to believe in our danger, & rejected all examination into the malady which destroyed us.'[19] Many other Friends, however, did not share his critical views or call him to their counsel.

In the crisis of 1856 it was not matters of structure which so much concerned him as faith itself. The challenge was existential rather than narrowly intellectual. He read about 'The Eclipse of Faith', but it was not biblical authority or scientific discovery which gave him anxiety. His problem was Job's problem. He read through the Book of Ruth and the Book of Samuel. Old Eli heard of the death of his two sons but was unmoved, he noted, but when he heard that the Ark of God was taken, he fell backwards. Was the Ark of God to be taken from John Bright too? If he brooded in this fashion, he did not confide his thoughts to anybody. His isolation was another aspect of his condition. He was not a recluse, but he was detached. He was not unhappily married, but for many months each year there was no companionship in it. Regular correspondence was no substitute. His wife, with their many children, either would not, or could not, come to London during the parliamentary session. J. B. Smith, he reported to her on one occasion, had taken a country house in Berkshire for this purpose, and there is little doubt that he wished to do the same. From time to time, a certain grumpiness creeps into the letters, though it is never predominant. In June 1855, for example, he wrote from the Reform Club that it was time that Elizabeth developed 'a little independence of action in travelling — for it will be a miserable thing for thee & for others, if thou should become as difficult in this respect as thy mother is. . . .'

He did not see very much of his children either. Helen remained his favourite child and the condition of her lungs gave him anxious moments; her mother had died of consumption. She was now at school in Brighton. By his second wife, he had five children, although being so fruitful did not gain universal approval. His brother Thomas wrote in October 1855 that 'John and his very numerous family (shortly to be increased unfortunately) are at Rhyl. . . .' Thomas explained that he had 'a particular objection to large families and I always determined not to follow in the footsteps of my parents on this point.' He clinched his argument by claiming that, however happy they might be when children, his experience was that in after years, the larger the family, the more numerous the quarrels. John was not deterred by such sentiments, perhaps because, as the eldest, he had himself come out on top. Nevertheless, the fact of such a large young family was an additional anxiety. Thomas really ran the business and prudently had only one child; John did not and had six. Precise figures of John's financial situation at this time are not available, but he could be described as comfortably-off rather than wealthy. He was evidently able to contemplate investing £1,000 in the projected newspaper without undue difficulty. There was even one curious consequence of his opposition to the war. An admirer left him a house and 27 acres of land in Surrey. He went down to look at the property and decided to sell. Since the Safety Insurance Company, in which Bright and Cobden had an interest and to which they lent their names, was proving far from safe, such a bequest was most convenient. In other respects, however, acres of fir, pine trees and furze seemed scant consolation for mental turmoil and physical distress.

The full extent of Bright's debility did not become apparent immediately after the January speech in Manchester. He went up to London for the new session in the belief that a change of scene would reinvigorate him. No sooner was he in town, however, than some 'unpleasant sensations' reappeared. They passed again, and he spent a pleasant evening with Cobden, Ashworth and others, talking politics. Shortly afterwards, on medical advice, he returned to Rochdale. After a few days at home, he went to the hydropathic establishment at Ben Rhydding in Yorkshire and endured its treatment for eight weeks.

> Our days are generally much alike [he wrote to his wife].
> Wake about ½ past 6. Dripping Sheet, standing in cold
> water at 7. Walk, Breakfast at 8. Letters ½ past 9 . . . Drill at
> 10 under our Prussian drill master. Billiards. Walk. Bath.
> Dripping Sheet or sitz or pack between 11 & 12. Walk.
> Dinner at 2. Rest. Write for the post. Walk. Afternoon bath
> at 5. Walk. Rest. Tea at 7. Billiards. Drawing Room 9 to 10 &
> then to bed — *sic transit* a Ben Rhydding day.

This regimen may have been exemplary, but Bright was not alone in submitting to it, and company made him 'excited'. His friends were unanimous in the view that he should eschew politics completely. Cobden urged this as strongly as any in letters with a high political content!

Bright took some of the advice that he was offered, though not all. The Free Trade London paper, the *Morning Star* had just been launched and he perused its editorials and contents avidly. As he explained to his wife, he did not seem to be very ill, though he did not really improve either. In early May 1856, he was back in Rochdale, claiming to feel a little better, though constantly in danger of 'exceeding his strength'. Accompanied by his brother Jacob and his daughter Helen for some part of his journey, he set off on an eleven-week tour of the Highlands, staying chiefly at lodges possessed there by Lancashire friends. He watched others fishing. Privately, however, Cobden continued to believe that it was[20]

> a mistake to treat his symptoms as altogether mental or cerebral. His bodily structure, sanguineous temperament & especially his short neck, indicate an *apoplectic* tendency; and I preach to him the necessity of counteracting this predisposition by abstemious diet & exercise out of doors quite as much as by diminishing his mental efforts.

At least as far as newspapers went, Bright did not diminish his mental efforts at all. He assured Cobden that the *Star* would be a good property within two years. Cobden was less convinced. It was, he wrote pointedly, 'far more difficult to start & sustain a successful daily London paper than a cotton mill.' Bright could hardly resist replying to such a remark, but Cobden realized that he was sinning against his own precept and, reluctantly, changed the subject.

Returning to Rochdale briefly, Bright was soon off to Scotland to join the covey of Lancashire exiles — Ashworth, Thomasson and others — at their shooting quarters. His comments as a guest were suitably censorious — 'what a monstrous extravagance this shooting mania is. It surely cannot last long' — but he himself stayed for a month. He left in mid-September to stay for the first time in the home of an aristocrat, Haddo House, the residence of the former Prime Minister. The occasion was no doubt as intriguing for the Aberdeens as it was for Bright. 'I have a beautiful bedroom', wrote Bright to Helen, 'looking on to the front, & below the windows is one of the most charming flower gardens I have ever seen.'[21] Eating proved difficult, for breakfast was at nine, lunch at two and dinner at eight in the evening. He lunched with Lady Haddo and the children but he reported that he had taken almost nothing at dinner and 'in future, I don't intend to go into dinner at all — for I cannot live in this way & must dine at a more rational hour, or I shall cease to dine at all.' Such an unappealing contingency no doubt accelerated his departure at the end of a week. His host had been most courteous and the deer in the park were most pleasant to see. 'It would be a great gain', Bright had written in March, 'to the country if a large portion, not of the woods only but of the parks of England, were brought into more productive use' — but perhaps Scotland fell into a different category.[22] 'The journey was of no apparent benefit to me', wrote Bright gloomily on his return to Rochdale, 'as I saw too many people — and talked too much.'

The next venture in search of health was to Llandudno with his wife and children, but this trip, too, was not very beneficial. He wrote to Helen that he had not improved of late and would have to go abroad for a time. Various destinations and companions were suggested, before it was agreed that he should accompany a Friend, J. C. Backhouse, to Algiers in November. Informing George Wilson of his decision, he added that something might have to be done about his parliamentary seat. Throughout the war, he had held that his 'moderate and rational views' would not injure him in Manchester, but this was wishful thinking. He knew that he had critics and also that even his supporters might not be prepared to go without effective representation indefinitely. The situation might arise, but Bright told Wilson that his medical advisers believed that a full rest would restore him to complete fitness. Nevertheless, he felt obliged to offer his resignation if Wilson felt that his constituents were dissatisfied. Assuming that he did recover, he hoped to continue to represent Manchester.

In Algiers, he was not altogether idle. He read Lyell's *Elements of Geology*, bought a French grammar and took drawing lessons. He strolled around the town, visited the Great Mosque, watched a Moorish ball and took a Moorish bath. He did not bathe in the sea, having heard the American Consul report that sea bathing so much excited him that he could neither sleep, nor write, nor indeed do anything afterwards. After a month in North Africa, he returned to Marseilles and then went on to Nîmes, where there was a school kept by Friends — a useful information centre. Eliza Gurney reported a recent encounter with the Empress of Russia who was wintering on the Riviera. The Empress, she related, had described Bright as 'a friend of theirs, or friendly to them, and had been just to them and to Russia'. He was joined by Thomas Bright and Helen, and the party travelled on to Italy. He was delighted to have his daughter, now seventeen, with him, and they enjoyed themselves en route, dining with such elements of the

British aristocracy as they encountered. At Nice, Lord Dufferin graciously offered the use of an 'excellent little nag', but Bright did not have enough time to exercise it. They did have time, however, to be received by the Empress of Russia. She told Bright that she had long wanted to meet a man who spoke from his conscience and, moreover, spoke the truth. Bright replied carefully that he had opposed the war 'in the interest of England and of truth, as well as in that of Russia, for I thought war as bad for England as for Russia.' Their conversation then centred on the Society of Friends, after which, they bowed and took their leave.

They then passed into Italy, reaching Rome by the end of January 1857. The usual round of sight-seeing began. Three hours at the Vatican Museum did not produce in Bright the enthusiasm 'which some men feel or affect for the "crack pieces" of sculpture, if one may use a familiar or almost slang word'. His interest in sculpture was not restricted to museums; after haggling over a price, a bust of John Bright was commissioned. The Roman Church could not be altogether avoided. Not even the presence of the Pope and the Cardinals at St Peter's could prevent the service from being 'rather tedious than pleasing' to Helen. Bright insisted on a visit to San Carlo Borromeo where Dr Manning, late of the English State Church, and later to be a cardinal, was the preacher. 'If I could have shut my eyes or ears, or mind, to the *matter* of the sermon', Bright noted, 'I should have spent an hour of enjoyment such as I could not easily forget.'[23] Various zealous English missionaries for the Papal superstition called on him and, with wonderful civility, invited him to take tea, but he showed no disposition to become what he termed a 'pervert' himself.

Then there was the Carnival, which Helen enjoyed immensely. Bright claimed to be glad when it was over, though 'the amusement has served to dissipate me a little, which, I think, is not without its use'. Lady Login, in her recollections, paints a picture of rather more energetic dissipation. 'He and I and his daughter', she writes, 'drove up and down the Corso, pelting strangers and being pelted with confetti and flowers — John Bright the most vigorous of them all, though gallantly *handing* bouquets to the ladies who took his fancy!' Two days later, she continued, he exchanged shots from the balcony of their hotel with Lady Knatchbull at a window opposite, 'putting her finally out of action with a terrific shot with a sugared almond'.[24] Bright also appeared at the Masque Ball, which he pronounced a 'dull affair on the whole'.

After Rome, there was fishing on Lakes Como and Maggiore. The gear was cheaply purchased in Milan, but it did not attract a single fish. Bright reported to his brother-in-law, James Vaughan, that he felt in better spirits, as if time, and perhaps not a long time, would restore the tone of his system. However, he could not 'banish home & wife & bairns & therefore a great distance from them only makes them a burden on my spirit.' In Turin, he had been rash enough to plunge into discussing the Italian question, writing afterwards to the British minister, Sir James Hudson, that he had to 'run away to save myself from undoing whatever good I have received from my five months' absence from England'.[25] Late in May, after Bright and Helen had left Italy, Elizabeth joined them in Lyons and together they toured through Switzerland, Germany and Belgium before returning to Rochdale in the early summer of 1857. He returned simply as John Bright, for in his absence he had ceased to be a member of parliament.

The Mediterranean sun had never completely banished thoughts of English politics. All along the Riviera, he picked up any political news he could discover, and read English newspapers. His first night in Rome had been distinguished by a dream that he was at the opening of the parliamentary session and heard Roebuck speak. 'My old labours sometimes seem to haunt me', he noted 'and I am very sad at being excluded from the field where so much is to be done or attempted.' The anniversary of his Manchester speech of January 1856 brought considerable melancholy. He reflected that he had always desired the true greatness of his country whereas the English oligarchy was characterized by selfishness and fraud. He looked with gloomy foreboding on the consequences of the follies and crimes of his countrymen. These reflections gained a certain strength from their Roman context. Surrounded by the ruins of Empire, he concluded that 'loud boasting, great wealth, great power, extended dominion, successive conquests, mighty fleets and armies, are not immovable foundations of national greatness.'

In his meditations on the English political scene, he turned increasingly to Gladstone as the one statesman with intelligence and conscience who might save the state. Early in March 1857 came news that Palmerston 'and his crew' had at last been beaten. The occasion was a vote of censure moved by Cobden with support from Gladstone, Disraeli, Russell and others. Sir John Bowring, Governor of Hong Kong, had ordered the bombardment of Canton, following the refusal of the Chinese authorities to apologize for their detention of a vessel, thought to be British registered, called the *Arrow*. It had in fact been owned by a Chinese who used it for piracy. Palmerston felt himself committed to supporting Sir John and defended him in the debate, to no avail. Bright sadly recalled that he had done his best to help Bowring with letters of introduction when he was first appointed, but now he rejoiced at the result of the debate: it showed that there was yet moral sense in Britain.[26]

Palmerston gained a dissolution of parliament and Bright, still in Italy, had quickly to decide whether or not to stand. On 8 March, he wrote to Wilson enclosing a draft address to the Manchester electors and offering himself as a candidate, stating that his health had sufficiently improved. However, far from the scene, he recognized that there might be difficulties and asked Wilson to do what he saw fit. Reports reached him that his old opponents were at work and were being joined by some previous supporters. He attributed this change to the war. Whatever happened, he told Cobden, he would not be disappointed. His wife and brothers were pressing him to retire from parliament, but he would not run away. If he were defeated, however, no one could complain if he took his leisure.

Of course Bright could not campaign and merely followed events in the English newspapers. On 30 March, the news from Manchester was telegraphed through: Bright came bottom of the poll, with Gibson just above him. The new members were Sir John Potter and Aspinall Turner. Bright had nothing good to say for either man. Potter was vain and had eaten and dined his way to a knighthood. Turner was a toady of the East India Company who had the temerity to oppose Bright's commission of inquiry into cotton growing in India. The defeated member sent off a defiant message to his old constituents and then continued on his round of museums and churches. 'Far better fall against', he wrote to Wilson, 'than rise with such a wretched cry as has been lately got up. . . .' He supposed that he would now be out of politics and could devote himself to his family and his business. 'If Cobden is thrown out', he concluded, 'the "School" may be said to have shut up, at least for a vacation, the discipline having been too severe for the scholars.' Cobden was indeed defeated, and Bright wrote from Venice to commiserate. He suggested that they had been ahead of their time and differed from other politicians in refusing to make politics a mere trade. In fact, however, Bright's defeat might well have occurred even without the special factors of the war and his illness. His representation had been, from the beginning, controversial. Prosperous Manchester men now wanted the seat for themselves. The surviving electoral machinery of the old League situated in Newall's Buildings provoked resentment and hostility. The social, political and commercial cohesion of the 'Manchester School' had broken in Manchester itself. Social aspiration, economic self-interest (a belief that jaunty anachronistic Palmerston could best look after Manchester's cotton interests in the Levant and Far East) and satisfaction with the political status quo ruined the hopes of Bright that Manchester and the 'middle class spirit' would swiftly become the ruling ethos of Britain. His career had ended in dejection and disappointment. 'John is free', was Thomas Bright's reaction, 'and I hope will *always* remain so. To throw a life away on a ungrateful people is a folly and in future if he is wise he will work for himself and his family. . . .'[27]

Part Four

The Birmingham Backbencher

EIGHT

The first Reform crusade: failure 1858-61

In the months that followed the Manchester defeat, Bright may well have been advised by his family to withdraw completely from politics, but he does not seem to have given this advice much attention. In the summer, Rochdale Liberals were frequently consulting him about constituency matters. There was a suggestion that he should fight Rochdale at the next general election. On 26 June 1857, he wrote to Smith that he had allowed it to be understood that

> if the Liberals are of opinion that to keep the Borough from the Tories & to unite the party, it is necessary for me to stand, they are at liberty to nominate me — on condition that I keep away from the Election & that I am not required to begin work before I am well enough to undertake it.

Bright had been telling his associates that he was feeling better and that 'another year of leisure & of health seeking will see me again ready for work.' Parkes was pleased, but urged him to take life steadily and refrain from so much animal food. He reported to Cobden that the invalid did indeed look much better. His complexion was clear and the heavy obesity had gone. 'He is "fined down"', he concluded, '— not so much fat. A weight seems to have dropped off his forehead & eyes and his mind is as clear as a bell.' In order to continue the good work,

129

Bright set off again for the north of Scotland to fish. He was pleasantly enjoying a picnic in Glen Lyon when he received an urgent call to Edinburgh. One of the members for Birmingham had died. Would Bright stand in the ensuing by-election? It was a challenge he could not resist. He travelled down to the Midlands and matters were settled to general satisfaction. The by-election presented no difficulty.

Bright was to represent Birmingham for over thirty years, though few at the time could have envisaged such an enduring relationship. Those who approached Bright were looking for a national celebrity. They knew that there was little likelihood that Bright would ever become, in any deep sense, a Birmingham man. He would keep his home in Rochdale and only make occasional visits to the city, usually for the purpose of making set speeches. He would take a decent interest in local matters, but they would be mistaken if they supposed they were selecting an assiduous 'local' member. The Birmingham men knew that in bidding for John Bright they had, to an extent, to take him on his own terms. From Bright's standpoint, the fact that he was clearly an outsider in Birmingham meant that he would be less likely to be involved in the social and political jockeying for position which had latterly characterized Manchester. Besides, as Cobden was quick to point out, though Bright knew it well, the class structure of the two towns was different. Gradations, rather than extremes of wealth, were typical of Birmingham and ideas of class-co-operation rather than class-conflict were prevalent. Municipally, the reformers were very active — and there were many Quakers among them, a fact which may account for the adoption of Bright appearing the natural course.[1] Even so, there was no suggestion that Bright had been approached specifically because of his 'anti-war' views — the industries of the West Midlands had more to gain and less to lose from war than Manchester's. What the Birmingham Liberals hoped for was a member who could project the reforming vigour of its local politics onto national politics. Bright also recognized that Birmingham could offer him a base for a new, more vigorous, campaign for parliamentary reform.

In the first place he had gradually to make clear the relationship of this major concern to those who still looked to him for support on other issues — India, Temperance, Peace and Dis-establishment. The great shock of the Indian Mutiny of 1857 clearly placed Bright in a quandary. He assured some of the Birmingham Liberals that though he had been critical of the Indian administration, his views were not subversive. He did believe, however, that when the insurrection was suppressed the political question would again come to the fore. 'A hundred millions of people tossed about between Leadenhall Street and Cannon Row', he argued, 'must some day or other get into chaos.' The rebellion had, in this sense, confirmed his judgment, but he was quite clear that it had to be put down, even if this confirmed the 'insufferable ruling people', as Cobden called his fellow-countrymen, in power. This view did not, however, please Joseph Sturge, now, of course, one of his constituents. He disapproved of all armed force and believed Bright should do so in this instance. 'It may be quite right for me not to oppose many things that I would not practise', he replied in September 1857, 'I would not have conquered India, if possessed of it, I would not have unjustly governed it and to keep it I would not reconquer it.' However, he claimed (rather oddly in view of the previous three years) that he only opposed evil when he saw a prospect of doing any good. Attacking the views of Southall, another Birmingham Quaker, he asked whether Southall believed that the British government should rest quiet and allow the murder of every Englishman in India. The British government, he argued, had to act on its own principles, since it admitted no others. Bright claimed that he had never advocated the extreme peace principle, the non-resistance principle, either in public or in private. As a parting shot, Bright doubted whether any statesman could leave India and abandon the overseas colonies. 'Let those who feel any act wrong, keep out of it', he declared, 'but let them not judge all else uncharitably. . . .' Here was the voice of the seasoned, if not cynical, Birmingham Bright.

He concentrated, not upon the drama of the rebellion, but upon its political repercussions. The British, he reminded Layard, were in India as conquerors, and were therefore necessarily disliked, indeed hated. With this natural hostility to contend against, the government needed to render much 'visible service' to justify its conquest and make friendship possible. In his judgment, nothing had so far been done to improve roads, navigation and irrigation. What was needed in India was a total change of ideas and policy; no more conquest, but a prudent use of revenue to benefit the cultivators. The only source of gratification to Bright was that most people seemed to feel that the rule of the East India Company would be ended.

Bright also tangled with Sturge on the subject of peace. Invited to attend a peace conference in Manchester in October, he bluntly declined. 'I am disposed to think', he stated, 'that all we have done as a 'Peace Conference' or 'Peace Society' of late years has been of no use. I am not sure that it has not done a positive harm.' It was, sadly, the case that the Peace Society's principles were totally repudiated as impracticable by almost everybody. He disliked working in an impossible cause and had come to the conclusion that *nothing, absolutely nothing* can be done in the direction in which we want our countrymen to travel.' He admitted that he was 'well nigh sick at heart', but confessed that he was 'only saved from a feeling of misery because I am gradually growing callous about crimes and follies which I cannot prevent.' Sturge was shocked by this letter, and urged him to reconsider, but Bright would not. Public opinion might change in their direction, but for the moment, in foreign policy, Palmerston stood supreme.

Bright was no more responsive to other calls for assistance. In 1854, for example, he had declined an invitation to lead the campaign of the Liberation Society, as the Anti-State Church Society had become, and he maintained this attitude.[2] His opposition to Church Rates and the privileges of the Established Church remained undimmed, but to have become simply a mouthpiece for militant Dissent would have been too restrictive a role. Similarly, he would not identify himself politically with the temperance movement, confessing to Sturge in May 1858 that he was taking a little beer and wine on medical advice and therefore did not wish 'to be paraded as urging others to do that which I do not always do myself. During my absence abroad last year I drank the wines of the country & I think with benefit, and here also I believe that I am the better for taking a little claret.' It was a comforting conclusion. A couple of years later, he told a correspondent that he believed that health and temperance might both gain from the introduction of light wines into the country. As far as legislation was concerned, he did not believe that it was the province of government to fix what people should drink. 'Law', he argued, 'must be founded on broad and general principles, such as are consistent with "political economy", but individuals may use their discretion as to what they may abstain from . . . .'[3]

In taking such views, Bright cut himself off, to some extent, from the men and movements of his early career. The member for Birmingham, who reappeared in the Commons in January 1858 was a rather chastened figure when compared with the young member for Durham in 1843. Although he had lost some of his recent weight, he looked older than his forty-six years. The welcome he received from members of all parties was genuine, although he remained a somewhat isolated figure in the House. It was a position which, to some extent, he had cultivated in the belief that to be a member of a group would too greatly restrict his conduct. In the first few weeks back, he was hesitant about speaking, but there was considerable excitement in the House. Early in January, a bomb was thrown in Paris at the Emperor Napoleon III. It was subsequently discovered that the explosives in the bomb had been made in England and that the would-be assassin had links with Italian refugees in London. The Emperor sent an indignant protest to London, asking that steps should be taken to stop the plots. Palmerston successfully introduced a Conspiracy to Murder Bill for this purpose, but declined to acknowledge the French protest. Gibson, newly elected for Ashton-under-Lyne, moved an amendment deprecating the attempt on the Emperor's life, but regretting the government's failure to reply to the dispatch before introducing its proposals. Bright seconded. It was, indeed, a curious position to find them accusing the Prime Minister of neglecting the honour of England — as Palmerston did not hesitate to point out. However, it did him no good. Disraeli led the Tories to vote with Gibson and Bright, and the amendment was carried. Despite his triumph at the general election, only ten months earlier, Palmerston saw no alternative but to resign.

Bright's delight overcame any qualms he may have had about enlisting anti-French sentiments to defeat the Prime Minister. He had remained in the House the whole night, he told his wife, but had not suffered from the experience, which was 'a great sign of recovered strength'. It was also his opinion, in April, that he could make a better speech than before he broke down. The overthrow of Palmerston, he claimed, brought a sense of relief in the public mind, though there was the danger that Napoleon might seek an escape from his difficulties by going to war with England. If he and Gibson were vindictive, he concluded, it could be said that they had had their revenge. Of course they were not. His future course, however, was not clear.

> I think [he wrote to his wife in May] few men in Parlt suffer so much as I do from untoward circumstances — worried so often about business & separated so much from my family — having a very advantageous position in the House & yet unable from my opinions on certain subjects, to avail myself of the rewards which meet other men in their political career. Never mind, I hear thee saying, perhaps all is for the best. . . .

One suspects, however, that John would have been happier if he could have believed that himself. He was aware that he did have a 'very advantageous position'; the question was how best to exploit it.

Lord Derby, as the leader of the largest section of the Opposition, now formed a government, with Lord Malmesbury as Foreign Secretary and Disraeli as Chancellor of the Exchequer. The new administration was not strong, being only made possible by the coolness between Palmerston and Russell, and the preference of Bright, Gladstone and their friends for almost any ministry not headed by Palmerston. Lord Derby had indeed offered Gladstone a post, but he declined it. No doubt he would have refused anyway, but rather to his astonishment, Bright wrote to him on the subject. In the most friendly spirit, the letter urged him not to join such a precarious government, because, if he did so, he would be linking his fortunes with a constant minority. That seemed to Bright to be very foolish. The future lay with the other side of the House and, for good measure, Bright added that he knew nothing 'that can prevent your being prime minister before you approach the age of every other member of the House who has or can have any claim to that high office.'[4] Bright had chosen his man. From this point on, despite Gladstone's unexpected departure to the Ionian islands, their contacts and correspondence increased. Many differences separated High Churchman and Quaker, but they were much of an age, and the old guard could not go on for ever. They both possessed a highly developed capacity for moral feeling, and their abilities might be complementary. Together, they might fashion a real Liberal party.

The strange party situation which prevailed can be illustrated by the fate of measures to deal with India after the mutiny. Two issues were paramount — the question of punishment and the new administrative structure. After some delay, Palmerston had given his support to Lord Canning in his policy of 'clemency' and, shortly before his fall from office, had succeeded in passing a Government of India Bill which transferred control of the Governor-General and his Council in Calcutta to Westminster; previously a system of dual control had been operated with the East India Company. The Tories had been critical of some of the details and the incoming government decided to introduce a new measure. Bright, who watched events closely, had no confidence in the new President of the Board of Control, Lord Ellenborough. He thought that the size of the Council now proposed by Ellenborough was too big and would lessen the chances of an effective role for the House of Commons. 'We must honestly do our best for India', he wrote to Smith on 31 March 1858, 'without reference to the result or effect upon this or any other Ministry. . . .' His dislike of Ellenborough grew and he took to journalism in the *Star* to destroy his scheme. In particular, Bright objected to the 'absurdity' of five members of the Council being returned by the five cities of London, Liverpool, Manchester, Glasgow and Belfast. In the event, the government backtracked.

Then came an unexpected turn in the contest. Ellenborough censured the Governor-General for his policy towards the small proprietors of Oude. Early in May, he was himself censured in the Commons for this dispatch and resigned. Bright was placed in an awkward position. The case of the Opposition was that the government had acted injudiciously in publishing the dispatch. In his own speech, on 20 May, Bright contended that if the motion were passed, it would inevitably be interpreted in India as approval of a policy which Ellenborough was right to censure. The Opposition move was simply an attempt to bring down the government. 'We are told', Bright said at one point, 'and the whole country has been in a state of expectation and wonder upon it, that two eminent statesmen have actually dined together.' He had little enthusiasm for what Russell and Palmerston might concoct.

The following month, a third India Bill was brought in. Bright made a lengthy speech in which he remained critical, though he did not vote against it. If it had not been for the East India Company, he argued, the proposed scheme would never have been introduced. He condemned the inadequacies of administration and development, while also criticizing the government for running up a debt of £60 million. However, while not excusing the luxury and extravagance which he claimed prevailed, he recognized the difficulty of governing India. Indeed, with its diversity of peoples, religions and languages, and its sheer size, it was impossible for a single Governor-General to govern the country. Instead, he advocated a policy of decentralization. Five independent Presidencies should be created, equal in rank, whose Governors should have direct access to the Secretary of State in London. The Secretary of State should be a man with a real interest in India, and if any Prime Minister appointed an inefficient man to the office, he would be 'a traitor to the throne of England'. Britain was in India, he concluded, and she did not know how to leave, so it was her duty to govern well.[5] Although his ideas were not accepted, Bright was pleased with his speech. Some of the papers sneered, he wrote, but the general impression on the House was most satisfactory.[6] Russell even said that he agreed with everything Bright had said.

Bright was justified in claiming for himself a certain modest authority on the Indian question, although, as he acknowledged privately, many of the leading ideas were not his own. The scheme for separate Presidencies, for example, was devised by John Dickinson of the India Reform Society. In the wake of the mutiny, that body gained a fresh lease of life and Bright took the chair at its meeting. Throughout 1858 and 1859, in association with Dickinson, Smith and others, he continued to address himself to the administrative and financial problems of India. His advocacy of decentralization brought him some support from Indian provincial officials who had commonly complained that too much authority rested at the centre. Bright was far from satisfied with the changes that had taken place, but he conceded that India seemed quieter, better governed and more prosperous than for years. The logic of Bright's position, of course, was that if, at some future remote date, the British did leave India, the Presidencies would emerge as separate, independent, states. Sympathetic though he was to Indian aspirations, he did not believe that India could form a nation-state — a view which subsequent events seem to have justified.

While Bright derived some prestige from his participation in the Indian question, and some great Whigs took elaborate steps to consult him on the subject, general public interest in India was very limited. The crisis of the rebellion had created an exceptional degree of concern, but when the danger passed, that concern diminished. It was time to turn to what he hoped would become the central issue of politics: parliamentary reform.

If a campaign to extend the suffrage and redistribute seats was to be mounted, it was clear that Bright would have to take the initiative himself. Cobden would not be drawn back into active campaigning and was sceptical of the chances of success. 'On the contrary', Bright replied on 9 April 1858, 'I think the fever is passed & people are everyday becoming more conscious of the folly of the past. In the House, there is a larger party willing to act against the old parties than ever before. . . .' He was thinking primarily of foreign policy, but he also thought it true domestically. The difficulty was that it was easier for reformers to oppose the status quo than to agree on the system to replace it. In any event, the existing basis of the vote — briefly, occupiers or tenants of houses worth £10 a year within boroughs and 40s. freeholders in counties (but with many local variations) — produced a great many variations in the nature of the electorate throughout the country. Bright's initial idea was to go for a £10 occupation franchise for the counties and a household suffrage for the boroughs. The ballot, he believed, was essential, since without it any changes could be nullified. If that was to be the objective, and he wavered on the point, he was not sure that he could stand the strain of leadership. 'Our old Liberal party is without a leader', he wrote to Sturge towards the end of April 1858, '& I am pressed every day to occupy that position — but my head will not bear it & I can only speak now & then *briefly* & even so I feel that I run some risk.'

There was an additional reason for Bright's reluctance. The family business had not escaped the effects of the 1857 commercial crisis. In that year, they had decided to go into the fancy coloured trade, requiring investment in expensive machinery and alteration to the looms. In retrospect, it seemed just the wrong time for such a commercial venture. At the end of 1857, Thomas Bright reported that 'to sell has been impossible, and to buy; nobody has any money'. Not since August 1842 had the mills been working so little. The firm was bound to suffer heavy losses, but it would survive. Many stupid follies, he commented, would be checked and 'after such a storm the commercial atmosphere will be clear and pure'. In June 1858, he further reported to his American cousin that 'our loss has been much greater than I like to mention and for many weeks I scarcely knew what it was to sleep. This I do not tell everyone, tho' I often think my very white head tells its own story.' Though they had come through, it would take a long time to recover their previous buoyancy. In these circumstances, though not so intimately involved, John was understandably reluctant to take on demanding new political commitments.

By the summer, the commercial future looked brighter. John retreated to the Scottish Highlands and from there wrote an encouraging assessment of his personal and business future. 'I am not feeble as I was when here two years ago & all our sweet children are well & *we* are not tired of each other after 11 years of living together.' As if to reinforce the latter point, he added that he had never before regretted so much that they could not travel together. He spent some time fishing, but the weather was wet and there was too much water in the rivers. While on holiday, he meditated on his forthcoming speech to his new constituents. He did not look forward to the occasion, claiming to dread the Town Hall and the thousands who would be there. Nevertheless, he was determined to put the reform question 'on the right track' if he could. The Derby government had announced a reform measure for the 1859 parliamentary session and was beginning to work out details. Bright was very sceptical. A Tory bill, he claimed, would be worse than nothing. He had to devise a real measure, while recognizing that many Whigs might be more attracted by Derby's proposals than by his own. It was a 'nice difficulty'.

Some six thousand people, standing shoulder to shoulder, cheered long and passionately when Bright rose to speak on 27 October. The press was installed in strength. He began by acknowledging the weakness to which he had recently been reduced and the comparative health to which he had been restored. It did not seem to him out of place to acknowledge 'the signal favour which has been extended to me by the Great Supreme.' When all present had joined him in rendering thanks, Bright warmed to his task. He defended his attitude towards the Crimean War and believed subsequent events to have justified his stand. Then he turned to his main theme. Lord Derby had in mind a Reform Bill, and indeed all parties now pretended to be in love with the question of Reform, though they said little in detail. It was abundantly clear that the existing system of representation was unequal and dishonest, and he gave a string of facts and figures to justify this view. The body of the nation had a right to decide and no one should be frightened by what the House of Peers would say. Stating that he was not going to attack the Upper House, he proceeded to do so, culminating in a sneering reference to 'that creature of — what shall I say? — of monstrous, nay, even of adulterous birth — the spiritual Peer.' However, he defended himself against the charge that he wanted to introduce any new subversive principle or novel theoretical opinion. A franchise based on those who paid poor-rate worked well enough in municipal elections, and he did not see why it could not operate for parliamentary elections. Such a scheme would not introduce fresh complexities when it came to registering voters — so much the heart of mid-nineteenth century elections. Such a franchise would not, he claimed, be directed against any class. It would not be perfect, and not for a moment did he claim that it was better than manhood suffrage, but he was only speaking of what a government might consider politically feasible. He also advocated an extensive redistribution of seats. It was a 'miserable delusion' that the 300,000 inhabitants of Birmingham should have only two members in the House of Commons. They should insist on a real Bill, a good Bill, or no Bill at all, and it should be rounded off by the ballot. He spoke, he said, with diminished fire and acted with a lessened force, yet he would be found in the ranks during the impending struggle.

Two days later he again spoke in Birmingham, chiefly on foreign policy. His lengthy remarks on this subject, however, can be summarized by stating that he was against foreign policy. He listed all the treaty connexions Britain had with the continent, and declared them quite unnecessary. While he did not wish the country to remain without adequate and scientific means of defence, he would 'repudiate and denounce the expenditure of every shilling, the engagement of every man, the employment of every ship which has no object but inter-meddling in the affairs of other countries. . . .' The British Empire was already large enough, indeed too large, for the highest statesmanship which any man had yet attained. The only permanent greatness a nation could attain was based upon morality, not power.[7]

People will make me of great importance in spite of myself. [he wrote afterwards to his wife, but then added] 'What am I to do but to assume that there is something in it, or that the world is mistaken? Other men, I mean our public men, must be *very* little, if I am so great.

His Birmingham speeches brought back his old confidence and pleased his constituents. His remarks about the franchise reassured the more conservative middle class while holding out to the working class that he would go further if left to himself. His remarks about the House of Lords did not cause dismay amongst his audience, although they infuriated the editor of *The Times* and many others. He would launch the 'New Reform Movement' even without support from other established politicians. Cobden had by now reached that happy condition in which he felt himself 'in such discord with every political party' and, indeed, with nearly all mankind, that unless he compromised himself, he could not find a plank to stand upon on any 'platform' in the country. The British people were little better than brigands, murderers and prisoners in their dealings with half the population of the globe. Gladstone would not help either, despite the fly that Bright had cast in his direction earlier. Gladstone, he wrote to Cobden, had courage at times, but it was spasmodic. Oxford and tradition held him back and prevented him leading a popular party. Russell was also supposedly in the Reform field, but Bright's remarks about the House of his fathers had aroused in him fears that Bright was a republican. 'I fear much more is expected from me than I can perform', wrote Bright to the Positivist Congreve, thinking of pressures in the other direction. The Positivists wanted at this time 'to show the public that men of education and reflection join heart and soul in John Bright's attack on the aristocrats.'[8]

Franchise reform and seat redistribution offered endless opportunities for discussion in these winter months, both inside and outside the government. Politicians tried to assess the likely consequences of any changes, bearing in mind that it by no means followed that a wide extension of the franchise automatically benefitted the Liberals. The self-respecting artisans might well support them, but less 'respectable' workers might be open to Tory tricks, particularly if there was no provision for the ballot. Two opinions could also exist about the merits of completely assimilating the borough and county franchises.

After his Birmingham speeches, Bright went on to London and at a conference of reformers on 5 November, his notion that they should themselves prepare a Reform Bill, was taken up. The details were left to Bright — which caused him some anxiety, since drafting was not his forte. Sturge suggested to him that his speeches had made such an impact that the time was ripe to suggest manhood suffrage at the age of twenty-five. Bright was not sure. In some uncertainty, he turned to Cobden with his first ideas. He suggested a rating suffrage for the boroughs, with a clause to exclude all whose rates were remitted on the ground of poverty. In the counties, he advocated the vote for £10 occupiers. Throughout the United Kingdom (Bright was sensitive to the situation in Scotland), 40s.

freeholders, copyholders and perpetual leaseholders should be enfranchised. As for seats, he suggested a population figure below which boroughs should be disenfranchised, or reduced to one member. The big cities — Glasgow, Liverpool, Manchester etc. — would benefit and new boroughs would be established in Lancashire and Yorkshire and two or three other counties. The ballot was a difficulty. He was annoyed to discover that the Ballot Society did not want him to include it in his proposals, though he admitted that its absence would make relations with Lord John easier. He was not averse to making some concession in his direction in return for general support.

It is obvious that Bright was much more confident about his redistribution than about his franchise proposals. He reported that he was thumbing through Locke King's return of the £10 occupiers in counties and seeking guidance from Sharman Crawford's abortive Complete Suffrage Bill. 'I hope you are giving your mind to the question', he wrote to McLaren, 'so that with your *head* and my *tongue* we may make something of it, as we are in strife.'[9] While considering these details, Bright agreed to widen the campaign by undertaking to speak in Manchester, Edinburgh and Glasgow. His return to Manchester, where he spoke in the Free Trade Hall on 10 December, was in the nature of a reunion. The grand organ played 'Auld Lang Syne' as he made his appearance. It was an emotional occasion, with some of the leading figures in tears. The main burden of his address was on the inadequacy of the existing system of representation, but the language and temper of the speech was more restrained than the Birmingham performance. The House of Lords was not praised, but he was prepared to give it its proper name rather than refer to it as the House of Peers. He reiterated, though briefly, his proposal that 'every householder, of course, because every householder is rated to the poor, shall have a vote. . . .'

If you wish to admit the working classes [he argued] — for that is the question — if you wish to admit them, you must bring your suffrage down to the point that will admit them, or else you are only practising upon them precisely the same sort of legislation that they complain of with regard to the Bill of 1832.

142

Although the tone was confident, Bright had to take care to rebut charges, made after Birmingham, that he was trying to 'Americanize' Britain. The charge was both absurd and irrelevant for was not representation an English custom and an English principle and were they not Englishmen who first took it to the United States.

In Scotland, Bright spoke first at a meeting in the Music Hall in Edinburgh before an audience of two thousand, with his brother-in-law McLaren presiding. He went over comparable ground though, suitably briefed by McLaren, dealt particularly with the peculiarities of the Scottish situation. The secretary of the London Reform Association also addressed the gathering and a resolution was passed to extend the franchise in boroughs to all inhabitants rated to the poor and in counties to all occupiers of houses of the yearly value of £10. *The Times*, on 18 December, noting the absence of any reference to the secret ballot at Edinburgh, thought that the orator was drawing back. 'No man of note or mark', it noted with satisfaction, 'not originally committed to the movement, has been prevailed upon to join it; and, though thousands naturally congregate to listen to and applaud an orator of Mr Bright's undoubted powers, the process of conversion seems to be to the last degree slow and laborious.' Some days later, however, in Glasgow, where he spoke for nearly two hours at a meeting in the City Hall, Bright was careful to reintroduce the ballot as an integral part of his scheme. He was, however, very careful to argue that a great measure was 'as much wanted for the security and for the welfare of the middle classes of society as it is for the operative classes'. His audiences were predominantly middle class. In Glasgow, for example, the rates of admission were 6*d*. and 1*s*. respectively, and *The Times*'s reporter had no doubt that 'the vast mass' of those present were there to satisfy their feelings of novelty and curiosity. The Lord Provost of the city had declined to take the chair. If the audience did expect entertainment, the applause and cheering would seem to indicate that it was satisfied. Bright, now no stranger to Scotland, showed a happy capacity to slip into his speeches, anecdotes and illustrations which he knew would have a local appeal.

His friends were effusive in their praise of these speeches, even the doleful Cobden expressing approval. Bright himself, on 1 January 1859, wrote to Wilson that what ought to be done was clear, but what could be done was dark. His investigations into borough politics continued and he corresponded with Crawford about the Irish franchise.[10] The outcry his speeches provoked amongst the aristocracy was something Bright anticipated and hoped for. More difficult to deal with was working-class criticism. A member of the London Parliamentary Reform Committee wrote to the moving spirit of the Northern Reform Union (later League) in Newcastle, Joseph Cowen, urging that it was 'most desirable to press Mr Bright to go at least as far as the programme of the London Committee in extending the franchise to *occupiers* not *ratepayers*'.[11] The point he had in mind was that in many parts of the country, not least in Birmingham, householders 'compounded' with their landlords for the payment of rates and would therefore not qualify. Indeed, a Birmingham correspondent wrote to Newcastle at the end of January that 'the working men of Birmingham dare not speak out or attend any meeting because their *Masters* almost to a man belong to our reform association which goes the whole hog with Mr Bright', yet he claimed Bright's proposals would leave nearly four million working men unenfranchised. He believed, however, that in his heart Bright did not really wish this. The Birmingham middle class had got hold of him. If, however, the working men made themselves felt, Bright 'would go for a franchise that would as near as possible enfranchise all'.[12] Similar comments about 'Bright's Committee' came from Glasgow, though the writer argued that if nothing better seemed likely to emerge, they should make a merit of necessity and back him.[13]

Throughout February Bright himself came to feel that he was too advanced rather than insufficiently radical. Meanwhile, the Derby government at last settled its own proposals. The county occupation franchise was to be made equal with the borough figure of £10 but there were to be special franchises designed to give votes to the superior working class, together with a small amount of redistribution. The 40s. freeholders in boroughs were to be deprived of their dual vote in the counties. Bright considered the so-called 'fancy franchises' an insult to the country. The crucial question, however, was whether the Whigs would support the measure or, if they refrained,

1a Jacob Bright and Martha Wood Bright
Bright's father and mother

1b Green Bank: Bright's birthplace

2   A country house – One Ash – in an industrial landscape

3   Bright as a young man

4   Bright in his prime

5a   The entente cordiale: Bright and Cobden

5b   Margaret Elizabeth Bright née Leatham

6 The proud parents c. 1870

7a   Priscilla McLaren née Bright

7b   Jacob Bright MP

8 Bright's study: books and bookshelves from a grateful people

9 Bright at fifty

10 A Quaker wedding: Helen Priestman Bright to William Clark at Rochdale in 1866

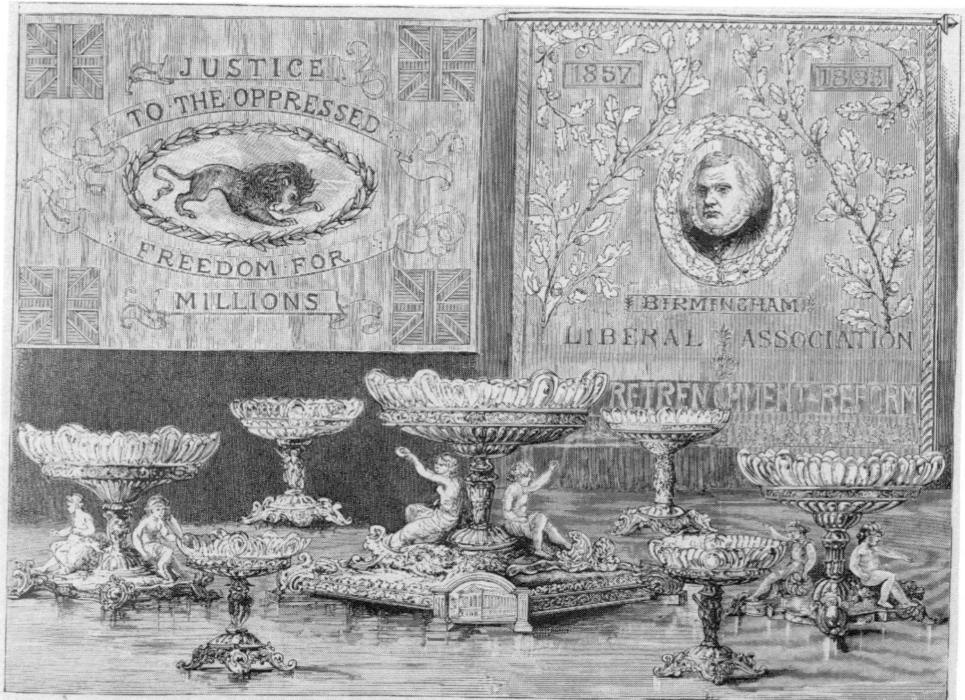
JUSTICE
TO THE OPPRESSED
FREEDOM FOR
MILLIONS
1857
BIRMINGHAM
LIBERAL ASSOCIATION

The "Banner of 1832."   Birmingham Liberal Association Banner.   Dessert Service presented to Mr. John Bright, M.P., in recognition of his Political Services to Birmingham.

THE BRIGHT CELEBRATION AT BIRMINGHAM.

11 Bountiful Birmingham

12a   Haddo House, Aberdeenshire: Bright slept here in 1856

12b   Inverary Castle, Argyllshire: Bright slept here in 1872

13   As others saw him . . .

RIGHT HON: J. BRIGHT.M.P. RHT.HON: W.E. FORSTER.M.P.
RIGHT HON. W.E.GLADSTONE.M.P. RHT.HON: R. LOWE.M.P. EARL GRANVILLE.KG.
LORD SELBORNE.   MARQUIS OF HARTINGTON.M.P.

14   Some members of the Cabinet, late 1873

THE MEETING IN THE TOWN HALL, ROCHDALE

MR. BRIGHT'S SEVENTIETH BIRTHDAY

15   Seventieth birthday celebrations

16a   Joseph Chamberlain

16b   William Gladstone

17 Taking the air

18 Advancing years

19   Darkness and light: Bright in ambivalent old age

20   The last photograph: Bright and his grandchild, Hester Elizabeth, 1888

whether they would offer anything better. On 4 March, he discussed the matter with Russell and found that he would oppose the Bill. So would Palmerston, although he agreed with it — as, incidentally, did Gladstone. Bright, mobilizing petitions from Birmingham and Manchester, warned Russell that it would be pointless if the Whigs defeated the government but did not produce a better measure of their own. When Bright spoke in the Commons on 24 March, he declared that the government's proposal was, in an electioneering phrase, a complete case of personation. Russell's amendment was carried by 330 votes to 291 and Lord Derby announced the dissolution of parliament.

John Bright had no difficulty winning in Birmingham; the two Liberals comfortably headed the poll after 'glorious' meetings. His voice had been in good trim because he had taken a glass of porter 'at the recommendation of somebody acquainted with the habits of singers'. Bright was also able to secure Cobden's nomination and return for Rochdale — a nice touch. Cobden was in the United States at the time but, on coming home, raised no objection. During the campaign, Bright spoke on parliamentary reform on a number of occasions. The *Morning Star* wrote him up handsomely. He reported to Sturge that the paper was doing well — no doubt a consolation before his sudden death a fortnight later.

In the general election, there was no disguising that the Tories had made small but significant gains. Bright was very disappointed, writing to Smith that the world was 'handed over to the sons of Belial in the shape of Emperors, Kings, Lords & soldiers and in our time we cannot hope for any sensible progress towards a deliverance from them.' It was not even the case that reform had dominated the election. Unfortunately, Napoleon III had chosen this moment to attack the Austrians in Italy, and the Tories had gained from the desire not to change the government in such circumstances. Bright had little enthusiasm for Italian unity; what concerned him, as always, was the possibility of Britain being drawn into the conflict. He feared that once again English blood and English treasure would be squandered. He reproached Wilson for organizing a 'neutrality' meeting at which Kossuth would be present. Neutrality, he argued, required complete impartiality.

The Hungarian was a standing menace to Austria. John would not come to such a meeting.

In the aftermath of the election, the political leaders man-oeuvred for position. Before the results were known, Parkes had suggested to Bright that Russell's position would be eased if he renounced office for himself, but he declined to do so. On 23 May, Bright's own view was that Derby could not survive, but there was no clear alternative. If Palmerston would take himself off to some place 'from which no traveller returns' — say the House of Lords — that might help. He feared that Lord John lacked the necessary firmness and resolution. If Derby and Disraeli would keep out of war, he would let them go on, but that could not be guaranteed. There was some talk of a Palmerston/Tory coalition — which might in turn make a real Liberal party possible. Parkes, however, argued that Palmer-ston would be most likely to keep the peace with France, and if Lord John were severed from the bulk of the Whig aristocracy, the split would not hasten reform. Writing on 27 May 1859, he urged Bright to think in terms of power for himself and to recognize that *combination* (whether nicknamed "Party" or "Graft") *is* an essential element in Public Life.' The game was rarely, if ever, successfully played by 'one Public Man in or out of doors'. Bright took the point, but was determined to strike a hard bargain in return for co-operation. He wrote to Russell that Radicals would need distinct assurances on reform and neutrality in the war. They would not be 'the cat's paw for the old concern'. He met Lord John on 3 June at Gibson's house. He explained the radical position and Russell confirmed that he and Palmerston would remain neutral in the war. On reform, they were proposing a £6 borough rental franchise. The ques-tion of the premiership had not been settled. On the whole, Bright was satisfied, but knew that his own chances of gaining office were slight, though Cobden and Gibson might be invited. 'Blind fools!', was his diary comment, 'They think Cobden more easy to manage and less dangerous than I am.'[14]

Nevertheless, Bright did attend the famous meeting at Wil-lis's rooms at which Palmerston and Russell announced their reconciliation and promised general co-operation. A few days later, the Derby government was defeated and resigned. The Queen tried to promote Lord Granville, but in the end had to call on Palmerston. Bright had been arguing with his associates that if the Whigs would only admit Gibson and Cobden, the 'independent' party should demand three representatives. If their demand failed, they should withdraw. However, in the haggling, it became clear that Bright was out of the running. The Queen was hostile and the aristocracy was incensed by his recent attacks. Russell was left to explain, on Palmerston's behalf, that he had been excluded not because he wanted to reform the Commons but because of his attitude 'to other institutions considered essential by the great majority of Englishmen'. His crime consisted in his attacks, not on individuals, but on classes.[15] Queen Victoria refused to sanction Palmerston's conciliatory suggestion that Bright might be offered a Privy Councillorship. 'It would be impossible', she wrote, 'to allege any service Mr Bright has rendered, and if the honour were looked upon as a reward for his systematic attacks upon the institutions of the country, a very erroneous impression might be produced. . . .'[16]

How Bright reacted to this exclusion is in some doubt. Some testimony represents him as being in high dudgeon at this final insult from Crown and aristocracy. In his diary, however, Bright recorded that even if he had been invited, he could not have served under Palmerston. In any case, he suspected that he would be miserable in Court dress and official fetters, speaking privately of his 'immense relief' at his exclusion. When Cobden returned from America, Bright tried not to influence his decision, though his own feelings against the new combination were hardening. He complained to Smith on 28 June that the Whig press was attacking him with more than its usual virulence, the *Scotsman* — 'that Scotch viper' — particularly. If Cobden read these papers 'he will see them at the bottom of the sea before he will have anything to do with them'. Cobden did indeed refuse, and only Gibson took office, first as President of the Poor Law Board and then of the Board of Trade. In practice, the 'independent' party had shown little cohesion and Bright had overestimated its ability to dictate terms. There was, indeed, something remarkable about Palmerston's survival capacity. If Bright could have known that he would still be Prime Minister in 1865, the year of his death, he would have been aghast.

THE REFORM JANUS.

Bright's own dilemma was now clear. His personal standing among the unenfranchised and among some sections of the enfranchised middle classes had never been higher. Office, however, was denied him by those very groups in society which he attacked with such zest. He could either accept this situation, continue his reform campaign, appeal to the respectable working men and then secure for himself an important role when a popular Liberal party finally emerged, or he could accept Parkes's advice that combination was indeed the essence of politics. He would have to compromise in the House of Commons and modify his attacks on the established order outside. It was not easy to decide between these two courses and he put off a decision, hoping perhaps that he would never have to make it.

The immediate danger remained the Italian situation and the state of Anglo-French relations. Bright had no faith in Palmerston, but knew that Russell, the Foreign Secretary, and Gladstone, the Chancellor of the Exchequer, were very Italian in sympathy. He wrote to Congreve on 20 June that there seemed less risk of conflict but he deplored what he termed the reckless arming of the previous administration. The bloody slaughter in the battle of Solferino horrified him. The peace of Villafranca, which brought the war to an end on 12 July, was a great relief. He believed that the government could promote commercial intercourse with France by a mutual reduction of duties, which would, in turn, reduce tensions and armaments. This idea was not new, but when Bright elaborated on it in the Commons, it had repercussions. Cobden eagerly responded to the notion of a commercial treaty which Chevalier, a French Saint-Simonian, had urged upon him. Enlisting the support of Gladstone, he was able to persuade Palmerston to let him go to Paris to negotiate. So long as he did not have to abandon his forts, the Prime Minister was not averse to the project and it was successfully brought to a conclusion in early 1860. Although he corresponded with Cobden throughout, Bright had nothing to do with the negotiations and the credit for the success must be Cobden's, though Bright's original stimulus need not be disparaged.

'I am tired of agitation', Bright wrote to Cobden in August, 'but I would give something to lift up our population into freemen & to bring down the lofty pretensions of the ruling class.' Only hoarseness and a breaking voice prevented him from eagerly responding to invitations to address another extensive round of public meetings. Meanwhile, he applauded the exposure of electoral malpractices, though he feared that parliament loved corruption as a child should love its parents. The subject of electoral misbehaviour was in fact a rather delicate one for Bright at this juncture. Two of his wife's brothers, William Henry and Edward Leatham, had been elected for Wakefield and Huddersfield respectively. At the end of July 1859 a petition against William for bribery was upheld and he was turned out. 'The agent', John reported to his anxious wife, 'seems to have acted like a fool — that is, if he thought bribery was a thing anybody might do openly. I am disgusted that W.H. should have been mixed up with such a mess. . . .' The incident caused Bright some embarrassment, though no lasting political damage.

Lord John was as good as his word, and pressed his colleagues at the end of 1859 to introduce a Bill which would reduce the county franchise to £10 and the borough to £6. Bright spoke in Liverpool during December, under the auspices of the Financial Reform Association. He warned the aristocracy, and even the monarchy, that the true interests of the people could not be ignored. If the opportunity was not seized, louder voices and ruder hands than his own would intervene in the future. It was a disappointment that his old associate, Villiers, thought the £6 franchise too liberal, though Gibson seemed sound. The latter, however, reported that the bulk of the government's correspondence urged caution, and Bright began to suspect that the ruling classes were stimulating the old military spirit in order to divert attention from reform. Cobden, however, detected a tendency in Bright to advocate the interests of the 'working class'. If he continued in this fashion, the middle classes would range themselves with those above them to resist a common danger. Possibly in response, Bright's speeches in Manchester and Birmingham in the next few months were more circumspect. This, of course, brought him criticism from other quarters. 'The field is abandoned to you', wrote Holyoake to Cowen on 10 January 1860. 'Bright's speech of last Friday at Birmingham is an abandonment of the right of the people. He is dead beaten by the critics.'

In March 1860, Lord John brought in a Reform Bill along the lines agreed by the Cabinet, but it evoked no enthusiasm. Bright considered the £10 occupation franchise for the counties and the £6 rental franchise for the boroughs not altogether unsatisfactory and he would support the bill, *faute de mieux*. 'What do you think of Mr John Bright now?' was one agitated reaction. 'The man of the people — a pretty leader indeed! he deserves to be kicked on his bare bottom through the streets. . . .'[17] The preponderant parliamentary opinion, however, was that Russell was going too far. A new proposal to substitute figures of £15 and £8 was considered, but in June the bill was withdrawn, ostensibly to await the 1861 census.

Bright saw Palmerston's hand in this procrastination, as he saw it in other matters. Despite the progress of the commercial negotiations, suspicion of France remained rife. French 'imperialism' in asking for the cession of Nice and Savoy was strongly denounced. At once Bright detected danger and 'Perish Savoy' was his response. Talk of a French invasion increased, and the Prime Minister pressed ahead with the system of fortifications along the south coast. Bright protested to Russell about the expenditure upon 'defence', but did not think he made much impression. 'I agree with you', he wrote to Cobden in early July, 'that we cannot & must not longer tolerate a *Liberal* Govt doing worse things than the Tories would dare to propose.'

Bright's despair at the government's behaviour was not quite complete. As Chancellor, Gladstone's help in the French commercial negotiations had been invaluable. His opposition to the fortifications programme also counted in his favour. He once again became the rising hope of the stern unbending Radicals, though they still had doubts about him. It was only the previous year that Bright had described the 'eccentric' Gladstone's acceptance of office as 'wholly unjustifiable'. Gladstone's defence of rotten boroughs in 1858 and his refusal to vote against the Derby government still rankled. In 1860, however, his 'fine conscientiousness' outweighed his defects, particularly as he wished to abolish the paper duties. Lord Clarendon was not the only one to fear that if Gladstone ever became Prime Minister he might be 'a thorough-going Democrat with Bright in his Cabt'.[18] Towards the end of May, the House of Lords rejected the Paper Duties Bill. It was an open secret that the Prime Minister disapproved of the measure. A Cabinet split and a constitutional crisis seemed possible. Bright was once more in a quandary. It went without saying that Palmerston's conduct was infamous, and he was tempted to help overturn the government at the first opportunity, yet he did not wish to embarrass Gladstone or Gibson. If the government remained, a Paper Duties Bill might yet be passed, whereas a Conservative administration would be unlikely to carry it. The crisis was temporarily resolved when Palmerston agreed that the whole matter should be referred to the Committee of Privileges. Bright spoke on the subject but in reply the Prime Minister 'lost his temper and spoke foolishly — but he is a foolish old man.'

It seemed that the only consolation 1860 had to offer Bright was a further visit to Paris. The French commercial treaty had been concluded and Bright did not think it amiss to bathe a little in Cobden's glory by appearing in the French capital. It was flattering to be treated with considerable respect by leading French personalities. There was even an audience of the Emperor on 27 November. It was very gratifying to learn from imperial lips that the work Bright had been doing to reduce tension between the two countries was appreciated. The two men then discussed the undesirability of passports. Bright returned to England with his morale improved.

Since the Reform Bill was still technically only postponed, Bright made some effort to keep the issue alive. Inevitably, Cobden was pessimistic about his chances, writing in August that sometimes he felt that there would be no further change in the franchise until it became universal. As things stood, 'with the people well employed & no pressure from below & no fear of the working class, there is no disposition on the part of the rich middle class to entertain the question of extending the franchise.' Bright's relative gentleness towards the government — Palmerston apart — did not go unnoticed. 'He wishes the government to act', wrote one critic, 'but if they *will* not, he shields them from opposition as far as he can.' Believing the 'French Treaty Business' to be the explanation, the writer was confirmed in his belief that the Liberal party would do no good until it emancipated itself from the Manchester School.[19] Bright dismissed these comments as the carpings of a man recently sacked from a Reform organization.[20] Even so, his tactical dilemma remained. He tried to goad middle-class employers by arguing that the workmen were 'great in numbers, growing in intelligence and their power of combination is without limit. They will contend for themselves, by themselves, if condemned to remain a separate and suspected order in our social system.'[21] A few weeks later, on 11 December, he consented to speak for the first time before a substantially working class audience. He told the members at the inaugural meeting of the Leeds Working Men's Parliamentary Reform Association that when he learned of the nature of the meeting 'he felt it was quite impossible to absent himself . . . without doing violence to his own feelings. . . .' At the same time, it was aristocratic gossip that Bright was a bad employer.[22] It was clearly impossible for him to please everybody. He did, however, try to please Gladstone with a new year message in 1861. Palmerston and Russell, he wrote, were men of the past and there was a feeling that his correspondent was destined to give the country a wiser policy and higher morality. Gladstone did not take up this point and in reply stated that, in principle, Bright's plans for Anglo-French talks to reduce armaments were sound.

'As to political meetings', wrote a dispirited and depressed Bright to Wilson in January 1861, 'I am refusing all the invitations I receive — for I cannot undertake the weight of an agitation which does not seem able to sustain itself.' It was a sad commentary on his efforts and somewhat galling to admit that Cobden's analysis had again proved correct. Palmerston was, of course, to blame, but it was Russell who bore the brunt of his criticism for his ineffectiveness and effrontery. It was almost best to hope for a Tory restoration, or a coalition with Tory support. He begged Cobden to come back from abroad to give him support since, with Gibson 'in the net', the government treated him insolently. 'Mr Bright', wrote the secretary of the Northern Reform Union, looking at his position from another perspective, 'is as brave as a lion, but he is obliged to keep within what are called moderate bounds by the rank and file of his supporters.'[23] It was a generous estimate, but the truth was that, at least momentarily, he had lost his sense of direction and was again in some danger of losing his self-confidence.

Inevitably, he wondered whether to continue in public life since the claims of business and family were so strong — he now had an even larger family and the mills were only slowly returning to full production. Requests for portraits and busts, he noted wearily, seemed to be all that he gained from the House of Commons and he had had enough of them. In the Welsh hills, there might be gold, and the mine at Dylefe, in which he had an interest, might relieve him of all his financial anxieties if he devoted himself to its operations. Why not forget politics altogether? The answer lay in his striving to justify the ways of God to man, as far as he understood them. 'I believe I am not moved by projects of ambition', he wrote to a Friend, J. B. Braithwaite, 'or by any idea of personal advantage or advancement. If I am not sorely in error, I feel a strong love of what is just & a strong sympathy for those who suffer. . . .' That there were failings in his character, he did not contest, but he was 'supported by the hope that he was sowing some good seed in men's hearts and understandings on great public questions and that fruit may one day not be wanting'.[24] The previous May, he had gone to see Holman Hunt's new picture, *Christ Found in the Temple*. It is not altogether fanciful to suppose that it was the notion of confounding the wise which gave Bright some satisfaction at this dismal point in his career.

NINE

The American civil war 1863-7

It was perhaps fortunate for Bright that the American civil war broke out at this low point in his political life. Like many men of his stamp, Bright had long admired the United States, contrasting its open society and political institutions with his own country. With its natural resources, its democratic ideals, its pacific foreign policy and lack of militarism, the country was bound to flourish. That there was truth in this picture cannot be denied, yet for Bright it was a judgment of faith rather than experience. The nearest he had come to crossing the Atlantic was in 1845 when, with considerable regret, he had to abandon the plan. Bright's impressions, therefore, were derived from his family, friends and visiting Americans. He was convinced that the United States substantially embodied the ideals he preached.

Enthusiasm for the United States was not universal in Britain. Conservative images of its progress and prospects were very different from Bright's. Commenting on Bright's Manchester speech of December 1858, Lord Clarendon spoke for many of his class when he wrote 'His may be the best and quickest route to America; but I don't wish to go to America.'[1] Observers of American expansion westwards, and designs on Central America, found it difficult to recognize the pacific country of Bright's dream. Bright insisted, however, that Britain should not meddle in these matters and he criticized any attempts to contain the United States in the south and west.[2] He was delighted to observe the growing *rapprochement* between Britain and the United States in the 1850s;[3] a close working relationship seemed natural.

Some shrewd British observers of the American scene, however, concluded that the rapid extension of the United States might increase the stresses and strains within. So it proved. Towards the end of 1860, the gravity of the situation across the Atlantic became apparent. *Punch* was not alone in asking Bright what was going wrong in his promised land. In the summer of 1860, like many others, Bright had assumed that W. H. Seward would gain the presidential nomination and wage a campaign against slavery. Lincoln's selection, and then his victory in December 1860, came as a surprise. His success was the signal for disintegration — South Carolina left the Union and other states followed suit. Bright admitted that there was a good deal of confusion but 'could not convince myself yet that there will be anything more'. He was worried for another reason. In the previous decade, something like 80 per cent of the cotton used in Britain came from the United States. He reminded Gladstone of this fact in a letter on 9 January 1861. Nevertheless, it was not war which alarmed him so much as the prospect of a discreditable compromise which would prove fatal to the Union. He agreed with Cobden that the idea of a separate Northern state was attractive, but it was also 'a noble prospect to see a great continent under one central republican govt'.

After months of uncertainty, war did break out in April 1861 when the President refused to acquiesce in the withdrawal of the Southern States. They formed themselves, not without difficulty, into a Confederacy, with Jefferson Davis as President. The North proceeded to institute a blockade. In a proclamation on 13 May, the British government proclaimed its complete neutrality, recognizing the belligerency of the Confederate States, but not their independence. It was far from certain, however, that the government would maintain this stance. There was some emotional sympathy for the Southern States in official circles, but more important, if Britain ensured their victory, a balance of power could be created in North America to its advantage. The possibility of intervention, therefore, could not be ruled out. The issue of slavery did not, apparently, arise for, however tactical, Lincoln's inaugural address in March 1861 had ruled out interference with the institution of slavery in the Southern States.

Bright later devoted himself to the war, but to begin with he was distinctly reticent.[4] His sympathies were undoubtedly with the North, but he refrained from public expression of them. Cobden, on the other hand, was sympathetic to the legal right of the South to secede. Writing in June, he cited Tocqueville on this point, and thought the North unreasonable in treating the Southern States as rebels. Bright's brother Thomas was not a strong Northerner, stressing his dislike of American tariff policy. It was this policy, he wrote, just before the outbreak of war, which 'has much changed the feelings of people here, and they all hope the separation will be complete and final.' With separation, the North would not have to bear the odium of slavery and the South could trade without the shackles of Northern protectionism.[5] If, of course, the Northern blockade of Southern ports proved effective, then the loss of cotton would be a great disaster. 'Lancashire is in tremendous peril', Bright warned Cobden, '& if Lancashire, then England.'

It was not until 1 August 1861, in Rochdale, that Bright publicly stated his firm commitment to the Washington government. 'If the thirty-three or thirty-four States of the American Union can break off whenever they like', he declared, 'I can see nothing but disaster and confusion throughout the whole continent.'[6] It is perhaps an indication of the tension that he was under, that Bright again felt ill and weary. Early in August he refused an invitation to fish from the Speaker of the Commons on the grounds that his brother was unwell and he was needed in Rochdale. He even made difficulties about the annual family holiday to Llandudno on the grounds of cost. It was also undesirable to go there too early because there would be too many of his Birmingham constituents in evidence. On 6 September he reported to Helen that the mills would, in future, only work three or four days a week. 'The American confusion', he explained, 'is gradually gathering round us, menacing us with great evils.'

The initial Northern defeats caused him much grief. In a letter to James Henderson, a New Yorker, on 4 September, he explained that he had hitherto abstained from much comment, 'feeling the difficulty of the question and fearing to do harm', but he thought, nevertheless, that certain points did stand out. First, slavery was an institution against which the *spirit* of the constitution revolted, though the practical difficulties in ending it were great. Second, he feared that if the South was indeed united, there was small chance that the North could defeat it, and little benefit if it could. The folly and guilt of the Southern leaders was enormous, but

> without a regular army, without skilled and experienced commanders, with the population of the Border States against you or divided in opinion & interests, & with so *vast* a territory in insurrection against you, there is little chance of anything like a conquest of the insurgent states.

There was also the possible danger from Britain. While recognizing the difficulties of an emancipation proclamation, he believed that it would make it impossible for the British government to side with the South. Public sentiment would go with the North and the constitutional issue would be overlooked 'in the effort to efface at one blow that which they feel to be the dark stain upon the character of your great republic.' Some lowering of the tariff would have a similar beneficial result.[7]

From this stage on, Bright began to meddle with the conflict at the highest level. He entered on what was to prove an extensive correspondence with the Chairman of the Senate Foreign Relations Committee, Charles Sumner. From the start, he did not pretend to be dispassionate, making plain his distrust of the British Prime Minister and Foreign Secretary. He warned Sumner that in his view the British ruling class would prefer two states in America. He thought the willingness of the British government to send extra troops to Canada was provocative. This ready condemnation reads a little oddly in the light of our knowledge that W. H. Seward, the American Secretary of State, believed that a war against Britain might be a way of bringing North and South together. At home, Bright devoted his efforts to trying to prevent intervention. He urged

Cobden to alert Gladstone to the possibility that, as in 1853, he might find himself drawn into war.

By November 1861, Bright felt compelled by the 'grossness of the misstatements' of others to make a public speech on America. Although he planned to make it in Rochdale, there was some disagreement in the family. 'If I were a Southerner', Thomas wrote on 22 November, 'I would either be free from the North or I would die the death. If the men of the South have any of the old blood left, they will win in this stuggle.' John, he added, was very strong for the North, but 'the North cannot win for all that, unless the Southerners prove to be curs.' There was an aggressiveness about John in these weeks which even seasoned observers of his pugnacity found disturbing. His brother-in-law, Samuel Lucas, in a letter to Harriet Martineau, believed that his exclusion from office 'by the Queen' still rankled.[8] In addition, no doubt, the *Trent* affair greatly agitated him. On 8 November, two Southern envoys, Mason and Slidell, had been taken from a British ship off the Cuban coast by a Northern warship. Although previously, British governments had never been impressed by neutral rights in this kind of situation, Palmerston was determined to give the North a lesson. On 30 November, Russell demanded the release of the envoys and an apology. The Prime Minister seemed to be ready for war if he did not receive a satisfactory answer. More British troops were sent to Canada. In its timing, therefore, Bright's Rochdale speech on 4 December 1861 came to have an unexpected importance. He argued that, in the *Trent* affair, the Northern captain had been acting without authorization — it was absurd to suppose that the North wanted to increase its burdens by going to war with Britain. In a very few years, he added, the North would exceed Britain in population and would not be well-disposed if the land of its fathers betrayed it in its hour of need. He made it clear in private that if war did break out, he would retire from parliament rather than wear himself out as he had done seven years previously. In the end, many letters from Bright, and many diplomatic dispatches later, Lincoln and Seward agreed to release the two Confederate agents, declaring that the captain concerned had acted without authority.

Although the dust had still to settle, Bright felt by early

January 1862 that the danger of an Anglo-American conflict had passed, though he still did not see the future clearly. Cobden was writing at this time that North and South could never lie in the same bed again and predicting that European Powers would soon recognize Southern independence. The only chance for the North was to mollify the Europeans by lifting its blockade of the Mississippi. Bright would not hear a word against the North and argued, on the contrary, that the speediest way through the cotton crisis was for the Washington government to win. He thought that the slave-owners had committed suicide by their insurrection. To acknowledge the South and to break the blockade, was war, without even the excuse of an 'outrage'. He wanted the North to capture New Orleans and Mobile so that the cotton trade could be re-opened. In February 1862, after an amphibious landing, New Orleans was in fact captured.

Bright's life now began to be dominated by America. While parliament held little interest, his role as a Northern publicist became increasingly congenial. He paid many calls on the American Minister in London and Northerners in Britain made a point of seeking him out. He corresponded with a wide variety of Americans — diplomats, scholars, clergy and businessmen. His message to them all was that there were two nations in England — the governing class and the toiling millions; the one supported the South and the other the North. He was frequently in and out of the *Star* offices, gleaning the latest news of the war, while confessing to his wife that it was 'sad to feel so much interest in transactions which have in them so much to condemn'. Writing to the American historian, Bancroft, on 29 March, he felt that the position within Britain had stabilized. Until very recently, he had been ridiculed for believing that the Union could be completely restored, but others now shared his opinion. He hoped that with the capture of New Orleans, the blockade of the Gulf might be raised and small supplies of cotton forwarded.[9] He painted a picture of suffering in Lancashire which, unless relieved, might harm the Northern cause. The Brights did their best to minimize the hardships suffered by their workers, but the business was doing badly. In his opinion, the Washington government should seek rapid and complete success. 'I want to hear that Jeff Davis is running for his life', he wrote on 10 April, 'tho' I hope no man will be put to death as a criminal for his share in the fearful guilt of this war.'[10] He found, with some satisfaction, that the inhabitants of beautiful houses in Kensington Palace Gardens were now seeking his views of American events.

In the late summer of 1862 Bright again retreated, without his family, to the Highlands for a month. Reports he received from Lancashire, however, caused him considerable concern. He had stated publicly that the workers of the country would willingly endure hardship, so staunch was their support for the North. He knew, however, that such support would be under severe pressure in the coming winter — indeed, it has recently been argued by Mary Ellison that it was never as deep or complete as Bright maintained. Thomas Bright, however, had now veered against the South and said that he was prepared to let the mills stand idle for years rather than work them on slave-grown cotton. 'Cotton is not "King"', he wrote, 'and the Planters will find that England . . . has no sympathy for Man Stealers and Woman Whippers.' He admitted, however, that there was much distress in Rochdale. The Brights were subscribing freely to the soup kitchen which supplemented the help available under the Poor Law. John believed that, as the situation deteriorated, the government would come under considerable pressure to provide relief. He recommended in July to his old associate, Villiers, now President of the Poor Law Board, that Guardians should be allowed to borrow money. The only drawback, he admitted, was that such a plan might interfere with voluntary subscriptions. However, he had to admit that, in this respect, 'some of the largest firms in the town in the Cotton trade had given little or nothing . . . towards winter some men may give in from fear who are not now to be moved by any nobler feeling.' The fact was, of course, that some who refrained from giving believed that a better solution was to recognize the South. Such men, Bright declared, were either fools or worse.

Because he feared that cotton famine might yet provoke European intervention, Bright again thought about the possibilities of India. The Manchester Chamber of Commerce, among other bodies, submitted memoranda urging greater public investment in India in order to stimulate supply. The eagerness of Manchester merchants to protect their own interests at the expense of their supposed commercial principles, provoked some amusement. Bright, for example, supported the idea that land on which cotton was grown should be exempt from tax. Yet, he did not take a very prominent part in the agitation — his pride forbade it.

> When there was a chance of averting this dismal state of things [he wrote to his daughter] I spoke as I thought might be useful — & nobody heeded much or thought the catastrophe could ever come. Now I feel as if speaking were of no use, & that others may find their way through it if they can.

He was sceptical whether the neglect of past years could be quickly made up. Half a dozen old fellows in Calcutta, as he put it, could not really claim to be an effective government. Merchants would be prepared to pay more for Indian cotton but a sufficient quantity would not be forthcoming. Bright therefore tried to influence Washington, believing that this would be more useful than attacking the British government in parliament. Moreover, he always believed that there was a good deal to be said for writing letters from the Scottish Highlands or North Wales! Cobden was somewhat peeved. 'I wanted you sorely in the House', he wrote on 7 August. 'I really think if we had been together the last six weeks we should have silenced the old fellow.' Bright was not perturbed. On 14 July he had written to Sumner stressing the need for cotton to come out of New Orleans, 'even at some sacrifice'. He had heard that the commanding Northern general was proving obstructive. Writing to Villiers a month later, however, he claimed that it was 'only the orders of the Southern government' which prevented the cotton coming. There was, clearly, no quick answer to the problem.

The issue which Bright most wanted to come into prominence, however, was that of slavery. Only if the black nation emerged into light and freedom, would there be any real compensation for the terrible losses of the war. In his view, every day the war lasted, black men became more important. He could not think that God had permitted the war without a plan for their redemption. If slavery came to the fore, it would be difficult for Britain and France to mediate. In September, the governments of Britain and France were indeed seriously considering offering mediation which, if it was refused, would be followed by recognition of the South. On 23 September, however, President Lincoln did issue the Emancipation Proclamation, to take effect from 1 January 1863. All slaves in states in rebellion against the United States would be freed. The declaration was not comprehensive — indeed, it only applied to those areas which Washington did not in fact control — but Bright welcomed it warmly. 'I begin to believe', he wrote to Sumner, 'that another crop of cotton *from slave labor* will never again be grown on your Northern continent.' There was, of course, the possibility that the Confederates might also declare for freedom, but if they did not, he wrote to the American Consul in Liverpool, 'their whole basis of industry and power will crumble under them.' He added that he hoped now for effective military action for 'it is what you do in America & not what people *think* here that will decide the contest.'[11] As if to endorse the point, Lee's invasion of Maryland was turned back at the Battle of Antietam, and the military situation began to look brighter for the North. The combined effect of these developments was to deter the British government from mediation.

The only politician to spoil what seemed to Bright to be an encouraging picture was the Chancellor of the Exchequer. In a speech in Newcastle on 7 October 1862, Gladstone declared that whatever views were held about slavery, it was undoubtedly the fact that Jefferson Davis and his colleagues had made an army, were making a navy and, what was more important than either, they had made a nation. Bright was shocked and angered. Before the speech was delivered, he had urged through Cobden that Gladstone should not say anything unfriendly to the United States, and speak liberally on home affairs, in order to show the public that he was the Liberal man of the future. He had done no such thing and his remarks only gave fresh hope to Southern supporters. Gladstone's reference to the Southern Navy inevitably redirected attention to the building of the warship, the *Alabama*, which had earlier caused a major diplomatic row between London and Washington, and which was to have even more lasting consequences in the future. Gladstone's mind, Bright concluded sadly, was too unstable for him to lead a party or a nation successfully. 'He was born of a great slave-holding family', was his verdict to Cobden, '& I suppose the taint is ineradicable.'

Gladstone's *faux pas* left the field for Bright himself. Early on, he had seen that enthusiasm for the North could perhaps be harnessed to revive the reform cause in Britain, and he now saw his opportunity. In the months after the Emancipation Proclamation, meetings were held in the big cities to celebrate this event and to revive the call for parliamentary reform. 'We shall have a general election in 1863, certain I believe', wrote Bright on Christmas Eve 1862, '& then the result of so much treason to the Liberal party & of so much incapacity will be seen. I suspect the result will be such as has not been seen since 1841.' In the previous week, he had made a major speech in Birmingham, blaming the government for the cotton famine and observing that the price for neglecting his past advice on India was now being paid. Bright's fellow-member for Birmingham took a different view of the war, but that did not deter him. His praise of the 'free' States reached new heights; everything there, apparently, was free. He offered his audience a vision of a vast confederation from the frozen North to the glowing South, from the Atlantic to the Pacific, in which there would be one people, one language, one faith; a refuge for the oppressed of every race and clime. It is little wonder that suggestions were made that he should emigrate at once. Bright, however, intended the old country to pattern itself of this elysium; he was regaining his confidence.

'I think in every town in the Kingdom', he reported to Sumner, 'a public meeting would go by an overwhelming majority in favor of President Lincoln and of the North.' At Rochdale on 3 February 1863, he denounced those who thought that it was still possible to be strictly and coldly neutral on such a great question. His most impressive performance, however, was at a gathering of London trade unionists in St James's Hall on 26 March.[12] Apart from the Positivist, Beesly, who organized the occasion, and Bright himself, the other speakers were working-class leaders. Karl Marx was in the audience and grudgingly conceded that on this occasion Bright had spoken like a real Independent. The orator declared that the issues had now become so plain that most Englishmen understood them, 'and least of all do I expect that the six millions of men in the United Kingdom who are not enfranchised can have any doubt upon it.' A few years later, the trade unionist, George Howell, gratefully reminded Bright that his presence on this occasion 'gave a great impetus to the political tendencies of the unions, and aided us greatly in our endeavour to bring them into the political arena.'[13] The Positivists, too, were well-pleased with the 'sort of reconciliation' which had apparently been achieved. It was on the strength of such gatherings that Bright assured Mrs Harriet Beecher Stowe, whose *Uncle Tom's Cabin* had greatly moved the British reading public, that in all but a limited aristocratic circle and its commercially corrupt associates, news that the Northern forces had taken Vicksburg and Charleston would cause great joy.[14]

In the next few months, Bright chiefly occupied himself with the naval-building question which again threatened relations between Britain and the North. Some more 'rams' were under construction at Birkenhead. 'If the Govt are in earnest', Bright argued, 'they ought to prosecute Mr Laird. He has admitted in the House that his firm built & equipped the *Alabama* & there is abundance of evidence to sustain a prosecution.' He urged patience on Sumner.

> Whether a ship more or less breaks the blockade is of no real importance to you or to us; but whether you should be interfered with in your efforts to suppress the Southern insurrection by a war with England, is of an importance to you and us that words cannot describe.

'Your fate', he wrote in a further letter on 2 May, 'seems to depend on yourselves, on your armies and fleets, and on the pressure under which the conspirators are suffering.' His remark was more apposite than he knew. The Battle of Chancellorsville had begun and Lee defeated the Northern armies. Once again, it seemed as if the South had made a decisive breakthrough as Lee prepared to move on the North. Not until early July, when Lee was defeated at Gettysburg and Grant accepted the surrender of Vicksburg, was the situation again optimistic for the North. It was a measure of Bright's apprehension and anger that he attacked Roebuck's motion that the Confederacy should be recognized with even more than his customary ferocity. Roebuck suggested that the United States would never be in a position to bully the world if they were divided and sub-divided. Bright dismissed his contention as groundless and unworthy; the issue of slavery was much more central.

While Bright maintained his public display of confidence in Lincoln and the Washington government, he was anxious in private. Frankly describing the Northern government as 'imbecile', Cobden considered there to be an utter want of central authority to direct, control or correct. Moreover, such deplorable incapacity reflected damagingly on democratic principles. 'I confess', he concluded, 'it has given me so great a distaste for the topic of war that I try to avoid it.' Bright understood these fears, but expressed himself more moderately in a letter on 9 July 1863 to his friend T. H. Dudley, the American Consul in Liverpool. 'There seems a strange want of foresight and of force at Washington', he wrote, 'and I fear this has bred *disgust* and helplessness among the people. . . .' He wondered whether the 'slavery poison' had polluted and enfeebled the free States so that they could not subdue the revolution which might destroy them. After the news of Gettysburg and Vicksburg, Northern successes, Bright cheered up at once. '"Secesh" in England', he told an American correspondent, 'must be out of spirits, as it is doubtless in America, & there will be lamentation in the hearts of those who wish ill to the great republic.'[15] He developed a different anxiety.[16]

I only begin to fear [he wrote on 31 July] that your cause may go on too fast, for I am not sure that the North is yet resolute & unanimous enough to be able to deal wisely with the great slavery question. To me it seems necessary to declare the Proclamation an *unalterable decree* and to restore no state to its ancient position in the nation until its constitution & laws are made to harmonize with the spirit of it. . . .

He deprecated any talk in the North of vengeance against Britain; there was enough to do to restore the Union. 'The most complete vengeance on the ruling classes here', he urged, 'will be to falsify their prophecies and to restore the unity and strength of your country.'[17] He did his best to silence any English aristocrat who ventured to doubt the North's capacity for this task. 'I do not think', he wrote to Lord Hartington on 17 December 1863, 'the terror of an approaching commercial panic will shake the resolution of the American people to preserve the integrity of their government & country & to make freedom universal over the continent committed to their rule.'[18] Talk of the South as a 'new nation' was certainly warning.

Most of Bright's American sources seemed to think that the war would end some time in 1864. He continued to follow its progress throughout this year, though with less excitement and exclusive devotion than previously. From time to time, he could not help expressing the view that it was all taking longer than expected. Politically, Bright was highly relieved when Lincoln was re-elected to office. 'If you become *sure* that Mr Lincoln will be elected', he had written, 'may I ask you to send me one line to say so; my anxiety is very great.'[19] Once the election was over, he urged on his American correspondents that the central issues of the war were not negotiable. Slavery, he wrote to Sumner, 'should be extirpated wholly and immediately throughout the union and without any compensation'. He advocated a general amnesty, except for a dozen or so leading rebels. Lands already seized and sold should remain with their existing owners, and in other cases there should be generosity and mercy. All debts contracted by the 'conspiracy' should be made void. He did not wish to be vindictive, but 'nothing should be done or conceded that lessens the idea of the CRIME which the slaveholders have committed'.

In late January 1865, he at last felt sure that the events of the war were 'tending towards peace'. He still hoped and believed that the President would consent to nothing but a full submission. Indeed, in all his correspondence at this time, he continued to stress that there was 'little to negotiate about & submission is the only condition on which war can be closed'. Writing to his wife at the end of April, he summed up the history of the previous four years in these terms.

What a good result, white and black are henceforth alike free on the American continent. I seem to have more reason to rejoice than most others for I have had more anxiety and more faith. It is another proof that He who made the world, still rules it & will not forsake it.

We shall feel 'less *intense* interest in the arrival of the boat' was his final comment on the Northern success.

Bright did have some grounds for satisfaction. A cause that he had supported throughout, had triumphed. It was such an unusual experience that he may be forgiven some exaggeration of the part he had played in the outcome of the war. Palmerston was not deterred from intervening in the conflict from fear of Bright's tongue, but from his own calculation of British interests. Power did not shift during the war from Palmerston and Russell to Bright. Despite all the flattery that Bright received from Sumner and Lincoln, the American leaders never lost sight of this fact. Yet the exchange of kind words, books and presents was something more than a highly edifying form of self-congratulation. It was helpful to some Northern leaders to find an Englishman who was prepared to clothe their actions from the outset in a cloak of righteousness. It was convenient to have the support of a powerful speaker whose admiration for America was so intense and uncritical. Indeed, Bright rapidly became an American hero. Poems, dedications, books, paintings, screens, walking canes and a variety of other interesting objects reached Rochdale from across the Atlantic. Many invitations were extended to him to visit the United States and it was made clear that both log cabin and White House would be open to him. Bright was careful never to accept any of them. It was better for the American dream to remain a dream, uncontaminated by actual experience. Besides, if he could summon up energy, he had his own civil war to fight at home.

TEN

The second Reform crusade: success 1863-7

The House *talks* Poland tonight [wrote Bright to his wife in June 1863] I take no part in it. I am sick of politics in truth & I suppose the mind cannot be greatly occupied on more than one question at one time. Till America is disposed of, I cannot feel deeply about English or European subjects.

In fact there were a good many other questions on his mind. His family was growing up, though only with the arrival of his eighth child in the spring of 1863 was it completed. 'Now, my dear, take all care of thyself, eight children are no small charge', he wrote, though perhaps his wife scarcely needed the information. The eldest boy, John Albert, was at a Quaker school in London, Grove House. His father stressed to him the need for financial prudence, writing that, 'the habit of spending all thy money will bring thee to much anxiety & to many troubles & must be corrected.' On another occasion, he wrote that while wine would not be likely to do him good, the schoolmaster had been informed that 'if thou would like half a glass of Bass's Beer to dinner, he may provide it for thee'.[1] Bass, after all, was good Radical beer. Although now twenty-three, Helen still on several occasions earned a rebuke. 'Thy note to Mama this morning', he wrote, 'is shabby in the extreme — hardly to be understood for its carelessness.' During the school holidays, he ordered his wife to stop Albert

169

shooting birds in the garden. Such were the responsibilities of a father, though exercised, for the most part, from a distance. In October 1863, he did consent to go on a family holiday at Llandudno, but since the weather was not very congenial, he was glad of the excuse provided by a law-suit to return to London.

For some time, the Brights had been engaged in a controversy with the Crossleys of Halifax concerning the patent of a particular type of carpet. The Crossleys were also Dissenting manufacturers and Liberals — Sir Francis was at the time MP for the West Riding — but when it came to carpets, business was business. It was a source of great gratification when, after a long court case, judgment was given for the Brights. In the end, however, carpets made Crossley more money than they did Bright. At his death in 1872, Sir Francis left £800,000; seventeen years later, John Bright left a tenth of that amount, the mid-Wales gold mine never having proved as lucrative as he had hoped. Even so, by the time of his death, Bright was very comfortably off, although he never showed much disposition to promote charitable works on a considerable scale in the manner of many of his Quaker brethren. He gave financial encouragement to a few poets whose work he believed to have merit, but their fame has not survived. He was prepared to make small sums of money available to help correspondents who wrote to him in distress — though, like any MP, he could not respond in such fashion to all. He also wrote to potential employers in the United States whenever any of his own workmen wished to emigrate. In general, however, he kept a tight grasp on his purse and expected others to do the same with theirs.

Even if he did have family and business matters to concern him, it is quite true that, politically, there was nothing to compare with America for interest. The Polish rebellion of 1863 stirred no enthusiasm, and, as always, his chief anxiety was that Britain might be drawn into another war against Russia. He at once plied Villiers with letters making it clear that no one would support such an absurd adventure, though claiming that Russell did 'queer & absurd things often & requires to be watched & kept up to the mark.' The questions disturbing to Europe only were so, he believed, with impeccable logic, because Europe would not let them alone. The Polish question, for example, would settle itself if France and Britain did nothing. In a further letter to Villiers, in December 1863, he repeated his hostility towards Napoleon III and urged a policy of disarmament. In the event, the Polish crisis passed, but Bright's contempt for Palmerston remained withering. He hoped, unsuccessfully, that a fresh touch of scandal, involving the Prime Minister, would unseat the 'hollow idol whom so many fools have worshipped'.

Some of Palmerston's greatest admirers did, in fact, concede that at eighty, his judgment was not as sharp as it had been. Radicals who sympathized with continental nationalism, criticized him for doing nothing to support the Poles. Bismarck was in power in Berlin and began to call the tune. Over Poland, Palmerston had alienated Russia by an ill-judged threat, which he could not carry out, and relations with France had also worsened. When Prussia turned her attention, in the ensuing months, to the Duchies of Schleswig-Holstein, Palmerston led the Danes to expect support, though in the end it was not forthcoming. After his military victory, Bismarck agreed to an armistice and to refer the problem to a conference in London. There, the Danes refused mediation, and fighting resumed, with Prussian troops advancing into Denmark. Lacking support in the Cabinet, Palmerston did nothing, causing Disraeli and Derby to attack the government for betraying the Danes. In the Lords, the vote of censure was carried by a small majority, but in the Commons it was narrowly defeated. Feeling that he could not both speak against the government and vote for it, Bright said nothing in the debate, but he drew some comfort from the outcome of the voting. He liked to believe that his ideas on non-intervention were having their effect.

The old Prime Minister was undoubtedly in difficulties, but whether the result was indeed a 'great triumph' for the Radicals is another matter. Certainly they remained acutely divided between 'non-interventionists' and 'liberationists'. The visit of Garibaldi to Britain in the summer of 1863 proved as embarrassing, in this respect, for Bright as it did for Palmerston. John was invited to meet the Italian hero, but felt, initially, that it was not his place 'to step forward prominently on such an occasion'. He had no 'solid' faith in Italian unity, though he wished it no harm either. As the days passed, however, Bright dithered over the invitation. Garibaldi, he found, was being taken up by the government and the aristocracy. The Duchess of Sutherland arranged a great dinner party at Stafford House, followed by an 'at home', to which Bright was invited. Feeling that the arrangements were 'so perfectly hollow', he did not intend to go and could only hope that Garibaldi would take the occasion to express the hope that English working men might soon be more free. In the event, however, Bright did attend the reception, finding the hall, staircase and reception rooms magnificent. He shook hands with Garibaldi and then saw him 'limping downstairs & across the hall, still leaning on the arm of his hostess — he so weather-beaten & simple, she so fair, so exquisitely dressed & apparently so loving to him as a daughter.' Such a charming picture apparently put ideas into Helen's head. 'Don't think & write nonsense, my dear girl', her father replied, 'about inviting Garibaldi to Rochdale & to our house.' A few days later, Cobden and Bright saw him at a less aristocratic gathering, and found that he 'wore the same kind face, exhibiting the same dreamy enthusiasm. He was pleased to see us & said "I am of your principles, for if I am a soldier, I am a soldier of peace".' They appear to have accepted this remark with equally dreamy enthusiasm. Shortly afterwards, however, Garibaldi left the country in a pique. Bright suspected the evil hand of Palmerston, but had to confess that he was not altogether sorry to see the Italian depart. He thought that excitement about foreign affairs did not help at home.

'I keep in Parlt', wrote Bright in March 1864, 'because I do not seem able to give a good reason for leaving it.' He also stated that as much as possible, he was withdrawing from meetings and platform work, limiting himself to the Commons. At the same time, he also repeated his desire to see the franchise extended and the secret ballot introduced, though the prospects were not good. In May 1864, however, in another of his surprising speeches, Gladstone made his enigmatic declaration that, unless incapacitated by personal unfitness or political danger, every man was morally entitled to come within the pale of the constitution. Bright thought that at last Gladstone was looking to the future and, as he put it, braving the aristocratic mob of the London West End. Since Gladstone's Newcastle speech on the American civil war, the two men had had little contact. Now, Bright felt that there might be some political way forward. Perhaps it was this development that made him feel it was safe for him to visit Gladstone's constituency, the University of Oxford. He had, hitherto, resisted attempts to interest him in university questions, having written to T. H. Green, the Balliol philosopher, in 1861, that in his case, 'any interference in the matter would be attributed to hostility to the Church & to its supremacy at Oxford.' As things stood, he claimed, the Dissenters could not be induced to be very interested in Oxford education. In 1864, Green met Bright for the first time — 'a great brick' was the philosopher's description — and, sitting on Goldwin Smith's lawn, the orator allowed himself to be overheard saying that it would be pleasant to be eighteen and coming up to the university.[2]

It was only in the late summer, that Bright began to explore the ground on the Reform question, writing to Villiers that the easy-going days of the government were coming to an end. The Whig leaders had either to move on or move off. 'As a party', he complained, 'we are going to the dogs, & we can only gain fresh life by adhering to the principles which distinguish us from the Tories.' Looking to Gladstone, he confidently believed that the Liberal party would very soon undertake a measure of parliamentary reform because the alternative was for it to be broken up. Nevertheless, he confessed to being completely bewildered about what he himself should say on the subject in a forthcoming speech at Rochdale. In the event, he did not speak there, not for want of a theme, but because of the sudden death of his little boy, Leonard, while the family was on holiday at Llandudno. 'I am in no mood for a public meeting', Bright wrote to Helen, 'so thou must forgive me as I feel sure all reasonable men among my friends will readily do.' Even the discussion of capital punishment in the Commons would not bring him up to London.

Opposition to capital punishment had always been one of Bright's most deeply held convictions. Early in his career as a MP, he had campaigned against hanging. He even braved what he termed the 'dodges and shuffles' of 'overprudent Friends' at the Yearly Meeting of the Society in 1847.[3] He rarely spoke at this gathering, but he was convinced that 'Friends could do more on this question than any other body . . .' In parliamentary terms, however, the cause made little progress. Bright on occasion urged the claims of mercy in particular cases, but could do little more.[4] Earlier in 1864, however, the subject had again come before the House of Commons. Although he had 'abstained from saying anything upon it for several years, seeing no disposition in Parlt towards anything just & merciful on any question', for a few months he did take a keen interest once more, hoping to 'teach something to people outside, who are often more easily taught than the hearers inside.'[5] In his enthusiasm, Bright even wrote across the Atlantic for information, quoting the replies in his speech in the Commons on 3 May; but he was right to be pessimistic about the outcome.[6] In subsequent years, Bright regarded this speech as the complete expression of his views and always referred correspondents to it.[7] He never changed his mind on the subject and its importance for him can be judged by the fact that he was always ready to leave a dinner table if a debate on capital punishment was taking place.[8]

It was not possible, without serious offence, to refuse to speak in Birmingham at his customary January meeting in 1865. On this occasion, he pronounced the theory of the balance of power pretty nearly dead and buried. He then turned to America and rejoiced that the shackles were dropping from the negro. This was his cue for a review of current proposals for parliamentary reform. He contended that in Canada and Australia, the wider franchises which prevailed there had not prevented men from legislating fairly. There was always, and rightly, a good deal of talk about the 'freedom of England'. Why, then, should her people not be free to vote? Having once more posed the question, however, he made no specific suggestions about the number of people who ought to be enfranchised. It was sufficient, for the moment, to draw attention to the incongruity and leave it at that. Admirers were told that extension of the suffrage was very near and that only old Palmerston barred the way.

Bright did not want to take matters further. He was beginning to worry about himself again. 'I seem less and less able to determine what is best on matters of no great moment', he noted in his diary on 19 February. Early in April, Cobden died and for days he was overcome with grief. As his coffin was being placed in the vault, he could not control himself, crying passionately. While their relationship had fluctuated in its intensity and intimacy, Bright could not fail to miss Cobden's advice and guidance; he was now on his own. On 16 April, his brother-in-law, Samuel Lucas, editor of the *Morning Star*, suddenly died and once again, there was a funeral to attend. A few days later, in mid-Wales on mining affairs, he heard the news of President Lincoln's assassination. 'The slave interest', he exclaimed, 'has not been able to destroy the nation, but it succeeded in killing the President.' 'What a sad month,' he wrote on 29 April. 'I feel at times as if I could suffer no more and grieve no more.' As a result of these events, he felt unable to be present on any occasion which could cause him to become excited. His head was 'uncomfortable', reminding him ominously of eight years earlier. Cobden and Lucas figured prominently in his dreams and he could not 'at present do anything in the political field'. He began to persuade himself that, at fifty-three, he was an old man, unfit for further action; in reality, however, he was on the verge of a remarkable burst of political activity.

In July 1865, Palmerston went to the country and increased his parliamentary majority. Needless to say, the Prime Minister had conducted the election as a vote of confidence in himself. Like most candidates, he eschewed reference to Reform, except in the most general terms. Radicals in the Liberal Party strengthened their position at the expense of the Whigs, but only marginally so, and the result therefore seemed another substantial endorsement of the status quo. Bright thought the results 'remarkable considering the state of our electoral system & the treachery of the Whigs.' The situation was, indeed, more uncertain than it seemed on the surface. There were some 150 new members in the Commons, among them intellectuals like Mill, Fawcett, Hughes and Trevelyan. Duncan McLaren had also been elected, and through him Bright made some contact with these men, though in general there was a good deal of mutual suspicion. He liked to consider intellectuals as clever children who, for all their sophistication, often could not see the obvious. Although both William and Edward Leatham were elected, Bright's three brothers-in-law in this parliament did not see themselves as his adjutants. Perhaps the most significant result of all, however, was Gladstone's election for South Lancashire after his defeat at Oxford university. Despite the scant reference to Reform in Gladstone's campaign, it was widely believed that he would support it in the Cabinet. Bright was still somewhat reserved about Gladstone. 'What fools the Tories have been to drive him from them & to prefer Mr Disraeli' — Bright's comment to Thorold Rogers — hardly suggests that Gladstone was, in his eyes, a real reformer.[9]

After the election, Bright wrote to Villiers that, Palmerston's survival notwithstanding, early attention should be given to Reform. Its supporters would not be 'cheated or insulted any longer, at least in the same way & by the same persons as before'. The new ministry would not be able to meet parliament without a bill at least as extensive as that proposed in 1860. 'I would not touch the *distribution of seats* in the Bill', he concluded, 'that question only doubles your difficulties & you can do nothing that will really settle it & it can be dealt with much better in a Parlt elected on the wider suffrage. . . .' He would 'keep the Govt right' on the matter. On 18 October, before parliament met, Palmerston died. As Bright waded through the 'world of trash' written about the departed, he spared no sympathy and looked only to the future. 'Russell & Gladstone are now the Govt', he wrote to Smith, '& it is quite impossible for them to go on without some honest attempt on the suffrage question.' He warned Villiers that the 'dawdling system' of the previous five years was quite inadequate. 'I am an "outsider" & a "pariah" among politicians' was Bright's private reaction to suggestions that he might come into a new government, ministers knew that they could afford to pass by anyone who would not wound them merely on grounds of personal dissatisfaction. Although he was weary of the platform, he did have 'something to say to the people'. That word would not be extremist. 'I have never said anything in favor of universal suffrage', he wrote at this time, 'and am not of opinion that it is or would be the best suffrage. . . .' Household suffrage, however, was 'the ancient franchise of this country' and he had no fears about its consequences. 'There is no reason whatever to believe', he added, '& indeed the contrary

THE POLITICAL " WALL-FLOWER."

Miss Bright. "NOBODY ASKS *ME*; AND IF THEY DID, I SHOULD CERTAINLY DECLINE."

is certain, that the working classes would act together, & that all power would be vested in them.'[10]

Russell, in close consultation with Gladstone, proceeded to form his administration, fully aware of the pitfalls. He first tried to bring in known opponents of Reform, like Lowe, but when this failed, Gladstone suggested he might try the opposite tack and ask Bright. Russell refused. If he could not get Lowe, he would not afford Bright. After much manoeuvring, and by abandoning his scheme for a preliminary commission of inquiry on Reform, the Prime Minister took W. E. Forster as a representative Reformer. Bright, however, kept his views before ministers in a series of letters to Villiers in November 1865. His message was that if a dissolution should prove necessary to carry a Reform Bill, then the government should not hold back. On the other hand, it should be made clear that if the Bill passed, there would not be an election. This was shrewd advice. The 1865 election campaign had been generally acknowledged to have been very expensive and MPs would not be anxious to fight again if they could help it. Bright himself confessed that he was 'lazy & tired of meetings'. [11] The government should also stress that what was in hand was 'not a *revolution* . . . but a *progress* on the old foundation, the mere granting of a wider suffrage, without much & possibly without any disturbance of seats. . . .' He also attempted to scotch a proposal to have a different suffrage in small and large towns, based on a £6 rental and an £8 rental respectively. Working men were most numerous in large towns and it was most unwise, 'when you are professing to let them in, to establish a limitation in the large towns that will shut the great majority of them out'. The Prime Minister, for his part, tentatively reopened contacts with Bright by inviting him to visit Woburn Abbey in December. He accepted, finding the family portraits on the walls and the house itself 'all one could wish for', except that all the doors and galleries seemed alike and he got lost. 'My room', he reported to his wife with satisfaction, 'is sumptuous, everything covered with a buff silk, furniture white and gold, sofa and easy chairs in profusion & a pleasant fire of course.'

The government knew very well that if he decided to take the question to the country, his campaign might prove crucial. He might get lost in the galleries of Woburn, but he knew his way on the platforms of Town Halls. Requests to speak were, indeed, already reaching him in considerable numbers. 'If you go to Glasgow', J. B. Smith wrote, 'surprise the world by your mildness — let the Aristocracy and *The Time* alone.' Smith added that in his judgment there was still little clamour for Reform. This time Bright was more confident. The Northern victory in the Civil War brought him credit as its leading supporter in Britain. His connexion with the trade union movement, established during the war, had not developed very significantly, but it served to lessen some working-class hostility towards him. In addition, he reminded leading Nonconformists that the position of the State Church would only be altered by an internal crisis or by a differently composed parliament. In a speech at Birmingham on 13 December he also revived the Irish question, claiming that there would never be, and never ought to be, tranquillity in Ireland while the Church remained established. Bright also identified himself with the critics of Governor Eyre of Jamaica who, they contended, had been far too severe in his suppression of a native insurrection.

Bright wanted Eyre brought home and tried for murder, contending that 'there was no rebellion or insurrection even of a general or political character in Jamaica'. He joined in the work of the Jamaica Committee and criticized Cardwell, the Colonial Secretary, as 'feeble to the last degree'.

The Cabinet was in some confusion. It found that more working men than had been suspected did in fact have the vote and on this ground some were inclined to delay. The Prime Minister tried to strengthen his personal position by promoting young Goschen to the Duchy of Lancaster, a move which annoyed other aspirants. Bright discouraged complaints that he might have been summoned. 'To me the notion of going into the Cabinet is repulsive', he wrote to Smith on 7 January 1866, 'as a matter of *inclination* or *will* I could not discuss it or deliberate upon it one minute.' The Goschen affair, and the fact that the Cabinet rejected the franchises proposed by Russell and Gladstone, filled Bright with alarm. He feared that the Prime Minister might abandon Reform. The Tories and the 'traitors' were talking of having the government out by Easter and replacing it with a 'third party' ministry. A great deal would depend on Gladstone as Leader of the House, and Bright hoped that he would 'do well'.

On 25 January, however, Russell and Gladstone agreed to abandon renting as the proposed basis for the borough franchise and to accept instead a £6-rating franchise. Bright was very angry, having written to Villiers a fortnight beforehand that such a step would be a 'fraud of the worst character', fatal both to the Bill and the government. When he learnt the way the Cabinet seemed to be moving, Bright at once saw Gladstone, urging the merits of £6 renting. 'The Reform question', he reported to Wilson on 2 February, 'is in a critical position & it will need all our efforts to keep the Govt up to the mark of a £10 & £6 *rental*.' Bright's wife and Gladstone received the brunt of his irritation at this time. 'Thy letters', he wrote to the former on 5 February, 'would be worth more if they were written more clearly — as they now come, they annoy me & I grieve that my wife writes so badly.' Five days later, Gladstone received a 'friendly, if not pleasant' broadside. 'You have had three months in which to frame a bill', Bright grumbled, 'which any man knowing anything of the subject could have done in a week. . . .' Reform was a great matter, and it was sad to see it being treated in a huckstering spirit, 'as if a few thousands of electors more or less were of the smallest consequence.' Russell tried to mollify him by an invitation to dinner, but Bright could not decide whether to accept. He did not wish to appear uncivil, yet he would not be silenced, and it was uncomfortable to be dining with someone he would shortly be condemning. He may also have been smarting from the fact that the House of Commons had laughed for three minutes when he committed the grave error of saying the Pickley Hunt instead of the Pickley Hunt during the debate on the Cattle Diseases Bill.[12] Bright found himself being singled out as the sinister figure behind the proposed legislation, now believed to be a £14-county and a £7-borough-rental franchise. 'I am the great "terror" of the squires', he wrote to his wife on 18 February, 'they seem to be seized with a sort of bucolic mania in dealing with me. . . .' The Prime Minister's son and daughter-in-law were at dinner with him a few days later and learnt that the 'terror's' first pleasure in life was playing with little children and his second, reading poetry. J. A. Froude, the historian, was also in the party and made it clear to Lady Amberley that he did not admire Bright very much. He was all talk.[13]

Eventually, in March, after a good deal of Cabinet argument, Gladstone introduced a Reform Bill based on the £14-county and £7-borough-rental franchise. In order to allay the fears of some government supporters, he explicitly stated that a £6-rental franchise had been rejected because it might well have produced working-class majorities in most urban constituencies. There was to be no redistribution of seats. Despite these gestures, objections to the proposals came from Robert Lowe in particular. He saw the existing electorate as a perfect balance between the interests of land and commerce. It offered a disinterested forum for the arguments of the political nation. Bright, however, suddenly found himself rather popular. 'I think I have never had so many invitations on at a time', he commented, 'I suppose I must have risen in the Market.' Yet he did not lavish praise upon the proposed Bill, reiterating that he still favoured household suffrage for the boroughs, and indeed only accepted the original £6-rental franchise because he did not wish to be obstructive. It amazed him that the government had quibbled with £6 and produced £7 instead. However, he remarked, beggars in the House of Commons, like beggars outside, could not be choosers, and it was in that spirit that he accepted the government's proposals. While rebuking the ministers, he chastised their critics, describing Horsman, Lord Elcho and others, in a phrase which afterwards became famous, as the 'political cave of Adullam'. While the bill was not perfect, he could not associate himself with those who spoke so contemptuously of the working classes. He concluded by warning darkly of the possibility of violence if there was further obstruction.

It was not until after this speech that Disraeli decided to ally with the Adullamites to destroy the bill. To its opponents, John Bright soon became the bogy man. According to Lord Elcho, his game had long been to squeeze the old Whigs or moderate Liberals between the Radicals and the Conservatives and then, with the new franchise, the Conservatives would smash, leaving Bright triumphant with the Radicals.[14] Lord Grosvenor moved an amendment to bring in a Redistribution Bill before the franchise was further considered, but Bright defended the government against this move. He reminded opponents of the Reform Bill that if the reformers were balked in the House, 'there still remains the nation outside this House.' While Russell would not give way to Grosvenor, he announced that the government would in fact produce its own Redistribution Bill. On 27 April, Grosvenor's amendment was pressed, and the government only sneaked home with a majority of five; thirty-five Liberals voting against the ministry, most of them being Whigs.

The Cabinet was startled by this result, some ministers wanting to withdraw the Reform Bill in consequence, while others were prepared to go to the country rather than do so. Russell tried to find a compromise which would satisfy the Adullamites and yet keep enough of the Bill to please Gladstone. Bright was depressed by the vote. The Whigs were obviously trying to remind the Prime Minister that they were still a force to be reckoned with. He believed, however, that some of the deserters, having made their point, would return to the fold. Writing from Rochdale on 30 April, he was still uncertain whether opinion in the country could be mobilized to influence the situ-

ation. 'The rich men', he told Wilson, 'are not yet moved sufficiently to come together to give any considerable subscriptions
& the organization of the multitude is not complete enough to
enable them to make a very effective demonstration of
strength.'

Over the next six weeks, the government struggled to produce a Redistribution Bill, while Disraeli concerted moves to
bring it down. Bright thought the right thing would be 'to pass
the franchise clauses & to postpone the *seats* till next year', but
few people seemed to agree with him. He was depressed by
the failure of Gurney and Overend's Bank, though he did not
lose money himself. The size of the bill from Marshall and
Snelgrove, £48, for his daughter Helen's wedding dress, was
also disturbing, though the wedding gave him pleasure. She
married William Clark, a Friend engaged in the shoe business
at Street in Somerset. In his frustration, Bright turned away
from the Commons to the 'people'. 'The future position of the
millions of working men in the United Kingdom', he told a
correspondent on 19 May 1866, 'is now determined, if the
opposition of the Tory Party is to prevail — it is precisely that
fixed by the Southern Planter for the Negro.'[15] There was, however, comfort to be gained from the defeat of the slave-holder.

On 18 June, Disraeli's manoeuvres at last paid off. The government was defeated by twenty-one votes on an amendment
to substitute rating for rental as the basis for the borough franchise. A period of confusion followed, with ministers unable to
make up their minds whether to resign or dissolve. Bright
urged dissolution. Writing to Gladstone on 24 June he pointed
out that 'A General Election for Reform & for a Reform Govt
would bring an immense force of popular feeling into the field
& I do not believe in your being beaten. . . .' Bright did in fact
have 'talks' with Russell, Gladstone and Halifax on the subject,
but it became clear that the Cabinet could not agree to dissolve.
Derby became Prime Minister and it seemed that the cause of
Reform had once again ignominiously failed.

Bright had no clear idea what to do next. He thanked George
Howell, the trade unionist, for the vote of thanks which had
been sent him, but made no suggestion about future action. In
a vague way, he hoped that when the next bill came it would
go as far as household suffrage.[16]

The working men want more organisation [he told Wilson] and more life, but whether thro' their 'trade unions' they can manage it, I cannot tell. The Tories care little for a middle-class call for reform. It is only numbers and the aspect of force that will influence them.

At the end of June, he wrote to T. B. Potter, MP for Rochdale (brother of the notorious Sir John) urging 'an attempt at a better organisation' during the coming autumn and winter but he was not very specific. Conferences, petitions and meetings, he admitted, all had their uses, but they would still not amount to a 'formidable organisation or movement'.[17]

If Bright could not create a movement himself, the Reform League wanted to make use of him. Its President, the barrister Edmund Beales and its Secretary, Howell, had already organized large demonstrations in support of Gladstone and against the Adullamites. They decided to hold a huge gathering in Hyde Park — supposedly an area to which the public only had access by royal favour. The Home Secretary, Walpole, decided that the meeting should not take place. Bright declined to come down from Rochdale to attend, but fully supported the right of the League to hold a meeting in the park. The government, he claimed, was defying the constitution in its refusal to tolerate the voice of the multitudes. The following day he had second thoughts about his remarks and telegraphed Howell to stop them being published. He may have anticipated the trouble which developed when Beales, at the head of a large crowd, attempted to enter the park. Although Bright contributed to a defence fund for those arrested, he kept away from the capital until the situation cleared. While he had warned of the possibility of violence, he had no wish to be implicated in it himself. The riots were, however, evidence to him that the working classes were unwilling to acquiesce in the social exclusion which Hyde Park symbolized; perhaps, after all, a real Reform movement in the country was possible.[18]

I have not yet wholly recovered from the effects of speaking for 10 minutes in the open air in Easter week [wrote Bright to Howell on 26 July] and I should destroy my power to speak for weeks and months to come, and even it might be permanently, if I were to attempt to speak to a large audience in the open air.

What he did would have to be 'in his own line', though he claimed to be in agreement with the 'fundamental principles' of the League. This was, at best, an exaggeration, for Bright never supported manhood suffrage to which the League was committed. After a short summer break, Bright prepared himself for the most spectacular series of meetings in his career. The press followed his words closely in a sustained campaign which lasted from August until the end of the year. He began in Birmingham in August before his own people where he could be sure of a large audience. The rest of the tour was not, however, left to chance. 'Preparatory meetings', he wrote, 'are the only sure mode of getting a great final gathering!' — though there was no precise formula.[19] In Manchester, he spoke at a dinner in late September organized by the northern department of the Reform League. Bright was delighted with the response to these first two engagements, for it was fully reported in the press that he was being flooded with invitations to speak elsewhere. He agreed to go to Yorkshire, Scotland and Ireland later in the year, making it clear that he had to refuse other requests. 'The great meetings are telling on the fools & rascals', he reported to Potter on 27 September, '& next session they will be more civil than we have lately seen them. . . .'

The theme of his speeches did not vary greatly, either now or later. The Reform Bill associated with Russell and Gladstone, he usually argued, had been so moderate that he was profoundly amazed both at the depth of the opposition and at the manner in which it had been mustered. The accession of Lord Derby amounted to a declaration of war against the working classes. It seemed that they might work, pay taxes, fight and die for their country, yet they were not considered fit to share in its government. They were treated like coolies or Chinese imported into the West Indies or California. Lord Russell, on the contrary, emerged as a man with no fear of freedom who, with Gladstone, acted upon the principle of trust and confidence in the people. Bright therefore urged that the people should demand Reform so that the British Constitution, with all its freedom, should be restored to them. In

THE BRUMMAGEM FRANKENSTEIN.

John Bright. "I HAVE NO FE—FE—FEAR OF ;MA—MANHOOD SUFFRAGE!"—*Mr. Bright's Speech at Birmingham.*

future, the government should be conducted in the name of the people, not by a privileged class in a sham parliament. The rich and the great would be forced to develop a better acquaintance with the necessities and feelings of their countrymen. His slogan, therefore, was 'Let us trust the nation', but he claimed

185

that by this phrase he did not intend to brush the middle classes aside. In reality, as things stood, they only had a semblance of power and therefore Reform was also in their interest. He discounted the possibility of Derby bringing in an acceptable Reform measure. The Tories could not, in one short year, swallow all their principles. The enemies of the 1866 bill could not become the honest friends of Reform in 1867. Only a future Liberal administration, basing its plans on the ancient borough franchise of the country, could give satisfaction to friends of Reform.

After Manchester, Bright moved on to an even bigger reception in Leeds where he spoke on 8 October to a packed meeting at the Town Hall. A huge gathering of a hundred thousand people had assembled on Woodhouse Moor in the afternoon to set the tone of enthusiasm. Bright had made it clear that he would not speak in the open air, but it was nevertheless clear that he was the great attraction. His chairman was Alderman Carter, the ex-Chartist coal-merchant who was also chairman of the Leeds Manhood Suffrage Association. Also on the platform were W. E. Forster, E. Leatham, Edmund Beales, Ernest Jones and others. On rising to speak, Bright was greeted with cheering which lasted for nearly five minutes. It was a similar story in Glasgow on 16 October. A reputed 150,000 people assembled on Glasgow Green under the auspices of the Reform League to pass resolutions in favour of another Reform Bill. Bright watched the subsequent procession from the windows of the Cobden Hotel and solemnly bowed in acknowledgment of the cheers which greeted him. A fortnight later, Bright moved across to Dublin to enlist the Irish for the cause.

Back in February, at the time of anxiety about Fenian outrages, the Russell government had introduced a measure to suspend the Habeas Corpus Act. Bright was not hostile to this step but he did deplore the apparent absence of any general policy for Ireland. 'There is no statesmanship', he commented, 'merely in acts of force and acts of repression.' J. B. Dillon and others, wishing to express their gratitude for his 'eloquent advocacy of the rights of our country', invited him to attend a banquet in Dublin. In declining a similar invitation, J. S. Mill added that there was 'no one who has better earned the gratitude of Irishmen than Mr Bright. . . .' For a while, the Habeas Corpus Suspension Bill apart, Ireland had disappeared from Bright's portfolio of subjects and the time was clearly ripe to renew his association. His reception in Dublin, from Catholics and Protestants alike, was very warm. His only private regret was that he was expected to stay up until 2 am on the night of the banquet. In his main speech, he dealt once more with the Established Church in Ireland, urging the ending of its privileged position. Such a step would contribute to civil harmony and be of benefit to all churches. As regards land, his chief proposal was 'to restore to Ireland a middle class proprietary of the soil'. In his peroration, rehearsing the miseries of the Irish, he linked their resolution to the triumph of the people in the Westminster parliament. The occasion was itself rather a triumph for Bright. The Dublin correspondent of *The Times* reported that he had never attended such a well-organized event in Dublin. He added that those who expected a vehement and fierce style of oratory were disappointed. Bright was 'remarkably calm and deliberate', though this may have been because he was suffering from a bronchial infection. In any event, the tributes paid to him were such as were 'never before paid to an English commoner in Ireland'. The banquet was an élite occasion — tickets cost 25s. — but, after visiting Cardinal Cullen, Bright followed it up by speaking before an audience of Dublin working men. He asked the men 'to open your heart of hearts, and to join hands for a real and thorough working union for freedom with the people of Great Britain.'[20]

Bright returned to Britain well pleased with the result of his trip. 'It is the first time', he concluded in a letter to Smith on 7 October, 'probably since O'Connell's days, that an open meeting could have been held in Dublin & the first for a much longer time that anyone could have spoken in favor of the Union at such a meeting.' Joining his family in Llandudno on the way home, he relaxed for a few days before returning to Rochdale and future engagements. There was one further huge banquet in the Free Trade Hall in Manchester in late November before the campaign came to its climax when Bright spoke in the capital on 4 December. He addressed a meeting in St James's Hall called by the London Trades' and Friendly Societies as a sequel to the parades and demonstrations of the previous day. Pointing out that eight years previously he had urged working men, through their trades' and Friendly

187

societies, to put pressure on the government, he was delighted to see that in the past few months his advice had been taken. He urged that there should be no jealousy between the Reform Union in Manchester and the Reform League in London. Co-operation was urged 'to bring this great national question to such a solid and final issue, that it shall no longer disturb the repose of this nation.' It was not clear, however, what the 'final issue' was to be.

This sequence of speeches, and the responses evoked by the campaign brought Bright a position of great importance. He had demonstrated his capacity to attract and hold huge audiences in the major cities of the United Kingdom. Looking simply at the text of his speeches, it is not easy to understand the secret of their success. A Bright performance, however, must be seen in its total context. First and foremost, his voice was strong and powerful, capable of penetrating to the far corners of a large hall. He also had the capacity to elaborate and improvise from the brief headings and titles which provided the basic structure of the speech. There was, of course, more or less disguised, a good deal of repetition but he relied little on verbal conceit. He took inspiration from his surroundings — from the banners, the organ-playing, the sustained cheering — and seemed capable of enthusing both middle- and working-class audiences with a direct appeal to the morality of their cause. His style was deliberately combative and uncompromising; what he opposed was always much more apparent than what he advocated. However successful the speeches were in their delivery and local reception, Bagehot was not alone in feeling that his approach was too partisan to convince the waverers. 'He will persist', he noted regarding the Manchester speech, 'in arguing so exclusively with those whom he calls Tories, those who object entirely to Reform.' His arguments perhaps did not reassure 'moderate Liberals, who really wish for a large infusion of popular strength, but do not want to see the flavour of the wine quite destroyed by the quantity of alcohol introduced into it. . . .' If Bright replied that his object was not to argue but to stir the people, Bagehot felt that the greatness of the effort was impaired by scarcely-veiled appeals to physical force, and by attributing to one party 'a monopoly of the right to do justice'.[21]

Lord Derby was indeed taking soundings on a Reform measure but, unlike Bagehot, Bright could not associate him with any 'honest measure'. If Lowe continued to express his frankly oligarchic views, he wrote to Villiers on 16 November, it would be easy 'to induce many scores of thousands of men to provide themselves with arms, to form something like a great national volunteer force which, without breaking the law, would place the peace of the country on a soil hot with volcanic fire.' He stressed that, without a remedy, there would be violence. 'I am not responsible for what may come', he added, 'any more than I am for an outburst from the bowels of Etna or Vesuvius. They are responsible who despise & insult 5 millions of their fellow countrymen. . . .' Some Quakers were rather disturbed and wrote to say so. 'I have never said a word in favor of force', he replied, 'all I have said has been against it, but I am at liberty to warn those in authority that justice long delayed . . . always provokes the employment of force to obtain redress.'[22]

It was not only Friends who were worried by the path Bright seemed to be following. Gladstone, considering himself 'better out of the way of politics during the recess', departed for Italy, having thoughtfully left the wounded Liberal party 'to the healing powers of nature'. At the end of October he noted that the Reform question was complicating that recovery. It was 'separating Bright from us, and in one sense clearing our way. But then it may become too strong for us; or at least too strong to be stayed with our bill of last year.' He did not like what he read of Bright's speeches, but consoled himself with the thought that the ex-cabinet had no claim on him and he would probably part company 'the moment he sees his way to more than we would give him'.[23] For his part, Bright was equally puzzled about Gladstone's future political moves.

There were some who suggested that the time had come for Bright to make his own direct challenge for political power, but if tempted, he was not drawn. It was simply impracticable, he replied to Congreve's suggestion 'to undertake a leadership & guidance & even a Govt which many are unwilling & none have the power to place in my hands.' Personal qualities apart, he was outside the class in which 'the Crown, Parliament, Church, Universities, Army, Navy, Land and Society form a citadel'. He favoured the slow, but very secure, route to the overthrow of aristocratic power by undermining its legislative supports and changing public attitudes. A revolutionary course[24]

> might fail & in any case would involve a great ruin & much evil every way. Accident may force on this violence & I am not sure that the aristocratic class will shrink from it — but I prefer to leave it to accident rather than to undertake to stimulate or recommend it.

Since Bright preferred to take one step at a time, he resisted suggestions that the Liberals were treating him unfairly. The fact that the London press was against him was no novelty and no cause for concern. In a magnanimous mood, he even made allowances for the difficulties many Liberal members found themselves in. They dared not be seen with the Reform League because some of their leading constituents were critical of it. Bright himself was disturbed by reports of 'foolish conversation' at the meetings of the Reform League Council and urged Howell to keep them out of the press. Russell and Gladstone would soon be home from their Italian tour '& then we shall see whether they are willing to *lead* or not'. He was afraid that many prominent families would not support them if they went for a household suffrage, but nothing less would be rational. 'I do not think that the prospects of the country are cheerful' was his Christmas message.[25]

The government took Bright's campaign seriously. Disraeli had agents mingling with the crowd during the demonstration which preceded Bright's London speech. The size of the audience may have led Derby to suggest to Disraeli that they should start the hare of household suffrage, but couple it with plurality of voting. Hearing such rumours, Bright felt that the more likely outcome would be that the government would destroy itself. Instead, to general surprise, by the summer of 1867, the Conservatives had passed a new Reform Act. The making of this measure has been meticulously studied, and it is unnecessary to rehearse the intricate events in detail.[26] Bright's own position, however, needs reconsideration, for it was a very individual one. His speeches still rankled with many former ministers and, on his return to England, Gladstone was so uncertain of Bright's status, that he refused to give the customary opening-of-session dinner in 1867. He could not bear to invite Bright or to omit him. Looking at the Liberal benches, Bright indeed saw 'scores of miserable fellows who seem to be able to comprehend nothing but the dread of dissolution & this makes them in one sense corrupt & in action treacherous to their constituents & to the cause they pretend to support.' It was on these members that Disraeli worked. On 25 February, he introduced his hastily concocted bill proposing a £6 rating franchise in the boroughs and a £20 in the counties, without plurality, but with various 'fancy' franchises. Bright thought the idea a 'wretched proposition' and joined Gladstone in denouncing it. The following day, at a meeting in Gladstone's house, Bright surprisingly described the party as more united than it had been for a year. Disraeli took fright and withdrew his proposal.

Bright thought that the Tory party was in chaos, an impression perhaps strengthened by a 'long & curious conversation' he had on 1 March with Disraeli. They went over old ground on the Reform question. Bright advised him to go for a £5 rating franchise, or household suffrage, in the boroughs and £10 or £12 in the counties. If Disraeli did the 'right thing' then he would not be factious. 'Well, whatever happens', concluded Disraeli sententiously, 'you and I will always be friends.'[27] Bright was probably not displeased to be seen during this talk by the Liberal Chief Whip; it would not harm the Liberal leadership to scent a conspiracy. At the same time, he encouraged the Reform League, writing to Beales that there were many, like himself, who were not committed to its precise programme but who wished to help financially.[28] He also wrote confidentially to Disraeli, urging that a Reform Bill had not only to please the Cabinet and the House but also 'so far content the people as to extinguish the associations now agitating the question'. The 'great work' of the Reform League was clearly to be kept within careful limits! Either household suffrage or a £6 rental or a £5 rating franchise would, he thought, mean 'an end of all agitation of the Suffrage Question for an indefinite, but, I believe, *a very long period*'.[29] It was a concern which did not altogether match Bright's public reputation.

It is difficult to be sure what game he was playing. He seems to have kept aloof until the shape of Disraeli's new measure became apparent. It was introduced on 18 March against a background of internal party dissension and general confusion. Disraeli's objective, at almost any cost, was to keep the initiative for the government and not to let it slip into Gladstone's hands. He proposed a household suffrage but insisted on the personal payment of rates, residence for two years, dual votes for property and a number of other 'fancy' franchises, all of which were designed to reduce the size of the groups to be enfranchised. There was also to be a small measure of redistribution. Bright did not speak at this stage, noting in his diary that he was 'not well, and head not clear'. He welcomed the household suffrage, but not the fancy franchises, though he recognized that they might be whittled away in debate. It was already becoming clear on the Conservative side that some of these provisions would be double-edged in their effect.

Gladstone took it upon himself to try to destroy the measure at the outset by opposing the Second Reading. He could not, however, carry his party with him in this attempt. The prospect of Bright in the government, if the Tories were defeated, was not universally attractive within the non-Tory ranks. The admittedly disaffected Edward Bouverie, for example, claimed that Bright's speeches and abuse of classes would destroy any Cabinet he entered. He would be utterly incapable as an administrator and his advice, as a colleague, worthless.[30] Gladstone, following this failure, now saw the danger that the limiting clauses would be abandoned in committee; the Bill that would be left would be far more sweeping than he — or Bright wanted. They both took the view that the franchise should be given to those whose 'condition of life and position of independence' gave them title to it. That meant, inevitably, the exclusion of the 'residuum' who lived in almost helpless poverty and dependence. Gladstone therefore decided to press an amendment removing the requirement that there should be personal payment of rates. He anticipated that if it was accepted, the House would insist on stipulating instead a minimum figure, perhaps £5, which would exclude the 'residuum'. Although such an amendment might be popular, for opposite reasons, with Adullamites and Radicals, Bright was not sanguine of success. 'One side', he told Helen on 28 March, 'is as rotten and broken up almost as the other . . .' This estimate was borne out by events for the 'Tea Party' emerged, a group which, from a variety of political and personal motives, was to ensure that when the matter was put to the vote, on 13 April, the government had a majority of twenty-one. Forty-five Liberals voted or paired with the Tories. Disraeli had succeeded in humiliating Gladstone. The latter admitted privately that he had received 'a smash perhaps without example' and contemplated withdrawing from public life. Bright could not withhold some admiration for Disraeli's dexterity, writing to Helen that he was 'such a good juggler that they don't know a real thing from a trick'. Nevertheless, he stood by Gladstone, going down to Birmingham and declaring that his audience would not be able to produce any statesman who could add dignity and grandeur to Gladstone's stature.

Discussion of the Bill resumed after this debacle and the Easter recess. On 2 May, Disraeli accepted the verdict of the House and reduced the two years' residence to one. On 9 May, he successfully resisted an amendment by the Radical Hibbert which would allow those who compounded for their rates to qualify by paying the composite, not the full, rate (local authorities generally allowed a reduction to landlords for block payment). On this occasion, some twenty-five Adullamites and Radicals supported the government. 'I have suffered a good deal recently', he wrote on 17 May, '& I know nothing more bitter than the desertion from a great cause of those on whom it seemed but reasonable to rely.' Even Smith and McLaren preferred the 'subtle wickedness of Disraeli' to the 'honest courage' of Gladstone.

One further major surprise remained. The vexed position of the 'compounder' still excited discussion and a number of proposals were canvassed before, on 17 May, Hodgkinson moved an amendment to limit the payment of rates within boroughs to the actual occupier. Amid general astonishment — for the effect would probably be to enfranchise about half a million occupiers — Disraeli accepted the proposal and household suffrage became the reality in urban seats in England and Wales. Bright then claimed, with less than complete justice, that the emerging Bill 'adopted the precise franchise I recommended in 1858/59'. In their disgust with Disraeli for taking this risk, Conservatives attributed to Bright the evil design which had made it possible.

The Bill had still some months to go before it assumed its final form. Bright remained assiduous in his attendance at the House of Commons, though he found the long discussion tiring. His weary condition may possibly explain his support for Mill's amendment which would have permitted female suffrage. 'The greatest triumph of all', Mill wrote, 'is getting Bright's vote: ten days before, he was decidedly against us.'[31] In general, Bright was satisfied with the new measure, though he could not quite understand how it was that the Tories were responsible for it. He urged the Reform League not to agitate the question any further, so far as the boroughs were concerned. Any further activity should centre on the secret ballot. Until that was introduced, corruption and intimidation would continue.[32] When the Bill reached the Lords, the peers treated it with a respect which concealed their real sentiments. The only amendment which passed into law was the provision that in three-member constituencies (like Birmingham), when all three seats were contested, the voters were to have but two votes. Lord Russell and a large section of the Whigs supported this change. For Bright, this insertion confirmed the bankruptcy of the Whigs and he even went so far as to claim that he would rather see the whole measure abandoned than see this odious proposal accepted. He had no patience with 'peculiar crotchets and dreamy propositions' designed to represent minorities, whether they came from Mill, Lowe or the Lords.

The session as a whole left Bright with mixed feelings. The manner in which Reform had been achieved was a great disappointment, yet, despite all his previous platform scorn of the Tories, he was pleased that it had been passed. Mr Cowling's verdict is just. He[33]

> probably did not anticipate the outcome of the action — at any rate in detail. He foresaw neither the defection of Radicals from him, nor the consolidation behind Disraeli in May. Nevertheless, Bright — of all the actors in the story — was the one who succeeded most abundantly in exposing

the raw nerves of the Liberal party, in imposing his opinions on its leader and in ensuring that, if there was to be a Liberal party in the future, he would be somewhere near its centre.

It is perhaps only the last suggestion that needs qualifying. In letter after letter, when the crisis was over, he expressed his weariness which he could only in part attribute to his increasing age. 'I can stand the hostility of opponents', he remarked, 'but I sink under the treachery & the feebleness of those who ought to be my friends.' He refused invitations to speak and claimed the need to catch up on business as the reason. 'Politically, I am snuffed out', he wrote to Helen in November 1867. 'I feel so weary of public life, that it would be the greatest relief to know that I was fairly quit of it.' It was time to relax in grandparental splendour.

He could not, however, throw off the social and political attraction of London life. There, he held court to fussy academics, anxious to be enlightened on the qualities and training required to make an orator, and eager Americans who were simply keen to make his acquaintance. He dined out regularly, though no host ever found the favour returned. At dinner, the platform orator was known to express views on the reasoning powers of dogs, the laws of primogeniture and the likelihood of miracles. What better tonic was there than to walk across St James's Park with Gladstone, speaking of the reckless and unwise character of the House — not what it used to be. Samuel Wilberforce, Bishop of Oxford, and Bright, found each other's company unexpectedly congenial. The presence of aristocratic and high-minded ladies in fact delighted him, though he sometimes ventured to find the trains of their dresses troublesomely long. It was strange, he thought, that women of sense should run into such extremes of fashion. Even if he thought himself 'snuffed out', therefore, it was most unlikely that John Bright would withdraw from politics at a time when his standing had never been higher.

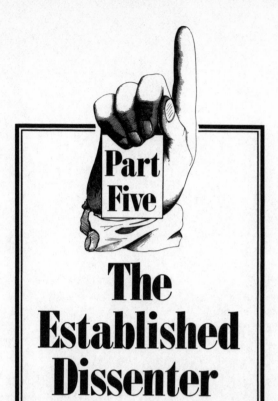

Part Five

The Established Dissenter

ELEVEN

The first Liberal government 1868-74

After the excitement of the Reform Act, there was a curious hiatus in politics. The Tory government continued in office, though it would not be long before an election took place on the basis of the new franchise. Politicians were left to speculate upon the likely impact of the new electorate both on their own individual careers and on politics generally. Bright's own position was particularly interesting. Would he remain somewhat detached from Gladstone as an independent voice? Would he come into the Cabinet if the Liberals should prove to be victorious in the election? A number of interpretations were possible, but Bright left few clues. It was, of course, clear that, the ballot apart, there was nothing further to be gained from Reform itself, the preoccupation of his immediate past. It was in these circumstances that he turned again to Ireland, both for support and for a cause.

The appearance of Fenianism upset the atmosphere which Bright had found so congenial on his visit to Dublin in October 1866. The Irish Reform League (of which he was a vice-president) made little headway. Bright's initial response was to interpret Fenianism as further proof that Ireland was misgoverned and required urgent reforms, but he could not appear to condone violence. By the end of 1867, he condemned the Fenians in strong terms, though he thought it folly to hang those responsible for the Manchester outrages. Writing to the

199

new editor of the *Star*, Justin McCarthy, he reiterated that such shocking events (a policeman was killed during an attempt to free two Fenian prisoners) were 'but the natural results of all that has gone before in connection with the Irish question'.[1] The changes Bright advocated to meet this situation were not new. In early December 1867, he sent Gladstone a copy of his 1852 open letter on the Irish Church. 'On reading it again', he commented, 'at this distance of time, I have nothing to retract or to change in it.' In reply, Gladstone choicely observed that in 1847, as a candidate for Oxford University, he had declined to pledge himself in principle to the Irish Church. He agreed that Bright's plan was the best he had seen in print. As far as land was concerned, Bright still pressed for the creation of an Irish proprietary class, if need be, by interfering with the normal processes of the market and establishing a parliamentary commission to buy large estates, particularly from English owners, and re-sell them, in existing farms, to their tenants on easier terms. The Church and the land were, he was certain, the heart of the matter, but he was sceptical of the suggestion that they might be struck down together in one blow. It had to be remembered that legislation would have to come 'through a Parliament which is not Irish, & in which every principle essential for the regeneration of Ireland is repudiated.' It would be best to advance by taking the two questions separately. He conceded that if the Liberal Protestants and all Catholics united they might induce a total change but, he confessed, 'looking to all past efforts among you, I am not very sanguine that you will succeed in bringing a strong & united pressure to bear upon our ruling class.'[2]

Bright did not believe that the Tories would tackle the problems, but he also remained sceptical about the Opposition. He had discussed the issues with Gladstone, now the Liberal leader, but he could not work without the Whig peers. Besides, though on 19 December Gladstone had publicly referred to the need to deal with the Church, the land and education in Ireland, Bright was still not sure that he comprehended 'the real nature of the case'.[3] Parliament was due to reassemble in February 1868, but he could not see any man or any party tackling the Irish difficulties. His mind turned constantly to Ireland, though 'from my position', he remarked to Helen on 11 January 1868, 'I can only *advise*: it is for those in office to act if they dare & can in this grievous case.' Sinçe, however, he believed that a speech in the Birmingham Town Hall was 'more read & tells more on opinion than a speech in a debate in the Houses', he took Ireland as his main theme there on 4 February. He declared that anyone who believed that if the Irish had their own parliament they could permit the minority political State Church to exist, must also believe that Ireland was 'no better than one huge lunatic asylum'. Far from being a support to the Union, therefore, its perpetuation would lead the Irish to separate.

When parliament resumed, Bright was summoned by Gladstone to a party conclave to discuss Irish policy. He professed himself somewhat embarrassed at being admitted to a 'sort of "Opposition Cabinet meeting"', since it opened the possibility of responsibilities which he did not wish, he claimed, to undertake. Nevertheless, a few days later, he joined in the debate then proceeding on Ireland. In his own view, his speech was a most successful effort, defending his land proposals from distortion and stating that he did not propose anything which would not be 'perfectly acquiesced in by both landlord and tenant'. The landlord would receive every shilling he could fairly demand in the market for the estate he proposed to sell. He had little patience with the 'grotesque and imbecile' plans of the Tory Chief Secretary, Lord Mayo, to set up a Catholic University and to increase the stipend of Presbyterian ministers. To do this, while maintaining the State Church, was nothing less than bribery, and would be ineffective into the bargain. Returning to his 1852 proposals, though aware that leading Dissenters were critical of them, he rejected the notion of a concurrent establishment of churches. The Irish church question should be regarded as *sui generis*. Presbyterians in Scotland, Anglicans and Dissenters in England, had 'no right to suppose themselves to be judges with regard to religious matters in Ireland'. They could declare that the State Church should be discontinued, and no others created, but they should not interfere further.[4]

Gladstone was engaged on framing 'resolutions' concerning Church and State in Ireland, and Bright was closely consulted. He dined frequently with the 'Opposition Cabinet' and was more freely accepted in society than at any time in the past. 'I am becoming "respectable" surely', was his comment to his wife on being invited to the Royal Academy dinner. The Prince of Wales confessed that he felt more nervous than usual at having to speak with Bright present. Despite this new-found 'respectability', however, Bright hammered at the attitude of the Tories towards the Irish Church. The parliamentary situation was very confused, for although the first of Gladstone's 'resolutions' was carried against the government, it did not resign, since the new electoral register was not yet ready. Bright's righteous indignation now boiled over. Lord Clarendon had suggested to him one evening at dinner that Disraeli was poisoning the mind of the Queen concerning the Irish Church question. In the Commons, on 7 May, Bright referred to the manner, 'at once pompous and servile', in which Disraeli had talked about his interviews with the Queen. The Prime Minister (Disraeli had now taken over from Derby), either in a rage and shaking his fist, or in the most gentleman-like manner (testimony differs!) challenged Bright to substantiate his insinuation that the sovereign was being involved in a great political matter. Bright took the affair no further. Both men believed themselves vindicated in this encounter. According to Bright, Disraeli's reply 'showed how hard I had hit him', while the Prime Minister considered the 'rabid rage of Mr Bright indicated a consciousness of failure'. Their strange relationship ended abruptly.[5]

Bright's usefulness to the Liberal leadership, however, was not so much in the set-pieces of debate as in his connexions with the Irish and the Dissenters. There remained a danger, which Disraeli might exploit, that Protestant feeling might get the better of anti-State Church feeling on the Irish question, and then the swelling unity of the Liberal party might dissolve. Bright, therefore, had a number of sessions with leading Nonconformist ministers in order to clear up misunderstandings about his own proposals — though there was, of course, no guarantee that a Liberal government would endorse them to the letter, if at all. Several of these ministers he knew personally — Dr Newman Hall, for example, was another summer visitor to Llandudno. The ministers were pleased and Bright, in turn, regarded them as 'favourable specimens of the ministerial order'. It was otherwise, however, with a delegation of Irish Presbyterians. He felt called upon to rebuke them for their miserable subservience to the Tory and Church party. He agreed, rather reluctantly, to take the chair at a meeting at Spurgeon's Tabernacle on the Irish question and managed to speak for half an hour himself. That was the pattern of his life; big meetings followed by little ones. In June 1868 he travelled to Liverpool and there addressed a major gathering of Welshmen, from the city and from North Wales. His address was largely on the Irish Church question. 'I hold you, I bind you to this', he told his audience, 'that you are for justice to Catholic and Protestant in Ireland, established on the voluntary principle.'[6]

However, he did not rest content with speaking in Britain. Peabody, the American millionaire, invited him to spend some time with him at Castleconnell on the Shannon. Bright found himself 'quite a lion everywhere' and treated, a little embarrassingly, as an authority on Irish matters. Bright wrote to Thorold Rogers, another of his Oxford admirers, that while the gentry clearly did not like disestablishment, there was no frantic hostility to it. In a speech at Limerick on 14 July 1868, which was aimed at Protestants, he stated that Irish conditions had clearly improved since his visit in 1849, though much had still to be done. He wanted deeds of generosity and justice to supplement the 'fraudful' Act of Union. The Established Church, he argued 'is anti-Protestant by reason of its unnatural position, and at the same time it is as much anti-English as it is anti-Irish, because it makes impossible that Irish people should be in perfect harmony with England.'[7] In general, Bright was well satisfied with the summer's work and, after a brief holiday, joined in the general election campaign.

On this occasion, Bright exerted himself more than usual, though the detailed canvassing was still left to others. In Birmingham, his main objective, in which he was successful, was to capture all three seats for the Liberals, thus confining the new-fangled minority clause to the 'Bedlam' from which it originated.[8] In Edinburgh, he received the freedom of the city and, in accepting the honour, referred at length to Reform and to Ireland. He appealed to his fellow-countrymen to 'get rid of prejudices and false notions about Protestantism and Popery'. He repeated his view that Ireland was a 'special case' and need not be a precedent for action against the Church of England.[9] This degree of solicitude for the State Church in England, however, did not signify a change of opinion. 'As to the Hierarchy', he told a clerical correspondent, 'I have never known its members do anything *politically* to expose or to remedy the grievous ignorance, sufferings, & poverty of so many of our people. Their course on the Irish question is in harmony with all their history.'[10]

While Bright was in Edinburgh, he also spoke to a gathering of working men, appealing strongly for the introduction of the secret ballot to crown the work of Reform. He went on to say that it was extraordinary, considering the wealth of the country, that so large a mass of pauperism was evident. He declared that no country could be called happy and prosperous when such a state of things existed. If government were just, if taxes were moderate and equitably imposed, if land were free, if schools were as prominent as prisons and workhouses, the people would gradually gain more self-respect and become 'more virtuous and more like what the subjects of a free State ought to be'.[11] The question, he assured his audience, would not be neglected.

The election gave the Liberals a majority of 110 and, though delighted, Bright was disgusted that Lancashire should go against the tide. Even Gladstone lost his seat, though he quickly found another at Greenwich. Bright attributed the county's poor showing to the ignorance and brutality of the Tory employers and friction between English and Irish. He forecast to Rogers on 23 October that, despite the majority, Gladstone might have difficulties 'as much from the unreasonableness of the Radicals as from the timidity of the Whigs'. He feared the aristocratic and democratic elements in the party would continually jar. As for himself, he had written to Helen on 23 September that he would soon be considered too slow and unfit to be a leader in the team. Nevertheless, he had been assiduous in informing Gladstone of the content of his campaign speeches. Now, with the election over, the Liberals would have a hard fight, and he suggested the Irish Church, education and the reduction of service expenditure as priorities for a Liberal ministry.

The Prime Minister summoned Bright down from Rochdale

with an invitation to join the government. John left him at midnight and returned to a sleepless night at the Euston Hotel. Rather daringly in view of Bright's expressed views on India, Gladstone offered him the India Office, but John declined because, primarily, he did not want an office which could have military aspects. He chose, instead, the Board of Trade, writing to Gladstone that he would do his best, but feared he would prove a disappointment. The Prime Minister must have had some anxiety because he put someone with 'special training' under him.[12] In letters to his family, Bright claimed that he resisted 'almost more than any other man ever did', but submitted because that was what his friends in the country wanted. It was, indeed, a grave step to exchange twenty-five years' experience as an independent backbencher for collective responsibility and executive office. It was a sign to some that he was sinking into complacency, indeed J. S. Mill felt that Bright could be safely included because he was not 'in what is *now* the advanced party'.[13] It was a judgment which was only partially true.

The new ministers left London in a special train for Windsor. The President of the Board of Trade's arrival was a source of aristocratic amusement. Lord Granville, the Colonial Secretary, urged a friend to come over specially to witness Bright entering Windsor Castle.[14] On the train, Bright got Lord de Grey to tell him the details of the ceremony — twice. The Queen, however, graciously conveyed a message that he could do as he liked about kneeling; she would not offend his Quaker susceptibilities. After the ceremony, he walked back to the station with Lord Granville. 'I am not sure that I was not more observed than any other of the party', he wrote to his wife, 'as indeed I deserved to be — for what can be a greater marvel than my appearance at Windsor Castle in such company & on such an occasion.' A few days later, he was observed at dinner 'chatting with everybody — very unlike a traditional Cabinet Minister'.[15] Goldwin Smith, however, now in America, feared that Bright was 'touched by Royalty which touched even Cromwell and that as a minister he would learn to be discreet.[16]

Shortly afterwards, Bright visited the Queen at Osborne, again chaperoned by Lord Granville. All passed off admirably. The royal hostility of a decade earlier had faded into oblivion.

The first Dissenter in the Cabinet seemed very much at home. Lord Granville reported to the Prime Minister that, apart from some probing into the expenses of the royal yacht, his charge behaved himself very well.[17] Bright admitted that he had only informed his wife of the royal invitation at a late juncture. 'It seems strange', Elizabeth wrote, 'that you should be going where I cannot follow', but Bright did not seem upset. He entered an extensive account of his stay in his diary because, naturally, his children would wish it. He was not, he stated, a 'courtier' himself, but he could respect an ancient monarchy and reverence a monarch whom monarchy had not spoiled.

Gladstone, recognizing that his political 'corps d'armée' was composed of Scottish Presbyterians, English and Welsh Non-conformists and Irish Roman Catholics, decided to tackle the Irish Church question at an early stage. Bright wrote to the Prime Minister that he was prepared to leave a disestablished Anglican Church its churches and parsonages, but not its lands, if it would be responsible for their upkeep. The Regium Donum — a grant to Presbyterians — and the Maynooth Grant, would, he assumed, cease. Bright's Irish associates felt that such a scheme did not even create religious equality because there was no equivalent for Catholics of the fixed property left to Protestants. Bright, however, warned against any corresponding concession to the Catholics, though he could see there was a case. He suspected that a mass of Scottish members would revolt 'if anything so liberal as I would consent to were proposed by the Govt'. If anything should upset the 'Protestant' Liberals, the House of Lords might be tempted to tamper with the measure. In the event, Bright had few reservations about the government's Bill, and his speech on the Second Reading was widely praised. When the Irish Church Bill went up to the Lords at the end of May, Bright warned the peers not to intervene, for if they delayed the measure they would 'stimulate discussion on important questions, which, but for their infatuation, might have slumbered for many years'. In the event, the principles were not touched, although the amount of money to go to the Church of Ireland was increased.[18]

While reflecting on Irish matters, Bright wrestled with the question of his attire. He objected to wearing 'Court' or 'full' dress, and a somewhat cool correspondence on the subject took place with Gladstone. In the end, it was made clear that a 'plain' dress of black velvet was allowed and he had no need to sport 'effulgent trumpery'. A man sacrificed his self-respect, Bright argued, when he consented to wear the livery associated with a Court.

After the Irish Church came the Irish land question. Convinced of his expertise on the subject — he had written a year earlier that Gladstone 'had not studied the land question, and knows little about it' — he kept up the pressure on the Prime Minister.[19] 'We shall find', he warned in May, 'all Ireland, North & South alike, united in demanding something on the land question broader than anything hitherto offered. . . .' Gladstone replied that he agreed, but he had doubts about the State taking a hand in large-scale land-jobbing and in any case wondered whether 'economical laws' might not again result in land returning to fewer hands. Bright would not be put off, urging Gladstone in July to send a suitable person to report on the Prussian land system. Having been directly addressed by O'Neill Daunt in an open letter, *Why is Ireland discontented?*, he confessed to being very anxious. If nothing was done, the future of the two islands was 'cloudy'.

It was not until October 1869 that the Cabinet met to discuss the proposed Land Bill. Bright, somewhat bemused by all the detail, explained to Kay-Shuttleworth on 18 October that the task was both to meet the expectations of the Irish tenantry and the opinions of the two Houses of Parliament.[20] As far as the latter were concerned, he wrote to Lord Clarendon in tones of studied moderation on 14 October confessing that, moderate as his plan was, the Cabinet might not find it acceptable. He stressed that he would go as far as political economy would 'sanction' but no further, while admitting that 'courage & the dark may turn out to be only rashness & mischief.'[21] Even Bright was becoming vexed with some of the Irish, complaining to his daughter on 20 October of 'evil men in Ireland who raise expectations which no Govt, acting in & thro' the English Parlt can fulfil & the natural difficulty of the situation is grievously increased by them.' To an Ulsterman, on 23 October, he explained his feelings about abolishing all free competition in dealings between landlord and tenant, a suggestion sometimes made in Ireland. 'Competition', he remarked gloomily, 'seems to have no value or virtue in the mind of an Irishman when speaking of land.' He wanted the whole system of entail and settlement to be reformed to ensure 'fair play' but the idea of a government inspector fixing a 'fair rent' did not appeal.[22]

Gladstone worked closely with his Irish Secretary, Fortescue, to frame a Bill to protect the Ulster 'custom' of tenant right by law, and to give evicted tenants in other parts of Ireland where the 'custom' did not obtain the right to compensation. He introduced a measure on these lines of 15 February, though, as a concession to Bright, he included some provision for land purchase. The Bill was passed with surprisingly little opposition, probably due to anxiety that Fenianism would be strengthened if it were obstructed. In the event, however, the Act was a disappointment in its effects. The so-called 'Bright clauses' were not daring enough and less than a thousand tenants took avantage of them. Bright might have made a more determined struggle for his viewpoint, but a week before the Bill was introduced, he had written sadly to the Prime Minister saying that he was quite unable to work and had to leave London for a time. 'Don't be unhappy about me', he wrote to his wife, 'I have no pain & am not in low spirits. I am only weak & unable to read or work.'

It is not easy to explain Bright's second breakdown. In June 1869, he had complained to Helen that he often felt very weary, though the office work itself was not very heavy. What was burdensome was the additional attendance at the House. If office work was not very heavy, that was because he chose not to make it so. He relied on his civil servants and did not display any particular executive or administrative flare. Throughout 1869, he had to decline invitations to speak at public meetings. As a minister, he found it impossible to speak freely without exciting expectations which could not be easily realized. He would not descend to the 'common place language which means nothing'.[23] In addition, he felt a tension between his present responsibilities and his previous commitments on such matters as Ireland, education and the United States. The strained relations with America were perhaps the most acute disappointment of all. Bright, of course, fully expected the British government to have to make some restitution for the damage wrought by the *Alabama*. His countrymen would have to pay for their folly in not agreeing with him about the war. However, Gladstone's willingness to submit the matter to arbitration seemed statesmanlike, but Sumner's remarks about his country's massive grievance being still untouched caused Bright severe embarrassment. In letters to the Foreign Secretary, Lord Clarendon, Bright first tried to claim that Sumner would be 'more astonished than any other person at the noise his speech has made', but by October 1869 he took a different line, arguing that the speech did not 'receive a cordial support from the most thoughtful of his countrymen'.[24] In December, he wrote, regarding the *Alabama* damages, that 'we might have agreed to pay them at first, but it is very difficult now. I do not think the U.S. can fairly ask it after having once consented to arbitration. . . .'[25] Anxiety about British-American matters may, therefore, have been the problem which finally broke his composure.

Fundamentally Bright had never been a member of a political team and found it difficult to accept responsibility for policies which were not his own. Beyond the tension between office and independence, however, there may well have been a deeper tension between his London life-style and his ancestral principles. In November 1869 he wrote that he was sorely troubled with so much separation from his family, yet he dared not admit to himself how much he enjoyed the social life of the capital and the gossip of political circles. In this context, his irritated outburst to his wife when he again became ill — 'I told thee something would happen & that we should not always be so much separated. . . .' — is perhaps revealing.

'Prostrate and helpless', was how Bright described himself in mid-March 1870 in a brief note to the Prime Minister. He saw no prospect of returning to the Commons for weeks. The railway company obligingly fixed a special invalid carriage on the train which took him to Llandudno. He stayed there through the summer months, disappointed and discouraged, suffering from what he described as nervous dyspepsia. Even fishing was too much of an effort. The news of the Franco-Prussian war roused him to write to Gladstone expressing his anxiety lest Britain be drawn into war on behalf of Belgium. If he had to leave the government, however, he hoped that it would be on grounds of health rather than policy difference. The question of his future was left in abeyance. In a way, Bright was delighted with the Prussian victory.

> France is deposed & Germany is exalted [he wrote to the Prime Minister on 11 September] a great gain I think for liberty & for peace. It will be a great gain too for Protestants & the imposture which is still throned on the seven hills will be less able to claim military support. . . .

Thomas Bright was even more forthright. 'The French', he wrote on 17 September, 'are the same disgusting breed as the Irish, mere dissatisfied disturbers of the respectable part of the world.' John, however, did believe that Britain ought to be helpful to France in her humiliation, though without incensing the Germans. Advice on the papacy, the Fenians and France 'as a contribution to your deliberations' continued to trickle through from North Wales but the author did not feel able to come to London. He reported some improvement but since sea bathing seemed to be remedial he was unwilling to discontinue it. By October, he had amassed a total of more than eighty dips. Billiards, too, was fitted in almost daily, affording, as he put it, gentle exercise to the head as well as to the body. Eventually, however, in December 1870, Bright decided that since he could not even fix a day for his return to partial work, he had to resign. Bagehot, in *The Economist* was one among many who wondered at the dispensation of Providence 'which mixed a fine, and to some extent incapacitating, thread of nervous delicacy in a mind so healthy, so vigorous, and on most points so emphatically robust.' While he trusted that Bright would never again attempt administrative labours, he hoped that his powerful tones would often be heard again in the life of the nation.

It was not until April 1872 that Bright reappeared in the Commons, and then only briefly. He had spent the interval at home and in Wales and Scotland. In that time, his former colleagues had been most solicitous. The Queen had invited him to Balmoral, but he decided that the state of his head ruled out such a prospect. During his convalescence, however, he gave the new Foreign Secretary, Lord Granville, the benefit of his advice on relations with the United States and other matters.

210

He sent his congratulations when agreement was reached with Washington on the Claims Commission. The renegotiation of the Anglo-French commercial agreement also, very naturally, engaged his attention. He urged the importance of renewal. 'How delightfully "conservative" I am become, you will say', he wrote to Granville. 'I was always "conservative" in feeling & in reality — as those who know me best will freely admit.'[26]

Before his illness overtook him, Bright had anticipated playing a full part in educational as well as Irish policy. Nonconformists, indeed, looked to him to be Gladstone's 'guide, philosopher and friend' in this field.[27] Perhaps fortunately for himself, Bright was out of action during the Cabinet's consideration of the Education Bill. The 1870 Act provided a dual school system. The existing denominational schools survived and their grants were increased, though they were not permitted to become a charge upon the rates. Alongside them were the 'board' schools which did have power to levy rates. They were to give religious instruction, but to exclude the catechism or formulary of any particular sect. Opposition to the measure was strongest in Birmingham where the National Education League operated. The critics, chiefly Nonconformists, included the Reverend R. W. Dale and Joseph Chamberlain. Dale was a leading Congregationalist with considerable influence in the city; Chamberlain was on the threshold of his national political career. The critics, however, were not absolutely united; some wanted a completely secular education system, while others objected to the grants to denominational schools. The clause relating to instruction in board schools was also often thought inadequate. A system of competing denominational schools also had its supporters. Despite being one of the members for Birmingham, Bright appears not to have played much part when the controversy was at its height, though in a speech in January 1870, he did express opposition to the denominational system in education. He argued that because the Established Church was one body it obtained the bulk of the money disbursed by the State and the divided Nonconformist bodies could not compete. Nor did he forget that a third of the population did not belong to any religious body.[28]

The passage of the act did not end Nonconformist opposition and relations between Gladstone and Nonconformist Liberals became strained. When it became apparent that Bright's health was slowly improving, Dale approached him in 1871 on educational matters. When Gladstone sounded Bright out on the possibility of returning to the Cabinet, he was told that the political situation had changed since the onset of his illness. Enclosing a recent speech of Dale's, he warned on 21 November 1871 that the Education Act had done a 'tremendous mischief' to the party. It was possible that the exasperation felt by Dissenters would bear 'evil fruit'. The Church had been pleased, but the Church would not maintain the government. A few days later, he complained that in practice denominational schools were being encouraged at the expense of board schools. He also warned against voting any money in Ireland for a Catholic college or university. Everything, he concluded, went to show what a great error had been made in preserving and even extending the denominational school system. For the moment, Gladstone took comfort from the fact that Bright was not addressing his constituents on the subject: it looked, he wrote to Granville, 'rather Ministerial'.[29] Bright did not see how the government could extricate himself from the muddle in which it found itself. It was strange that the man who had misjudged the Nonconformist temper, Forster, had himself been brought up as a Quaker.

Early in January 1872, Bright wrote to Dale offering his services, in effect, as an intermediary. He described himself as a 'looker-on', a Nonconformist and friend of the administration, but not uncritical of both. He warned Dale that unless the ground chosen for contention was broad, he would not get the support of the working classes, because they would see the contest as one between Church parsons and Dissenting parsons in which they had little interest. The Act had only got through in the first place 'as much by the folly of the "Noncons" as by the pretensions of the Church'.[30] Partly in the hope that Bright's presence would help to mollify the Nonconformists, Gladstone tried to get him to rejoin the government. To his daughter, however, Bright wrote that if he could slip out of parliament, he would do so 'by the first post'. He was now very tired of public life and had no appetite for any further part in it. Even the least-worked office in the government was beyond his capacity. It would be 1873, at least, before his doctors would contemplate the resumption of such responsibility.

It is clear that Bright had every intention of sustaining a lengthy recuperation. His visit to London in April 1872, when he called briefly at the House, and had the pleasure of dining en famille with the Gladstones had been chiefly with the purpose of buying a handsome barouche at the handsome price of 147 guineas. Having achieved this end, he departed once more for Scotland. After a few months, he was induced to return to Rochdale where friends and admirers from Staffordshire presented him with an elaborate cabinet and pottery.'To a most eloquent and patriotic man', the Latin inscription read, 'these examples of most beauteous but not very ancient art.' In his speech of acknowledgment, Bright rehearsed the story of some of the movements in which he had been active. His style, thought the *Graphic* of 27 July 1872, was perhaps a shade 'too self-conceited and gratulatory'. Bright had done much for the country but 'we can hardly imagine that the political world would have stood still without him.' While he was in England, Gladstone enticed him down to London to discuss the possible prosecution of Irish bishops and priests: Bright was against it. He declined a further invitation to rejoin the government and departed again for Scotland. Accompanied by the Bible and Milton, he posted himself from fishing lodge to fishing lodge, culminating in a fortnight with the Duke of Argyll at his rather superior lodge — Inverary Castle. He followed up this visit with a correspondence on the Sacraments. The winter was spent at home 'without excitement'.

Enjoyable though these diversions were, Bright was aware that his abstention from politics could not continue indefinitely. 'My friends in Birmingham have been & are very kind', he wrote to Dale at the end of November 1872, 'but I am afraid my long absence from my duties must have made some of them weary of me.' He began to believe that he could return, but only in a minor role. 'I have had my part in some great questions', he wrote to Villiers, '& other parts must be left for other men.' Nevertheless, when the parliamentary session resumed in 1873, Bright came up for it, though his attendance was not very regular. He was not, however, a very contented man. Fresh issues were coming into politics and he did not find them very congenial. He found, for example, the growth

of trade unionism very disturbing and the idea of female suffrage was no more attractive.

> I see you go in for all the 'fads' and 'crazes' just now afloat
> [he wrote to Thorold Rogers]. For myself I have little
> sympathy with the score or two of women who are
> miserable because they are not men. My gardener says that
> there is nothing he dislikes so much in his poultry yard as a
> 'crowing hen' and men-women are not a pleasant addition
> to our social arrangements.

The death of J. S. Mill prompted further, slightly more
restrained, reflections on this topic. Within the family, he
advised his wife not to get into discussion on the matter with
their daughters. In the certain knowledge that his convictions
on the role of women annoyed both his daughters and his sisters, Bright made a point of stating them openly. Helen
lamented that her father seemed to forget that women made
up half of the population.[31] Bright also opposed many of his
relatives on the drink question, since he was against a Permis-
sive Bill which would allow a local veto on the sale of alcohol.
'These fanatical promoters of well-intending but impracticable
measures', he wrote to his wife, 'are doing much harm. It is
always so when great questions get into the hands of weak
people — weak heads are liable to be run away with. . . .'
Whatever the condition of his own head, the only subject
which Bright consented, in a mild way, to take into his hands,
was education. Discontent with the 1870 Act was still sapping
the unity of the party. It was upon this subject that he entered
into correspondence with Joseph Chamberlain, a man who was
not yet a close acquaintance. Controversy centred upon the
twenty-fifth clause which empowered School Boards to pay the
fees of poor children in denominational schools. After receiving a deputation from Birmingham, he urged Gladstone to
repeal this clause. His impression was that the amount of
money involved was slight, so that the Nonconformists could
be satisfied without much actual loss to the Church party. On
the same day, he wrote to Chamberlain in an optimistic frame
of mind about healing the wounds in the party. When he
spoke publicly on the subject a few months later, Bright did so

once more as a member of the government, Gladstone having conceded that 'to a certain extent' the education question could be an open one.

Throughout the summer of 1873, the Prime Minister had been dangling office in front of the elusive Bright and in August his appointment as Chancellor of the Duchy of Lancaster was announced. He did not have extensive departmental duties in this position. Gladstone brought Bright back to try to restore his government's popularity, but some of his colleagues felt that his influence was already 'much diminished'.[32] In a letter to the Prime Minister on 12 August, Bright warned that in taking office he could not break with his 'Noncon' friends, but he would try to do something (as Gladstone hoped) to alleviate the situation. What was wanted, he wrote a little later, was some definite willingness to recover the goodwill of the Nonconformist leaders. Gladstone tried to be conciliatory and, as a personal gesture, urged that they themselves should omit 'Mr' when addressing each other in correspondence. This familiarity was followed by an invitation to stay at Hawarden the following month. Part of the time there was spent by Bright observing the Prime Minister and his three sons working hard with their axes, part in church where Bright thought that what took place was 'only fitting for a very ignorant people', and part in political discussion. Bright played his role by writing to Chamberlain that both electors and non-electors were in favour of some religious teaching and therefore 'neither Mr Gladstone nor any other minister can hope successfully to contend with this feeling & we may resign ourselves to what cannot be prevented.' Lest Chamberlain did not care to so resign himself, he added that 'on a clear issue of excluding the Bible from the schools I suspect you would be beaten in Birmingham.'[33] Nevertheless, the Hawarden conversations did not solve the problem.

Late in October, Bright made his first major speech for years in Birmingham when he sought re-election consequent upon accepting office. He stated that he had been out of action when the original Bill had been under consideration. What should have been introduced, he argued, was a Bill to establish board schools and to offer inducements to denominational schools to put themselves under the control of the Privy Council. Speaking for himself, he declared that no sectarian system of education could ever be truly national or truly good. The real questions of education were neglected in bigoted squabbles between church, chapel and secularist. Bright's attempt to disclaim any responsibility for the 1870 Act brought down the wrath of Forster upon him. In a long letter, he went through the details of the situation as it existed in November 1869 before Bright's illness incapacitated him. Forster argued that, if anything, the Act was less rather than more denominational as compared with the original memorandum which the Cabinet had discussed. In his reply, Bright both defended himself and attacked the later decision to increase the annual grant to denominational schools. Forster sent a copy of the correspondence to the Prime Minister, complaining that Bright's intervention made his own position 'hardly tenable'.[34]

In the event, this dispute became absorbed in the various other problems which upset the Liberal government and led to a dissolution at the end of January 1874. Education had not been the only subject on the mind of ministers. Bright's views were sought by the Home Secretary, Robert Lowe, on the subject of 'the laws affecting the condition of labouring men' which he thought in an unsatisfactory state. Bright's chief anxiety, however, was not this problem but the tendency of the government to get involved in foreign adventures. He was not slow to communicate his worries over the Eastern Question and Afghanistan. The operations of British troops on the Gold Coast gravely concerned him. He warned Gladstone that 'promotion is so often their object & revenge & example the pretext for operations & cruelties which are needless & dishonourable.' Within a few weeks of this protest, however, the government came to an end and Bright's scarcely onerous second term of office was over.

In the conventional sense, in his early sixties, Bright's 'career' was over. For whatever reason, he had been unable to sustain his position as President of the Board of Trade and could never expect advancement to any of the major offices of state. Yet, Bright's career had never been conventional and he remained a powerful, if unpredictable, element in politics. Reflecting on Bright's position, Bagehot argued that nothing was more difficult 'than for a popular leader of the first rank so to act, *outside* a government, as to give it any real assistance'. In the government, involved in all its responsibilities, Bright was 'a very powerful auxiliary'.[35] It was for this reason that Gladstone was so anxious to have him back. He remained a vital symbolic figure whose white hair gave a benediction to the Liberal legislative programme and a representative character to the Cabinet. It was a role which Bright seemed prepared to accept. Largely without his direct assistance, his colleagues in this Liberal government had dealt, in considerable measure, with many of the questions which had first brought him into politics. The Church of England remained established, but its dominance was curbed. The ancient universities were opened to Dissenters. The Civil Service was proceeding along the road to open competition. Even if Bright would have preferred it to have been abolished, the army was at least reformed. The interlocking aristocratic order was in process of dissolution. It is conceivable that if Bright had never accepted office in 1868 he might, by external pressure, have pushed Gladstone further in these directions than the government did proceed. His health might not have suffered. These are imponderables; what is clear is that he no longer had the energy or taste for a big speaking tour like that of 1866 and that was the only independent activity at which he excelled. He had, in short, reached that satisfying stage of life when drastic change seemed unnecessary.

TWELVE

Opposition

1874-80

If he had known what would happen, Bright wrote to Helen in the aftermath of the 1874 general election, he would not have offered himself as a candidate. He had no difficulty in Birmingham, but elsewhere the Liberals did badly and Disraeli was able to form a Conservative government. 'Enormous lying', was Bright's verdict, 'for three years past or more has done much to change the result of the elections — the *state* preachers of the Gospel have gone up to the poll arm-in-arm with the dealers in delirium tremens.' He concluded, sadly, that a large portion of the newly-enfranchised working men had 'a sore want of political knowledge & do not understand what is meant by political principle.'[1] The Liberal leadership reacted gloomily to the defeat. 'Our forces are scattered', Bright wrote to an old friend, W. H. Northy, in December 1874, '& there is little *sagacity* among the most earnest men.' He feared that the fanaticisms and crazes of the various sections of the party would prevent any combined action. The following month, Gladstone resigned the leadership. Bright, who had been pleasantly travelling round the country for many weeks, wrote both to sympathize with the decision and to express himself strongly on the 'gang of priests' who prevented the reform of the papacy.

In the choice of the new Liberal leader, Bright was given a role to play. Granville had hastened to reassure him that party feeling would be consulted, and Bright presided over the meeting which selected Lord Hartington ('a strong-headed, sensible fellow'). The Quaker did his best to exclude the ex-Quaker, Forster, stating that his educational measure had divided the party. Moreover, he cared 'nothing for expenditure, as you know, & he is very fond of Factory Bills & the rotten legislation which has come so much into favor of late years'. It was safer, apparently, to place one's trust in the Duke of Devonshire's heir. 'I hope & believe', he wrote to Hartington, knowing that it was not very likely, 'you will find yourself supported by a strong and loyal party . . . .'[2]

The position of a senior statue in the Liberal party now suited Bright admirably. The routine of his life was well established. He regularly visited Birmingham each January and unloaded himself of the expected speeches but his constituents did not expect too many performances at other times. Apart from occasional visits and correspondence, the city's affairs could largely be left in the energetic hands of its current mayor, Joseph Chamberlain. Bright now often stayed with Chamberlain on his visits, though they eyed each other warily. Bright eyed most new men warily. He told Henry Broadhurst, the trade unionist, that he had no objection to any man being sent to the Commons if deemed worthy by his constituents. He would then be elected on general grounds, 'not because he is what you term a "working man", which I presume he will cease to be as soon as he takes his place in parliament'.[3] He had become very jealous for the honour of the House.

In February each year, shortly after parliament resumed, Bright normally complained of the demands made by social life. He had come to town, he wrote to Mrs Rathbone, intending to take great care of his health and was therefore abstaining from 'dining out' except 'in cases which are in some sort "official"'.[4] He told his wife, similarly, that he was declining invitations to late parties. His power of resistance was, however, limited and the social round soon became a busy one, even if he tried, on occasions to restrict his consumption to whitebait and lemonade. His political behaviour was equally forthright. He refused to talk to his sister Priscilla about female suffrage. 'She, dear creature', he commented, 'is almost too passionate & enthusiastic to reason on such a question . . . .' The family temperance clash also continued with Bright disputing 'the wisdom of insisting on the impracticable' where prohibition was concerned. Late in 1875, he had numerous discussions on the problem with Sir Wilfred Lawson, but he still did not see his way 'to propose anything new or likely to be useful on the great "Drink" question. The more it is looked at the more perplexing it seems . . . .'

Political life had, in any case, ceased to be all-absorbing. The Tichborne case greatly interested him and he followed the career of the claimant with considerable credulity. Other landmarks of the session included the introduction, by Bright himself, of the Duke of Bedford's heir, the Marquis of Tavistock, into the House of Commons; lunch with Moody, the American evangelist; dinner with the Prime Minister of Canada and a visit to Lord Russell at Pembroke Lodge. He also kept himself up to date with the latest medical opinion on consumption. He declined, however, an invitation to accept office in the Society of Friends. 'The labors of my life have taken me out of the way of service for our little Church', he wrote, 'I feel that there is nothing above the humblest office — shall I say that of doorkeeper? which I could properly undertake.'[5] He rounded off the session with a sentimental visit to York and then stayed quietly at home in Rochdale, concerning himself with family and business matters.

The new year, 1876, began inevitably with the Birmingham speech. This time, unusually, his wife wanted to come with him, but he told Helen that he hoped to dissuade her. 'I do not like so many going to our annual gathering', he wrote. 'It hinders me & it throws additional burden on my hospitable friends to whom I am so much indebted.' On this occasion Bright criticized a speech Lord Derby had recently made to an audience of three thousand working-class Conservatives in Edinburgh. He took leave to doubt whether there were three thousand such beings in the city. He took exception to the Foreign Secretary's claim that 'popular' politicians never gave any man better wages or a better house to live in, and rehearsed in reply the Tory obstruction of Reform. Attacking the landed wealth of the Tories, he urged his audience to 'give to the people who are now excluded that freedom which the Constitution has given to you.'

Although, on this occasion, Bright claimed that there were faithful Liberal working men in his audience, he made no attempt to pander to the supposed interests of the urban working class. It did still annoy him that so many of them had apparently taken advantage of the secret ballot, established by the Liberals in 1872, to vote for the Tories. His opposition to trade unionism was deepening rather than lessening. Declining an invitation to address the North Wales Quarrymen's Union in 1876, he wrote that he did not approve of '"combinations" for the purpose of improving or maintaining wages, nor of giving into the hands of an "Executive Council" of a district the power to "decide whether the members of the Union in the district shall leave work or not" — that is whether they shall strike or not.' There was, he believed, a natural law which determined the rate of wages much more justly than an Executive Council. Combinations, either of workmen or employers, to raise or lower wages, seemed to him to involve a condition of menace and warfare. Commenting on the activities of trade union agitators over the previous five years, he thought that the misery they caused in fomenting strikes could not be measured.[6]

> Had there been no trades' unions dealing with the question of wages [he commented] there would have been a gradual & certain rise & the highest point might or might not have been reached — but the fall would probably have been less sudden & less serious. The labor markets would have been more steady & the enormous loss caused by strikes would have been avoided. . . .'

When parliament reassembled, Bright felt more confident in the House than he had done for years. His attendance was more assiduous and he showed himself eager to be found in the company of the ex-ministers. Early in the session, he dined with the still-retired Gladstone, where he met Lord Rosebery for the first time and formed a 'very favourable impression' of him. He attended the Court where the Queen asked after his health, though in general he could not decide whether the occasion was humiliating or amusing. In March, he was a member of the party conclave to decide what should be the

Liberal attitude to the Royal Titles Bill which proposed to style the Queen Empress of India. Bright thought the proposal a fraud, a typical exercise by the frivolous and mischievous Prime Minister, but that did not prevent its passage. Naturally, the dinner question had again to be considered. This year he did not think the dinners did harm. He told his wife, 'sometimes they refresh me evidently — but they take up the evening . . . They are pleasant enough — only they come too often.' A little later, he added that although greatly troubled by them, he took the dinners 'mildly', eating little and drinking nothing. The fact was that this social life prevented solitary introspection. 'My rooms are *superb*', he commented sadly to his wife, 'only they want somebody else in them — perhaps they would suit thee.'

His social life was indeed very vigorous. He had so many invitations to lunch or dinner that it was difficult to prove accommodating to the many sculptors anxious for a bust. His devotion to the House of Russell was conspicuous, advising the Duke of Bedford to send his second son into the House of Commons on the unimpeachable ground that the breed was so good. He was present at the wedding breakfast in the Grosvenor Hotel after the marriage, in a Meeting House, of a daughter of Lord Charles Russell to a Friend. The case was curious, perhaps unique, but he added, referring to the Russells, 'it is a good family'. The occasion symbolized his own accommodation with the Whig aristocracy. He even felt more at home in their company than in that of the new school of Radicals in the Commons — men like Fawcett, Cowen or Dilke — and when they asked him to move a vote of censure on the government, he declined. It was a source of joy to him that, after a chat, Fawcett withdrew his Women's Suffrage Bill. Bright had spoken against the principle once more, knowing that his 'masculine sisters' would be sorely tried.

In addition to political dinners, Bright's face was also frequently to be seen among literary men and intellectuals — Jowett, Lecky and Trollope are among those whose presence at the same table he records. In late June 1876, he dined at Stafford House to meet the Minister of the Nizam of Hyderabad, in the company of Dukes, Duchesses and, unfortunately, Disraeli. It was a fine party, he remarked, with grand rooms, much music and plenty of light. The Duke of Sutherland, the host, then invited Bright to accompany the Indian to his house at Trentham and tour the Potteries. They would then go north, to Dunrobin (his castle), Glasgow and Edinburgh — thus seeing the sights of Scotland in order of importance. Though Bright found much in the invitation that was tempting, he declined for fear of the fatigue and excitement. When the Duke pressed, however, he agreed to travel on the first part of this grand tour and set off for Staffordshire by train in the Duke's own private saloon carriage. At Trentham, everything was comfortable. Bright spent a couple of hours in talks with the Indian and a couple of hours in the bowling alley. After Crewe, where the railway workshops were inspected, Bright hurried home to Rochdale where Prince Arthur, Duke of Connaught, had arrived to inspect the mills and take coffee at One Ash.

The only political excitement was the rather uncertain news of atrocities in the Balkans. The day after his return to the capital, on 14 July 1876, Bright agreed to lead a deputation from the Peace Society to the Foreign Secretary urging him not to react hastily to this information. Bright professed himself satisfied with the reply and throughout the rest of the month steered clear of protests against Britain's apparent acquiescence in the Turkish misdeeds in Bulgaria. He returned to Rochdale as soon as he could at the end of the session, and then disappeared to Scotland in September. In doing so, Bright escaped the burgeoning campaign in the north of England on the issue of the atrocities. Potter, however, Rochdale's MP, wanted to know more about Bright's feelings, implying that Gladstone's willingness to campaign against the government was being cold-shouldered by his former colleagues. Gladstone had, indeed, spoken at length about foreign affairs on 31 July, though his specific reference to the Bulgarian horrors was slight. On 23 August, however, he had committed himself to the view that Disraeli's treatment of the question was 'inadequate and unsatisfactory'.[7]

Bright replied to Potter on 27 August, stating that if Gladstone was in the cold it was because he had chosen this position. He did not believe that Gladstone wished to return, nor would it be possible for him to do so successfully because of the hostility his attitude to the Vatican had aroused among

Catholics. Bright declared that he had been chairman of the meeting which had chosen Lord Hartington and he would not act against him. He conceded that if there were an active committee campaigning on the Eastern Question, the government might be toppled, but it had to be remembered that 'in his recent great speech, Mr Gladstone still adhered to the integrity of Turkey & argued that the Crimean War had succeeded in its great object of overturning the Russian Protectorate of the Christians in Turkey & conferring it upon the European Powers.' A week later, he wrote from Scotland that he thought meetings on the Turkish question would 'do good'. He wrote to the citizens of Rochdale, since he could not 'keep silence', that the subject should not be 'treated hastily' and that the Crimean War had been wicked.[8] The same general message characterized his speech at Manchester a month later when he argued that[9] 'the vote of our government, the vote of England, in the parliament of Europe, shall be given in favor of justice and freedom to the Christian and Moslem alike, and the Ottoman power shall be left hereafter to the fate which Providence has decreed to corruption, tyranny and wrong.' He was equally anxious, however, that Gladstone's freshly attuned moral sensitivity should not lead the blood and treasure of England to be wasted *against* the Turk. Writing to Gladstone a week before this speech, he attempted to devalue the agitation by saying that he lacked confidence 'in popular fervor in a matter of this kind'. Even if a petition to recall parliament succeeded, which he doubted, it would be difficult to know what policy to urge. 'I advised the Cabinet 22 years ago not to get into a hole', he concluded, '& how to keep out of it, but it is difficult, when once in, to show them how to get out.' Gladstone's attempt to involve Bright failed. The orator retired to North Wales with his family.

'I am becoming more & more weary of political life', Bright wrote to Chamberlain on 7 November, '& yet I should much like an evening's talk with you on the present & future of public affairs.' Since Chamberlain joined him in the Commons in the summer, Bright regarded him as a protégé. 'Foreign policy in the hands of Disraeli is a great danger', he warned a week later. 'He is attempting to bully Russia & to raise a war feeling at home. I hope he may fail in both.' Another war on the Eastern Question would be disastrous. 'Fortunately for us', he wrote to Goldwin Smith on 19 November, 'we have no allies & our cause is so transparently selfish, that no European Power can sympathize with us or will be willing to help us.'[10] Neither the army nor the navy could contemplate a conflict on their own. To a large extent, therefore, while condemning the 'foolish and wicked jealousy of Russia' which the Tories were fostering, he kept apart from the main thrust of the agitation. Disraeli's Guildhall speech on 9 November, however, with its open support for Turkey, brought Bright into the fray at a great meeting in Birmingham Town Hall on 4 December. Again, he referred back to the Crimean War and to Cobden, and urged that in no circumstances should Turkey be supported. At the same time, his own ambivalence on the question of war and peace was apparent. He had to confess that he had sometimes thought that the government had been 'rather too much in favour of peace. They are in favour of peace, if not at any price, at least at a price which some of us would scarcely wish to pay for it.' At another point, he admitted that, while no defender of 'sanguinary struggles', they could not sometimes be avoided. There could be no arbitration unless the parties concerned were willing; Constantinople and its suffering subjects were not willing.[11] Having made his point, however, Bright took no part in the national conference held to discuss the atrocities at St James's Hall a few days later.

The international conference at Constantinople broke up unsuccessfully on 22 January 1877. Partly to escape from Gladstone, Bright disappeared to the South of France before parliament resumed. It was still not certain whether war would break out. In March, on his return to London, Bright was at once taken into the counsels of Granville and Hartington. After listening to Gladstone on 23 March Bright recorded uneasily that he spoke 'at length, but occasionally under unusual excitement'. Throughout April, the Eastern Question figured prominently at the dinner tables; war between Turkey and Russia was seen as inevitable and, in some quarters, desirable. When war did break out on 24 April, Gladstone announced his intention to move a series of resolutions condemning the Porte and asking that British influence be exerted on behalf of local liberty and self-government.

On the morning of 26 April, Bright breakfasted with Gladstone and Lord Granville and they discussed the situation. They were joined by the poet Tennyson, not Bright's favourite, whose comment that the Turkish religion was a very good religion did not seem very helpful. Bright preferred Lewis Morris, whose poem *The Epic of Hades* he had recently read. Everybody at this breakfast was in an emotional mood — Bright had just returned from the funeral of Mrs Cobden — and agreement proved difficult. After a private conversation with him, Bright came away convinced that Gladstone was burdened with a sense of responsibility connected with the Crimean War and for this reason would take his own line whatever his former colleagues thought. Fortified by another reading of *The Epic of Hades*, Bright attended the meeting of ex-ministers at Granville's the following morning. They agreed that Gladstone, who was ill in bed, ought not to proceed with his resolutions, and Bright was deputed to report in this sense to him. For over a week, the Liberal party was in difficulty and Hartington's resignation was talked of. In the end, Gladstone satisfied Bright and his colleagues by moving an amended resolution.

In mid-May, Gladstone accepted an invitation from Chamberlain to go to Birmingham to attend the inaugural meeting of the National Liberal Federation. Granville, and other Whigs, had been assuming that Gladstone would not attend because he would not wish to associate with a body which would seek to impose the style and methods of Birmingham politics on the party at large. Once more, Bright was in a difficult position and turned yet again to *The Epic of Hades* for inspiration — he urged the merits of the poem on George Eliot at dinner. He could hardly fail to appear in Birmingham, yet he did not want to seem an ardent Gladstonian. On 22 May, he wrote to a prominent Birmingham Liberal that he hoped Gladstone would not 'lead our friends into any wild cry for war with Turkey. He was wrong in 1854 & in my view is wrong now — *he* has turned round but it is not necessary that *I* should do so also.' Bright felt that Russia was 'the only real friend of these Christians' and she would deliver them if Britain did not interfere. There might well be a feeling in Birmingham in favour of the resolutions, but there had been a feeling in Manchester in 1854; it was mistaken then, it was mistaken in 1877. The day before

Gladstone was due to speak, Bright wrote again urging that a hint should be given to Chamberlain, Collins and Dale that if they sought to urge upon Gladstone the leadership of the party, or a section of it, 'they will place him in much difficulty & will compel him entirely to repudiate it & *they will show how little they are able to estimate his character.* I do not make this suggestion without reason.'[12] Gladstone spoke on 31 May and Bright addressed the dinner which was held in his honour. 'You have among you', he stated, 'the most eminent man of the statesmen of our country in this generation', but then went on to recount his own unhappy experiences during the Crimean War. He had then fought against public opinion but now could afford to be 'and think, perhaps, I ought to be tranquil and in some degree a spectator, for I see the policy that I approve is successful and triumphant now.'

There was no change in the party leadership after Birmingham, yet, for all his disclaimers, Gladstone was back in the field, eager to spread his new vision of Liberalism, however awkward it might prove to former colleagues. Bright, however, amply justified his claim to be a 'spectator' in the months that followed. He spoke again in the Commons on capital punishment, and discussed with Sir Joseph Whitworth his very curious invention of a new kind of wheel for carriages, made of steel with flexible spokes, each one, apparently, being a spring. There was a garden party at Marlborough House to attend and conversation with the Queen; dinner at Kensington Palace to meet the American General Grant; dinner with Lady Waldegrave at Strawberry Hill; dinner with Childers to meet the French politician Waddington, and so on. The Eastern Question certainly did not dominate his life.

At the end of July, he departed for Yorkshire, where he made a series of speeches in Bradford. The occasion of the visit was to unveil a statue to Cobden. In his address, which was not without a touch of exaggeration, he dwelt on their friendship and on Cobden's achievements. Richard's enduring monument, he claimed, lay in the steadier employment, higher wages and more solid independence which now obtained among the people. But just how enduring was Free Trade? He addressed the Chamber of Commerce on this subject and, predictably, declared that for this country now to return to Protection under any form, to reciprocity, which means to a war of tariffs, would be in reality to bar the progress of the world and, I should say, to destroy our hopes for future peace.

He was well aware, however, that the climate of opinion was changing and that Free Trade was not as self-evident a principle as it had once appeared. Bright himself remained quite convinced. The idea of retaliatory duties seemed to him quite absurd.[13]

> The only way to lessen the injury of Foreign Tariffs [he argued] is to reduce, or, if we can, abolish our own Tariff. In the depression of the last 2 or 3 years, we have suffered less than other countries & have had more scope for selling what we produce.

Devoted though they were to commerce, the citizens of Bradford would not let him escape without making some reference to foreign affairs. Bright discussed the scale of British colonial possessions and warned of the constant presence of a war party in parliament. The great majority of them were not on the Opposition benches, '& yet I sometimes think there are few even on our side whose language and whose conduct are not strongly in favour of peace.' In his conclusion, he again stressed his opinion that the policy of neutrality was best for Britain.[14] There was nothing to be gained from an interventionist foreign policy.

Bright was now in high demand as a speaker on civic and ceremonial occasions. He did his best to oblige, though without enthusiasm. He was present at the official opening of the Town Hall in Manchester and, in his address, expatiated on the political and economic development of the city during the century. Yet there was a gloomy note; referring both to foreign competition and combinations at home, he reminded his distinguished audience that 'great cities have fallen before Manchester and Liverpool were known'. A message delivered to the Science and Art classes organized by the Rochdale Co-operative Society was more cheerful. He discoursed upon the inventions and discoveries which had occurred during his lifetime; it had indeed been an era of improvement, though much still needed to be done. There was little bite in addresses of this kind; they represented rhetoric to order rather than the expression of deep feeling.

The State Church, however, still upset him, though he was now no stranger to Bishops and Deans. In a speech in Rochdale on 7 November, he attacked the new Bishop of Truro and found it shocking that his main purpose seemed to be to recapture Cornwall from Dissent. When a correspondent pointed out that the Bishop had said no such thing, Bright did not waver.[15]

> I did not pretend to quote the Bishop's words [he replied] but to describe his spirit and object. It is time that all earnest men should consider the position and claims of the State Church, so long as it continues a *State* Church, all other Churches must endure the humiliation to which they are now subjected.

Bright's personal humiliations were, in fact, few. He went to stay with Lord Halifax in November with 'a pleasant party' and even while there, received an invitation from Lord Hartington, on his father's behalf, to stay at Chatsworth. 'This will alarm thee', he wrote to his wife, 'but I can hardly avoid going as some of my late colleagues are to be there & the Duke has been civil to me before & I have been unable to accept his kindness.' Devonshire, on closer inspection, did indeed prove to be a very agreeable duke, worthy, in Bright's view, of the great respect in which he was held. The ladies of the party were intelligent and charming. Bright's general attitude did not go unnoticed. In August 1877, Goldwin Smith commented that Bright seemed restored to health but 'time and perhaps social influences' had mellowed the Great Tribune. Apart from his speeches at Bradford, 'he has been silent and apparently apathetic.'[16]

There was one subject in these months which did reawaken a real interest — the famine in India. 'With this gorgeous banquet before us', he told his Manchester audience in September, 'in this magnificent hall, let us not forget our responsibilities.' While individuals should be as generous as possible, only a new policy in India could really help. The famines could have been avoided if one-third of the money spent on railways had instead been spent on navigation canals and irrigation. Reverting momentarily to his enthusiasm of twenty years earlier, he chaired a meeting in Manchester in December at which Sir Arthur Cotton put forward proposals for preventing future famine in India. Bright spoke at some length on the subject himself and argued that it was Britain's duty to govern well in the present and to prepare for the day, which might be distant, but not remote, 'when India will have to take up her own government, and administer it in her own fashion'. In private he was more pessimistic about India. The question was so big, he wrote to Potter in December, that he was appalled at it. The statesman who could tackle it had not yet appeared and might never appear. England might 'receive her greatest humiliation the way in which she has boasted of her greatest triumph . . . .' When India came up in the House in late January 1878, his pessimism caused him not to take part. 'If others will say what is wanted,' he wrote to his wife, 'let them say it . . . I seem to have no desire to talk in the House.' Parliament had been recalled unusually early, but Bright was not optimistic about the session.

Appearances notwithstanding, the war in the Near East was never far from his mind. The Russians had done well initially, but in the high summer the Turks resisted stoutly, creating considerable public sympathy for themselves in England. Although apprehensive that the government might intervene, Bright did not think it very likely. Disraeli would be cautious because he knew that he had no allies 'except the Turks & they will probably be worth little to him before long'. It remained against Britain's interest to quarrel with Russia. In December and early January, the war turned decisively in favour of the Russians, but Bright remained calm. 'I have been against all the interference as not falling within our duty', he had written a few months earlier. 'I advocate no war, but if war exists I am at liberty to express an opinion upon it, & to wish, what seems the right side, to win.'[17] The early recall of parliament reflected the concern about the Balkan situation. Speaking in Birmingham, a little earlier than usual, Bright condemned the government unreservedly. 'No nation', he declared, 'has been in dis-

230

position more friendly to this nation than Russia. There is no nation on the Continent of Europe to whom we are less able to do harm than we are to Russia.'[18] In a letter to Chamberlain on 8 January 1878 he declared that Disraeli had no case and no allies, though the government might even claim support 'on the ground that they have kept us out of a war they could not venture to get into!' He was worried that the Queen might be meddling too much — she was in fact contemplating abdication — and lamented that she should have Disraeli as her adviser.

As the Russians advanced, Bright became more and more agitated. The government asked for a vote of credit after meetings between 21 and 23 January. The Cabinet also agreed to begin negotiations with Vienna and to order the Mediterranean fleet to sail through the Dardanelles to Constantinople. For a brief while, Derby resigned, but returned when this order was countermanded. So occupied was Bright's mind with the prospect of war, that he could not sleep, and at a quarter to three on the morning of 25 January, he got out of bed, lighted a candle, and went into the next room to make notes for a speech. It was delivered in the Commons a week later, reiterating the case against intervention. The Liberal party as a whole was in a divided state. Hartington refused to lead against the government, believing that circumstances might arise in which it would be the duty of Britain to fight. Although privy to the discussions of the Liberal leadership, Bright kept his own counsel, intervening later in the debate to quash suggestions that the Russians were violating the precariously established armistice agreement with Turkey. Gladstone's speeches at this time aroused his admiration. 'There is a noble earnestness about him', he wrote to his wife, 'which the Tory party & insincere men among us cannot bear.' Even so, the government had a comfortable majority at the end of the debate. Hartington abstained, but Bright joined Gladstone and Chamberlain in voting against. Though there was a great deal of talk about war, Bright still thought on balance that it was unlikely. The British government was in a hole, but it was unlikely that Russia would take advantage of it. 'We shall probably hear', he concluded, 'that both sides withdraw rather than resist & commit any act of hostility.' Great meetings were being held to counter the ravings of the 'Jingoes', but having 'an increasing dislike of the excitement & disturbance of great crowds', Bright was now content to resign his role as public orator to Gladstone. As the crisis rumbled on, however, he did speak at several public meetings, both in Rochdale and Manchester. His message was always the same. He did not believe that war was necessary and the divisions within the Cabinet showed that the government had a bad case. As he left the Free Trade Hall in Manchester, Bright was jostled and his hat received a considerable indentation — it was unpleasantly reminiscent of 1853 and 1854. Apart from these speeches, and a few public letters, he regarded the government's performance with a certain melancholy resignation, which the appointment of Lord Salisbury as Foreign Secretary did nothing to dispel. He had no sympathy for the difficult and delicate course pursued by Disraeli and Salisbury over the coming months. In a letter to James Bryce on the Armenian question, he wrote simply that if [19]

the Powers [would] agree to get rid of the Turkish Govt, both in Europe and Asia, something might be done for them — but they can agree upon nothing good & broad in policy & the English Govt is not the most willing to help the subject & suffering populations.

He had concluded, in short, that there was not much he could do about anything.

Suddenly, a new and different crisis occurred. On the morning of 13 May 1878, he received a telegram from his eldest son urging him to return to Rochdale at once. Albert met him at Crewe and told him the news that Elizabeth Bright was dead. She was fifty-six and her apoplexy was quite unexpected. A fortnight earlier, they had been on holiday together at Llandudno and there had been no premonition of death. In one of his last letters to her, Bright had written 'I write once in the day but I think of thee much oftener'. So much of their marriage had depended on the postage stamp that it is not easy to assess its significance. John and Elizabeth maintained the outward and visible signs of harmony and attachment, yet it is difficult to avoid the feeling that the pattern of their lives had become so different that complete mutual sympathy was

absent. He had been forced to discover that Elizabeth had a
mind and will of her own, and he did not much care for it.

> He could praise women [Priscilla wrote to Helen after
> Bright's death] but not Woman — he could worship what he
> called charming women, but he could *never* bear women to
> assert themselves — he could bear this less after his second
> marriage which taught him what a resolute woman could be
> and what she could not be — one who would assert her
> power over a £5 note to even a postage stamp, not to
> mention the comfort of a smoke in his own home.

Grumpiness, on his part, is not an infrequent note amidst the
expressions of devotion in their correspondence. When sending his wife a cheque in January 1878 he told her that she
'should learn not to complain so much, especially on matters
thou art not well acquainted with'. Yet, if there was a strain in
their relationship, the sense of loss he suffered was real and
lasting. It accelerated his already well-developed consciousness
of growing old. Scarcely a month passed without news of the
death of old friends — Thomasson, James King and others —
and by carefully attending to the matter of his own will, he
began to prepare himself for his own.

His family was some comfort and consolation, but not all his
children showed a fervent desire to conform to his wishes in all
particulars. Helen, his daughter by his first marriage, had her
own family to look after in Somerset. John Albert, as the eldest
son, had become to some extent his father's political confidant,
but his own political ambitions were strongly discouraged. He
should stick to business. The difficulty with the second son,
Willie, seems to have been in persuading him to stick to anything. 'Tell him how anxious I am about him', Bright had written to Albert in 1870, '& that I wish him to give up so much
joking & nonsense & to become a sensible fellow — he must
strive now for a character above that of a laughing schoolboy.'
In later life, like Albert, he became a member of parliament.
His daughters all showed a disconcerting tendency to marry.
Mary, a semi-invalid, became the bride of a schoolmaster who
had the misfortune to be the son and grandson of admirals.
Within a few years, Bright was successfully recommending his

name to Mundella for an Inspectorship of Schools.[20] Lillie married a surgeon and, within a few years, Sophie had also left home. That left Philip, who was a mere fifteen. Bright took his youngest son's education seriously, sending him off with a tutor to Darmstadt to improve his German. He later sent word that the quality of the coffee there had to be improved — Philip had complained that it was not to his taste. He also wished the boy to have 'some exercises that would give a greater breadth of chest'. Bright urged that it would be better for his son not to go to the theatre unless to refrain would make him seem particularly odd in the sight of his companions. Finally, almost inevitably, he commented that 'Philip has had too much money', but, unusually, 'I fancy his disposition is rather to keep it than to spend it.'[21]

Bright received hundreds of letters of condolence after his wife's death, and it was not clear whether he intended to stay in politics. He declined to go to Birmingham to celebrate the twentieth anniversary of his election there. Domestically, locally and nationally, everything seemed to be going wrong. In the house, he wanted someone else 'for it seems only a woman can deal wisely and constantly with half a dozen women servants'; in Rochdale, Fenton's Bank failed; internationally, no sooner was the Eastern Question settled, though not to his satisfaction, than a new crisis arose concerning Afghanistan. He had evidence which showed that, as usual, the government had been 'deceiving the people & they are solely responsible for the war'. Despite Gladstone's urging, however, he refused to take part in the parliamentary censure of the government in December. If he had spoken, he feared that he 'must have said some things not quite in accordance with the views of many of our side. . . .' To Helen, moreover, he described himself as being 'too ill' to venture to the House. He was on the verge of resignation, seeming 'to grow sick of the world' for its loneliness was 'something hardly endurable'. Trade, too, was bad, and Bright professed to see this as retribution. 'We have all gone too fast', he wrote to Potter, 'spent too much, been in many ways improvident & now we must retrench and suffer for a time.' Amidst this gloom, there was one curious incident. Lewis Morris, the author of *The Epic of Hades* wrote to ask Bright's permission to dedicate to him his forthcoming poem;

by a strange quirk, it was to be called 'Gwen' and was to be a love story set in Wales. Bright consented and his memory must have raced back nearly fifty years.

His mood before the resumption of the 1879 parliamentary session was little better. He regretted to Helen that he had to go to London at all 'and yet I seem without employment here & if there were no "session" for me & no Parlt I should have still less to do.' He stressed how old he felt and how he carried such a heavy burden that all 'vigor & elasticity' seemed to have vanished. The only remedy, he knew, was active work, but he appeared to lack the necessary energy. Even Philip now disappointed him. 'I am afraid', Bright complained to his tutor, 'he makes rather free with his Father's money.' Hostesses, Lady Granville among them, expressed pain that they were being dropped by him and he had to make excuses. Gradually, however, he emerged from his seclusion, and within a few weeks social engagements were nearly back to their normal high level. At length, he did go down to Birmingham in April to make his annual speech, postponed from January, and there liberated himself to general satisfaction on Russia, India and England. He again stressed how stupid it was to fear Russia. Britain had foolishly undertaken the responsibility 'for almost the whole ground from the Gulf of Venice, all round the Eastern Mediterranean to Egypt, to the Persian Gulf, through Persia to Afghanistan, and the confines of British India'. If Britain and Russia co-operated, Englishmen could forget about Constantinople, Asia Minor, the Euphrates, the Persian Gulf, Egypt and Cyprus 'and go to bed and sleep in peace even though Roumelia were delivered from the Turk'. What was needed, Bright wrote to Broadhurst on 4 June 1879, was that men

> should regard war with abhorrence & should deem it
> criminal until it is proved to be necessary, that is
> unavoidable. Now, war is looked upon as a reasonable
> thing, usual & in the common course of events, to be
> regretted perhaps but not without its advantages. . . .

Nevertheless, he thought that the Eastern Question, the Afghanistan affair, and the South African disaster (when British troops were defeated by the Zulus at Isandhlwana), were not without effect. 'I suspect', he concluded, 'that there has never been so much opposition to a war policy as during the last two years.'

In London, he soon settled down into a routine which differed little from his previous customs, except that he chose the moments for his attendance at the House with more care. He talked temperance with Sir Wilfrid Lawson, congratulated Edward Miall on his seventieth birthday, presided over an 'Indian' meeting addressed by a Calcutta lawyer, visited Stoke Poges churchyard, lingered in the Bodleian Library, and dined with Chamberlain, Fawcett and Morley at the Star and Garter, Richmond. In the Commons, he spoke on flogging in the army, which he did not favour; otherwise, apart from occasional references to India, he intervened little. In August, he declined another invitation to visit the United States where, this time, he would have been the President's guest at the White House. Instead, he escaped to Scotland, particularly to Aberdeenshire, where he paid another visit to Haddo. In the smoking room there, after dinner, a warm discussion took place on the Land Question. Both in Aberdeen and Inverness, his arrival was the signal for a deputation from the local dignitaries offering him civic honours — which he declined. In October, he was back in Rochdale, bracing himself for the departure of his youngest daughter, Sophie, who had just announced her engagement.

At the end of the month, however, he did his duty by the Liberal party in sharing a platform at Manchester with Lord Hartington. In advance, he indicated to Hartington his dislike of great meetings and revealed that he would 'probably never undertake to attend or to speak at another of the monster kind'. The only consolation was that their friends were not as 'mobbish' as their opponents. They drank less and thought more. When the audience reputedly exceeded twenty thousand, however, Bright could not resist the belief that the meeting was a wonderful one. The 'Fine Old English Gentleman' (played by the band to greet his arrival) then launched into an assault on Lord Salisbury for complaining that on the subject of tariffs and commercial treaties Britain was being asked to make bricks without straw. Bright would not let him get away with that, giving a glowing account of the 'Gladstonian Era' and contrasting it unfavourably with that of Beaconsfield. He scorned the Artisans' Dwelling Act, but his chief target was foreign policy. If Gladstone had remained in office, he confidently stated, there would have been no danger of war with Russia, no war between Turkey and Russia, no Zulu war and no war with the Emir of Afghanistan. He had heard that the government was toying with the idea of appointing a Minister of Commerce — an absurd project. It was impossible to have two ministers negotiating with foreign governments. What was wanted, rather, was for the Foreign Secretary to abandon all those miserable matters in which he was constantly interfering abroad and leave himself time to become Minister of Commerce. The speech — 'severe on the Govt, but *just* I am quite sure', — was well received. The incidents were, of course new, and the asides were up to date, but the message had not changed for forty years. People needed to be told that same truth over and over again, not to be presented with novel but specious proposals. It was, indeed, distressing that young countries seemed to be adopting protection, but it was a false solution. In the United States, he claimed, 'they have had five years of tremendous difficulty and suffering — all among their protected interests'. Rather than copy America, in this respect, the British should note that the States had '50 millions & almost no army or navy & no spirited foreign policy & we fancy we can compete with them'.[22]

On 8 December, as Bright settled down to writing a narrative of his early life for the benefit of his children, Gladstone returned to Hawarden, tired rather than refreshed by his recent visit to Scotland. He had been campaigning in Midlothian, and what he had said and the manner in which he said it indicated that battle was near. Although he had told Bright that he would not be resuming the party leadership, Bright was content to let time and the 'necessities of the case' decide. 'Our friend at Hawarden', he commented to Potter on 9 January 1880, 'is full of honourable feeling & he has no idea of playing false to his successor. I rely with perfect confidence on the honor of Granville, Hartington & Gladstone.' He sensed that what was 'moral' in political life was coming more to the front. He returned to London for the 1880 session with renewed interest and hoping for an election.

THIRTEEN

The last phase

1880-9

Beaconsfield announced a dissolution of parliament in March 1880. 'Mr Gladstone's Govt died rather of too much virtue & of the lying of its opponents', Bright wrote to Chamberlain on 1 April. 'The "Jewish" dispensation in our time will die of its vices & of our telling the truth about it . . . .' His forecast proved correct. The Liberals had a majority of 137 over the Conservatives, though there were also 65 Irish Home Rulers. It was not clear how the Liberal leaders would react to their electoral success. Gladstone, who happily likened the downfall of Beaconsfield to the vanishing of some magnificent castle in an Italian romance, determined not to serve in any position other than as Prime Minister. Although Hartington had increased his speech rate respectably, there was no denying that Gladstone was the man, and he made a graceful, though reluctant, concession of the leadership. Before this outcome became quite clear, Bright visited Hawarden on 16 April for discussions with Gladstone. Reporting to Chamberlain, he stated that Gladstone looked rather thin and worn after his recent speaking labours. 'Cabinet making', he wrote to Albert, 'is a wonderful business — how it gets done is wonderful & how it holds together when done is not less so.' Ten days later, Bright was once more on the train from Paddington to Windsor in order to kiss hands on his Cabinet appointment, again to the Duchy of Lancaster. Claiming to be 'very desolate & low in spirits', he had hoped that Chamberlain's admission to the Cabinet might mean his own exclusion; he could already sense that his head would not stand the excitement.

Initially, Bright led a full ministerial and social life, without apparent strain. The novelist Henry James was a fellow-guest with Bright at Mentmore in the autumn. He found the politician in extremely good form. 'He gives an impression', he noted, 'of sturdy, honest, vigorous, English middle-class liberalism, accompanied by a certain infusion of genius, which helps one to understand how his name has become the great rallying-point of that sentiment.'[1] In the first few months of the new government, the House was preoccupied with the question of whether the newly elected Bradlaugh, a noted atheist, should be allowed to take his seat. Both Gladstone and Bright were in favour, but they were obstructed by such noted Christians as Lord Randolph Churchill and Sir Henry Drummond Wolff.[2] It was not until July that Bradlaugh was allowed simply to 'affirm', but by then Bright felt that the House was 'in a bad state'. 'We have two sets of opponents on one front', he continued, '& a few who were elected to be our friends who stab or try to stab Mr Gladstone in the back.'[3] He would be happy to be out of politics, but it was not easy to run away, although if 'we muddle into another Eastern war I must stand by my own principles & refuse responsibility'.

Even more serious than the Near East was the Irish question. Parnell had assumed the leadership of the Irish Home Rule Party in 1878 and his obstructionist tactics in the Commons had contributed to the undermining of Disraeli's government. The Land League was formed in 1879, building its strength on the widespread distress in the Irish countryside in these years. Disraeli had tried, not altogether successfully, to raise the spectre of Home Rule during the election campaign, but it was a problem the Liberals could not ignore. Bright did not relish the consolidation of an independent Irish party. 'I do not see any chance for a better govt', he had written in April 1878, 'so long as the Irish members refuse to unite with English and Scotch Liberal members.' In a letter to William Rathbone in December 1879 he explained that if any grievance were brought forward as a reason for granting Home Rule, he would seek to remedy it, but he opposed a parliamentary committee to discover whether Irishmen wanted a parliament sitting in Dublin. North and south would probably be at variance and who would then decide? An Irish Court might save expense, but the idea of a restored Irish House of Lords was absurd. Could anything, he continued, justify 'the creation of an Irish House of Commons to have power only in those things which the Imperial Parlt would surrender to it?' He could understand an Irish independent nation, but 'an Irish Parlt with Lords & Commons, and Irish Cabinet, & still union with Great Britain & under the English Crown, seems to me of all schemes the most "unworkable" that can be imagined.' He still adhered to the belief that the land was the great question in Ireland and, if it was to retain the initiative, the government would have to deal with it. If the 'purchase clauses' of the 1870 Act were brought into effective operation, he told an Irish correspondent, 'discontent would be banished from your country & those who encourage discontent & in a political sense, trade upon it, would find their occupations gone.'[4]

When the Liberals took office, the situation did not seem quite so simple. A Royal Commission on relations between landlord and tenant in Ireland was already in being. The government also set up one to investigate the operation of the 1870 Act. It would take time for these bodies to report and, under pressure from Ireland, ministers agreed to bring in a Compensation for Disturbance Bill. Bright thought it best to keep silent on a subject 'so difficult and inflammable', but he supported it as a means of calming the Irish countryside. However, the measure was rejected in the Lords in early August and, with the Prime Minister temporarily seriously ill, the government let the matter rest. The consequences in Ireland were grave. The membership of the Land League increased, 'boycotting' was instituted and Parnell suggested that the future land measure would be influenced by the strength of feeling shown in the countryside. From the League's standpoint, the campaign proved successful — the number of ejectments dropped sharply in the last quarter of 1880. It meant, however, that the question of law and order moved to the fore.

In the last months of 1880, the Cabinet spent many sessions debating Ireland. Bright still seemed to be in the conciliatory camp. In a speech at Birmingham on 16 November, he condemned, as usual, the misgovernment of Ireland and the system of land tenure, stating that coercion should not be used lightly. He ended with a rousing attack on the Lords for rejecting the Compensation Bill. The speech caused a rumpus the following month when Lord Carnarvon criticized it in a letter to *The Times*. It seems that the Queen thought that Bright was going too far. Bright stood his ground, but privately he was much less sanguine about a solution to the Irish problem. He confessed to Gladstone that he was 'almost "muddled" with reading letters and plans on Ireland', but gleaned little from them. 'It is evident', he continued, 'that Parnell & Co only want men to provoke a revolt, & that their purpose is more revolution than a mere reform, however broad, of their land system.' Eddie Hamilton, Gladstone's private secretary, on reading this letter, thought it rather rich. 'If this is so', he commented in his diary, 'he might consistently be a little less sentimental about suspending constitutional rights.'[5] Bright, meanwhile, was deep in the evidence submitted to the Irish Commissions and the fruit of his meditation was a memorandum which he circulated to his colleagues on 17 December.[6] He advocated the appointment of four commissions, sitting in Dublin, Cork, Belfast and Limerick. The commissioners would 'after full inquiry, buy and sell, and be the medium of the change by which one owner might disappear and a hundred or five hundred owners come upon the scene.' Funds were to be raised by a system of debentures. Under this scheme, he believed that more than a quarter of Irish land might change hands. If Hamilton is to be believed, Gladstone could not get over Bright's 'wild land schemes', describing them as, at best, most naive. Bright, however, was undeterred and continued to press his case on the Prime Minister. He also stressed that it would be a great mistake to suspend Habeas Corpus in Ireland. The boycott was not increasing in power, and the war against rent and landlords would wear itself out if a really good Land Bill were forthcoming. The well-disposed tenants, who were the vast majority, could then show their satisfaction and the Land League's power for evil would then be broken. A few days later, he again urged Gladstone not to think of 'force'. He, however, was under pressure from Forster, the Chief Secretary for Ireland, and others, to introduce a measure of coercion.

The violence and unrest in Ireland did not abate in the new year and Bright gave this fact as the reason for his own change of mind. He found the behaviour of the Irish at Westminster most distasteful, particularly when they knew that the government was anxious to bring in a new Land Bill. After a conversation on 14 January 1881, Dilke reported that Bright now 'almost willingly' favoured suspension of Habeas Corpus. 'We have not only a *foreign* element amongst us', Bright wrote to Helen two days later, 'but a *rebel* party, with whom we must reckon.' Some sort of crisis in the business of the House could not be far off. February was indeed an uproarious month in the Commons, with the Irish members doing everything they could to obstruct the passage of coercive legislation. After one session had lasted over forty hours, the Speaker was forced to use the closure. Such tactics by the 'rebels', as Bright now described them, angered him greatly, but he believed that the House was resolved to free itself from their 'offensive conduct'.

The government tried coercion with one hand and conciliation with the other. The reports of the Commissions were available and the Cabinet now settled down to the drafting of its Land Bill. When introduced in early April 1881, it substantially conceded the 'three f's' which the Land League had demanded — fair rent, freedom for the tenant to sell, and fixity of tenure. Bright was in agreement, but still felt the proposals to facilitate the purchase of land by tenants were inadequate — as again proved to be the case. He had, however, grown very pessimistic about Ireland, and was ceasing to believe that even such an elaborate act could really help.

> Ireland is in a bad way [he wrote to Helen on 5 April] & I am almost in despair about it. Not one of her Parly friends of the rebel Party says one word in quieting the excitement which prevails & I fear we shall have much more trouble.

While he wished that he was not in a position of responsibility, he could not desert Gladstone.

Throughout the summer, Ireland was in a feverish condition, with Parnell trying anxiously to assess the strength of conflicting forces within the country. Despite his long association with Ireland, Bright was losing patience with the Irish. Noble men were trying generous measures which, he believed, through no fault of their own, could not have been introduced earlier — yet the situation only got worse. While hatred was being expressed and foul deeds committed, Irishmen expected additional assistance. He criticized an Irish correspondent for having the general Irish notion

> that Govt & Govt money must do everything for her country. To build mills, to fill them with machinery, to obtain skilled workmen, to buy wool, to find customers, to conduct a business, how is this to be done by Govt & its servants?

Even to pose the question was to show its absurdity. Ireland had many assets, indeed, he concluded sadly that Irishmen had 'everything but habits of business & enterprise & these not even Govt can give them'. He did not dispute that the land system was answerable for much evil 'but not for all that is seen in Ireland' and he proposed to say so, whatever insults from Ireland it brought him.[7]

When the question of arresting Parnell was under serious consideration early in October, Bright took no stand in principle against it. Parnell's objective, he considered, was 'a break-up of the United Kingdom for he hates us & England even more than he loves Ireland.' The question which had to be considered was that to single out Parnell might only increase his popularity. Bright found it amazing and discouraging that no Irishman had denounced the rebel faction led by Parnell. To denounce him without promising support to the law-abiding Irish would be very foolish. He conceded, however, that 'unfortunately when disaffection takes the shape of passive resistance it cannot be successfully met by troops or constabulary . . .' A few days later, Parnell was arrested and incarcerated in Kilmainham prison where he remained until the following April. Bright accepted the necessity of this action, though convinced that it did not offer a permanent remedy.

In the matter of Ireland, Bright in the end gave Gladstone full support, but on other questions he had distinct reservations. He had supposed that the Liberals would speedily reverse that forward imperial policy which he labelled Beaconsfieldism. In the event, extrication was not as easy as Bright imagined. In South Africa, the Zulus had been defeated, but the future status of the Transvaal Republic was far from clear. War broke out between the Afrikaners and a British force under the command of Sir George Colley. Bright was appalled and when, at the end of January, British troops were defeated, he was afraid that the demands for punishment would be irresistible; a fear that was heightened when Colley was defeated and killed at Majuba in February 1881. 'I am in trouble about the Transvaal', Bright wrote to Helen. 'I fear Colley preferred to fight rather than to suspend hostilities as *he was told* to do & to allow time for negotiation for peace.' He did not criticize Gladstone, who always meant well, but was not omnipotent and needed his support. However, another round of fighting did not occur and the 'Pretoria Convention' recognized the self-government of the Transvaal subject to British suzerainty and control of its foreign affairs. Somewhat prematurely, Bright wrote that 'the Transvaal difficulty removed is a great relief & I feel less unhappy in my Parly work.'

Bright's satisfaction at the Transvaal settlement was completed by the news in April of Disraeli's death. Learning that he was ailing, Bright wrote to Albert that he thought the matter was 'of no importance to the public affairs & politics of the country'. He kept away from the Commons when Gladstone moved that a monument be erected there — not being able to support such a resolution. Alarmingly, if Beaconsfield was dead, the same could not be said of 'Beaconsfieldism'. It manifested itself, Bright considered, in the behaviour of the Liberal government in the early summer of the following year, 1882. Arabi Pasha, an Egyptian nationalist leader, had seized control of the government from the nominal ruler, the Khedive. The Anglo-French financial involvement, which had developed through the later 1870s, now seemed threatened. There was also the more general problem of the security of Britain's route to the East. Diplomatically, the matter was complicated by Egypt's technical status as a part of the Ottoman Empire, and by the need for Britain and France to appear to march in step. At a critical moment, there was a change of government in France and it became clear that if Britain was to act it would have to be on her own. As Arabi Pasha consolidated his position, the British fleet took up station off Alexandria. In May, Bright had not appeared too disturbed. The Cabinet was divided but Bright was reassured by Gladstone's 'moderate and wise' tone.[8] At the end of the month, Bright claimed to have made it clear that he could not be party to the invasion or occupation of Egypt; any solution was 'better than occupation and war on or with Turkey . . .' Time and patience, he believed, might solve the problem.

About a month later, on 10 July, Bright met Gladstone in the lobby, finding him dispirited and without adequate support. He again stressed that he could not acquiesce in a policy which was at variance with the teachings of his public life. The next day the British fleet bombarded the Egyptian forts at Alexandria. Hamilton seems to have supposed that if a short sharp blow was followed by peace, Bright might be persuaded to stay on. His resignation would damage the government for he represented 'the Peace party, which is a large and increasing party, and which is numbered among the most trusty supporters of the government.' On 11 July, Bright wrote three letters of resignation, but put off sending any of them until the following day, and even then Gladstone wrote asking him to delay. Bright admitted that he might be placing too high a value on his own consistency at the expense of the government's welfare. Eventually, despite further attempts by Granville and Hartington to get him to change his mind, he did resign on 15 July, warning the Prime Minister that his Egyptian policy would destroy the government and break up the party. 'I am driven to the conclusion', he added, 'that there is a wide gulf, wider than I had supposed, between your views and mine.' As Bright wrote to Albert, it had 'taken me nearly as much trouble to get out of a Cabinet as it takes others to get into one . . . .' The disagreement with Gladstone was a source of regret. The two old men, after the vicissitudes of nearly fifty years, had reached a position of mutual esteem. It was now ruptured.

Bright never forgot the bombardment of Alexandria and the subsequent military defeat of Arabi Pasha. Although Albert wrote to Helen expressing the wish that at some stage their father would rejoin the government, Bright himself had no doubt that his Cabinet career was over. He did not, however, mobilize opposition to the Cabinet — it was agreed in Gladstone's entourage that his short explanatory statement on resigning was 'in the best possible taste' — but he absented himself from the Commons because he 'could not listen to the wretched excuses offered for the Egyptian policy of the government.' It is possible, as Chamberlain suggested, that Bright might have brought the government down if he had embarked on extensive public criticism. He convinced himself, however, that he was in no condition for such a campaign. 'I feel as if I was ready to resign everything & to run away', he wrote to Helen in September. 'If I were not so desolate and lonely in the world I should do so — I have no one at home & no one to go from home with me . . .' The prospect of speeches in Birmingham and at Glasgow University (where he was Lord Rector) filled him with horror. 'I seem as if I had almost lost the habit or the power of bending my mind to think of matter for a speech' he wrote in October. 'There are no subjects which I can feel with the force & heat of days that are past.' He confined himself to letters to Gladstone urging that Arabi and his friends be treated with some leniency. When the Prime Minister invited him to Hawarden in October, he declined. 'I prefer to keep away from him and them whilst this miserable business is being transacted', he wrote to Albert, 'and I do not want to be induced to join the Govt again.'

His feelings did not lessen as the months passed. 'I object to the slaughter of some thousands of Egyptians on such grounds as have been offered in defence of our policy', he explained to Lord Ripon, the Viceroy of India, in October, '& I think this war, had it been undertaken by the Tory Govt would only have added to the weight of the condemnation which was passed upon them at the late General Election.' The Prime Minister's personal popularity had prevented adverse reactions by the Liberal constituencies, but he was 'convinced that amongst them there is little — perhaps no honest feeling in favor of the war'.[9] The loss of life never seemed to affect the deliberations of statesmen!

> Mr Gladstone is a religious man [he wrote to a Friend in January 1883] & has said & thought much, I do not doubt, against war — but he was in the Cabinet which made the Crimean War, the most bloody in our days & he feels no

difficulty, or seems to feel none, in defending the recent deplorable war in Egypt.[10]

Christianity, he believed, as commonly taught and held, would not put an end to war. In Birmingham, matters were complicated by the disagreement between Bright and Chamberlain over Egypt. In a letter to George Dixon in December 1882, he stated that he did not see how he could share a platform with Chamberlain as things stood. He sent a critical letter to the Birmingham Liberal caucus, but the officials contrived to minimize it, for Chamberlain was in the ascendancy. In a letter to Chamberlain in January 1883, Bright emphasized the gap between them. It was wrong, Bright argued, to suppose that the policy of 'non-intervention' and that of 'peace at any price' had any necessary connexion with each other. 'Non-intervention' was neither unworthy nor ignoble. To speak, as Chamberlain did, of the 'honour and interests of England' was to talk the language of the Jingo school. Although Bright claimed that events had amply justified his opinions, he preferred to treat the Egyptian incident as a 'deplorable blunder' rather than a 'crime'. He ended by hoping that they might still work together on other matters.[11] For the time being, because Birmingham matters were rather 'mixed', Bright consented to the postponement of the January meetings. A year later, rather unexpectedly, Chamberlain agreed that Bright had been right on the Egyptian question. 'I wish', he wrote, 'with all my heart, that you had pressed your views more decidedly — even to the point of resignation, in the earliest stages — as it would have forced all of us to give the subject more careful consideration . . . .' Bright was not greatly encouraged by this confession. 'I shrink from the idea of public life after the present Parlt', he wrote to Helen in January 1884. 'The Egyptian blunder has blunted the edge of my regard for much further public labor & service.'

In May 1883, he returned to a theme of his youth when he spoke at a Liberation Society meeting at the Metropolitan Tabernacle on 'The National Church and National Righteousness'. He rehearsed his own long connexion with this question and again directed attention to the voting record of Anglican bishops in the House of Lords. The Established Church did nothing to guide the State in the way of righteousness and only weakened its own principles by its attachment to the State. The Church as an Establishment would certainly perish.[12] His cabman on the way to the Tabernacle was so honoured to have such a passenger that, initially, he refused his fare. 'I am a Christian', he stated, 'and I hope we shall meet above.' Bright thought the incident 'worthy of being remembered'. Mr Gladstone, fresh from a triumph on the same night at the National Liberal Club, could not resist an ecclesiastical discussion and, a few days later, the two men had a meal together for the first time since Bright's resignation. It was a source of considerable pleasure that, a couple of years afterwards, he received a most eirenic letter from Mr Gladstone's son Stephen, Rector of Hawarden, affirming that some day God would bring together all those who had striven to do good.[13]

In the Metropolitan Tabernacle address, Bright had stated that the future lay with the Free Churches of England. It was, therefore, a source of disappointment that his son Willie was married in church. Albert, too, was not married after the manner of Friends, but in a Unitarian chapel. Bright accepted that the wishes of the brides had to be respected, but he was disappointed. He did not like preachers and scholars who seemed to think that Christ had only lived to teach men to be kind. He did indeed do this, 'but this teaching is not all that Christianity has brought into the world'. He had no sympathy with Unitarians, much preferring 'the authority of the Gospels & of the writers of the Epistles . . . '.[14]

Brooding on religion and righteousness in these months, Bright could not keep his mind off Egypt. It became for him a symbol of British national decadence. He found the subsequent emotions roused by the plight of Gordon in the Sudan quite nauseating and again censured Gladstone for his weakness — 'if he had been strong enough to have taken my advice' he would have saved himself a great deal of trouble. He was horrified by remarks made by the American Quaker poet, John Greenleaf Whittier, whose work he much admired, in praise of Gordon's heroism. Gordon's employment, Bright wrote to Whittier, was a blunder as every member of the government would admit. He was 'a strong fanatic, bordering on the insane, drawing his justification from the horrible stories of the Old Testament wars rather than from the New Testament & Gospel narratives.'[15] The whole affair was another example of the Gladstone government's fall from grace since 1882. 'I am afraid', he wrote, 'the thanksgivings of some Church dignitaries for recent transactions in the Soudan would not have received the benediction of the great Apostle of the Gentiles.'[16] Nevertheless, although asked to speak at or attend meetings concerning Gordon, he refrained from doing so. 'It seems to me', he wrote to Chamberlain on 7 April 1885, 'as if Mr Gladstone had lost his control over his colleagues & that he is involved in courses that must be torture to him . . . .' Although criticized for his silence, he defended his conduct in a letter to Moncure Conway. A thorough change in notions of foreign policy was needed, but he could not bring it about. Perhaps, he concluded ominously, 'some great catastrophe is approaching. I sometimes suspect it. Earthquakes come without noise or footstep. Europe is nearly ready for one, and its nations, we amongst them, may need a lesson.'[17] As for the Empire, he wrote to Goldwin Smith that some day it would be 'in difficulty & the people of these islands may grow weary of the burden they now sustain.' At a dinner, in discussion with Lord Rosebery, he looked upon the idea of Colonial Federation as 'utterly chimerical'.

Prophecy apart, there are a few events which afforded Bright a modest satisfaction. In June 1883, the Birmingham Liberal Association organized the 'John Bright celebration' to commemorate his twenty-five years as their member. The Committee proudly declared that it had not 'spared trouble nor expense in order to suitably fit up the Hall for the accommodation of the many thousands of persons who will be present.' Processions of local Liberals, accompanied by mounted police and the Birmingham fire brigade, filed past and saluted at the 'prominent window' at which Bright stood. He was presented with a dessert service and informed that both a portrait and a statue of him would find their way to the Birmingham Art Gallery. At a subsequent grand fête and garden party, Messrs Brock were responsible for a mammoth fire portrait of Bright — a salvo of Crystal Palace Shells, twenty-four inches in circumference, with stars of light blue, dark emerald, pearl streamers, opals and golden rain, amethysts and rubies, silver rain and turquoise, emerald-headed snakes, scintillating meteors, fixed stars, brilliants, and comets were released in fitting tribute. The fireworks were also verbal. Hamilton noted that on this celebratory occasion Chamberlain had fired off a speech which was sure to frighten people and was not in the best taste. He unfolded 'the Radical programme of the future — universal suffrage, equal electoral districts, payment of members . . . .' Granville, who had gone down to give a 'ministerial *éclat*' to the Bright rejoicings, reported that Chamberlain's speech had not been well-received, 'being in effect an attempt to supplant Bright as the hero of the occasion'. If so, Bright does not seem to have shared this feeling and was quite happy to be associated with Chamberlain when the Tories criticized the speeches.[18]

Although Bright's parliamentary role was somewhat spasmodic, he was again dining quite frequently with the leaders of the Liberal party. He gave general support to further extending the franchise, speaking 'very briefly' on this theme at Leeds in mid-October 1883. On the whole, however, he was content to let Chamberlain make the running. 'I thought & think of speaking not on reform, & certainly not on Egypt', he wrote to Chamberlain before his January 1884 speech in Birmingham, 'but rather on the grounds on which the Tories ask for the confidence of the country . . . .' He was content to let the government be 'the best judge' of a future Franchise Bill. He had a number of conversations with Gladstone and pronounced the Bill 'large and complete and satisfactory' when it was introduced at the end of February 1884. Bright was asked to speak in the debate towards the end of March, to answer Lord John Manners who moved a resolution in favour of adding redistribution of seats to the proposed measure. 'He had not his old fire', Hamilton recorded on 23 March, 'and wandered from the point. But it is not given to everyone to keep intact their oratorical powers when the allotted age of man is passed.' Gladstone, however, besides possessing a general interest in upholding the merits of age, had a particular interest in resurrecting Bright. It helped him to keep the junior member for Birmingham in his place. It comes as no surprise, therefore, to read of the Prime Minister remarking, after visiting Bright (who had been suffering from 'congestion of the lungs') that he was 'a really splendid old fellow — so rounded off by mature age'.[19] On 21 July, a franchise procession passed outside Bright's windows in Piccadilly and he stood there for three hours, receiving the cheers with 'such courtesy as I could show the multitude'. In Hyde Park, it was Gladstone and Bright who were singled out for special favour by the crowd. Unlike the Prime Minister, however, Bright did recognize the limitations of gerontocracy. 'I feel now', he wrote to Gladstone, 'that my political life is nearly over & that this Parlt is probably or possibly the last in which I shall appear. I hope I may be able to give some help to the great questions of next year . . . .'

The immediate difficulty before the government resulted from the Opposition tactics on the Franchise Bill. After passing the Commons, an amendment was accepted in the Lords that it should be accompanied by a Redistribution Bill. Bright claimed that he had always favoured dealing with Franchise and Redistribution in separate measures. Despite criticism, he believed that there was 'no mode of dealing successfully with the Reform question but that which the Govt have adopted'. Speaking at Birmingham — 'my voice not so good and clear as usual' — Bright rehearsed the failings of the Upper House and confessed that he had come to feel indifferent about the need for any kind of second chamber. Since abolition, however, was not practical, he suggested a limitation on the power of the upper house as regards general legislation. There was no confrontation between the two chambers and a Reform and Redistribution measure was effected which met with his general approval. He was not very keen on the proposed single-member constituencies but rejoiced that proportional representation had been ignored.

Despite the Reform legislation, Bright was not happy with the government's performance — still arguing, however, that it was better than the Tory alternative. In January 1885, he made his customary journey to Birmingham.

> It is not a pleasant time [he commented to Helen] for everything seems out of square — Egypt, the Fenian outrages, bad trade in some districts & my weariness of public life. I do not wish to damage the Govt so I keep away

251

from Egypt but I must say something on the Jingo
spirit . . . .

As he watched the increasing disarray in the government
ranks, largely over Ireland, he was upset but continued to feel
that Egypt had been the source of all Gladstone's subsequent
difficulties. Liberal abstentions and Irish opposition led to his
defeat on the budget in June 1885. Lord Salisbury formed a
minority Tory government on the understanding that he would
go to the country before the end of the year. 'If I were not so
lonely at home', Bright wrote, 'I should be one of the crowd of
retiring members in November next.'

In the event, Bright did stand again as candidate for one of
the newly segmented Birmingham constituencies — the
Central Division. He had a stiff fight because the champion of
'Tory Democracy', Lord Randolph Churchill, was his opponent, but he kept the challenge at bay. The result of the election, on an increased franchise of some five million, was a disappointment to the Liberals. They had a majority of eighty-six
over the Tories, but the Irish Home Rulers emerged with
exactly the same figure and were thus in a position to exert
unparalleled influence. Bright continued to argue that, sad
though it was, the Liberals had brought this setback on themselves because of the Egyptian blunder. There were, however,
more reasons for the verdict than moral revulsion from the
bombardment of Alexandria and subsequent events. The Irish
question came to the fore since Parnell had been co-operating
with the Conservatives and most Irish voters (including those
in Birmingham Central) had voted for them. In its short life,
the Tory government had passed the Ashbourne Act, institut-
ing at last an effective scheme of land purchase. The issue of
Ireland's future was now wide open.

> The Irish Question must come to a crisis [wrote Bright to
> Helen in November 1885] & perhaps the sooner the better &
> what the crisis will be & what it will do, I cannot even
> conjecture — but it must bring forth something better than
> what now exists.

It would be tempting to see in Bright the prophet of the end of colonialism, the seer at loggerheads with his own generation but in tune with a later epoch. His attitude to Ireland, however, demonstrates that, strikingly different though some of his political convictions were, he was not immune from the passions of his own time. The Irish had nearly exhausted his patience and sympathy after a lifetime in which he had endured many taunts for his willingness to see problems through Irish eyes. He could rightly claim to have visited Ireland more often than any other leading British politician. Although his dislike of violent agitation in Ireland stiffened, he was still prepared to consider what he felt to be reasonable administrative arrangements which might meet Irish grievances. At dinner with Lord Dalhousie in April 1885, for example, he suggested that besides thirty-two county boards for thirty-two counties there should be a Central Council in Dublin with sixty-four representatives. It should deal with education, and local taxation and control but not deal with foreign affairs, the army, the navy, import duties or the police.[20] Chamberlain was thinking on similar lines at about the same time. At the end of 1885 after the election, talk of Home Rule was in the air and Gladstone brooded on the matter at Hawarden. On 17 December, the 'Hawarden Kite' was released, purporting to disclose Gladstone's conversion to Home Rule, though it was promptly followed by a disclaimer. Two days earlier, on 15 December, Bright wrote to Chamberlain that the situation was very 'mixed'. It would be possible to grant Home Rule in the shape of an Irish Parliament, or to refuse it. In many respects, it would be a 'blessed thing' to get rid of Ireland as far as the English Parliament was concerned — with the corollary that Irishmen would no longer deal with English and Scottish internal matters. The more he considered the question, however, 'the more do difficulties start up & yet I try to judge it without prejudice, or if I have prejudice it tends to favor something very like what the rebel party say they want.' He had some ideas which he wanted to discuss with Chamberlain privately. In general, however, he kept his own counsel, waiting to see what Gladstone, if he formed a new government when parliament reassembled, would propose.

There are times [he wrote] when silence is wisdom & when

it is difficult or impossible to see the way, it may be best to
stand still. I feel this with regard to the Irish question, of
which I see no solution in any of the declarations hitherto
made by our public & political characters.

The new year, 1886, began for Bright with a visit to Rochdale
from two leading Dublin Friends who were alarmed at the idea
of concessions to the 'rebel' party and he responded sym-
pathetically. But, since he was not 'called in', as he put it, he
did not offer advice. He did visit Gladstone on 13 January in
London but found him uncommunicative — 'not much talk
with him'. He went back to Rochdale and was there welcoming
back his boy Philip from a trip to the United States when the
Salisbury government was defeated. Chamberlain accepted
office under Gladstone but told Bright that he feared he might
not sail with the Prime Minister for long. Hartington declined
to serve. No offer came Bright's way. 'The House seems likely
to become a political chaos' was his comment to Helen on 1
February. 'If the *rebel* party were not rebels', he had remarked,
'something might be done but the difficulty must be almost
insuperable. Nothing that Gladstone can offer or give them
will content the extreme men — the Fenians & Irish American
enemies of England — & we may see Parnell & Co forced to
refuse what is offered by the discontent & violence of their
followers.'

It was not until early March that Bright went up to London
again. He found a letter from Hartington, asking for a chat.
Hartington wrote that he could not believe that Bright would
approve of what Gladstone seemed to have in mind, though
he quite understood that Bright might not want to take any
active part in opposing the Prime Minister. It was still far from
clear, in fact, what Gladstone did have in mind. Bright called at
Devonshire House and found Hartington 'very reasonable' on
the Irish question. Two days later, however, on 12 March,
Bright did have a long after-dinner talk with the Prime
Minister. He found that Gladstone wished to get rid of Irish
representation at Westminster and noted in his diary afterwards that he agreed — if the scheme was feasible. The following day, at the Cabinet meeting, Chamberlain unsuccessfully
demanded a declaration against a scheme for an independent

legislature. Two days later, he and Trevelyan resigned, though no public announcement was made. Chamberlain told Bright what he had done and 'in the main' Bright thought him right. In his account to Helen, however, Bright's comment was stronger. 'I think he is quite right', he wrote, ' — I should do the same thing were I unhappily in the Govt . . . .' Mr Gladstone's scheme seemed 'extravagant and unnecessary'. Ironically it was not so much the Home Rule Bill which excited him as the Land Bill with which it was coupled. For years, Bright had urged Gladstone to settle the land question by transfer of ownership along bold lines; now the position was reversed. Gladstone's proposals, he considered, virtually amounted to buying out the landlord class and he could not accept 'this wholesale surrender to the rebel party'. On 20 March, he discussed these points with the Prime Minister, making it clear that he was as much against his land purchase proposals as he was against a Dublin parliament. Neither man gave ground. A week later, Hartington sent on to Bright a delegation of Ulster Liberals. 'I fear they will be shocked at the measures of Mr Gladstone', Bright commented. 'I sympathize much with them & tried to offer them some consolation.' At the end of March, he still sat on the fence. 'The "outs" condemn the Gladstone plans as almost lunacy', he wrote to Albert, 'the "ins" profess warmly to approve. I wait & hold my judgment in suspense . . . .' After a further conversation with Gladstone on 3 April, it became clear that he would not be deterred. 'He is in for a great attempt', Bright commented, 'which I fear must fail & after that, what next & next?'

The Prime Minister introduced his Home Rule Bill into the Commons on 8 April. It provided for an Irish executive responsible to a legislature, but with the Imperial parliament retaining control over matters relating to the Crown, defence, foreign policy, customs and excise, trade and navigation, the post office and coinage. It was Gladstone's original intention to exclude the Irish from Westminster, but he later indicated that he would be prepared to discuss the issue, since there were those who thought that control would prove difficult if Irish representation at Westminster ceased. Bright did not speak in the debate that followed, though in the evening of 12 April he dined with the Gladstones, who found him querulous. Bright was dismayed that the exclusion of Irish members might be reconsidered — it was the only good point in the Bill. Earlier in the day, he had received a letter from Hartington urging that if he spoke the Bill would be rejected. Perhaps fortunately, Bright was distracted by the death of his brother-in-law, Duncan McLaren, and escaped to Edinburgh for the funeral and then home to Rochdale. On 6 May, in a letter to Benjamin Armitage, MP for Salford, he made it clear that his own opinion was hardening and he brought forward the Ulster problem as the chief reason for his anxiety. 'To hand over the million and a half of Protestant & loyal people of the north of Ireland', he wrote, 'to the tender mercies of the ruffians and rebels who sat opposite us in the late Parlt is more than I can consent to.' He hesitated to become an assailant of Mr Gladstone, but his policy was insulting to the party and injurious to the country.[21]

A week later, he received a request from the Prime Minister to come up to London to discuss the matter. Both sides, in fact, were anxious to enlist his support in the split that was developing. In his reply, Bright stated that he felt outside all the contending sections of the Liberal party since he did not favour Home Rule, a Dublin parliament or any kind of Federation. He could not agree to the exclusion of Ulster Protestants from the protection of the Imperial parliament. He could not bring himself to vote for the Home Rule Bill and he would vote against the Land Bill. Gladstone was disappointed, and through an intermediary, offered the possibility of delay — if the Bill received a second reading. Meanwhile, on 14 May, a meeting was taking place at Devonshire House of the dissentient Liberals, with Chamberlain urging that the withdrawal rather than the postponement of the Bill should be their objective. Bright did not attend the meeting, but after it he received an appeal from Chamberlain. 'I have hesitated to press you,' he wrote, 'but the situation is so desperate that I feel bound to implore you to intervene in the debate & to say what you feel on the great issue that has arisen.' He was confident that Gladstone would listen to Bright as to no one else. In a letter on 17 May, intended for the Prime Minister's eye, Bright did make an appeal for the Home Rule Bill to be withdrawn. Even if it could be carried at all, it would only be by such a small majority that it could not continue. It would be better to withdraw and indicate that the problem was open to further discussion. Talk of a dissolution if the government were defeated seemed to Bright quite irresponsible, creating by far the greatest wound since the Liberals became an effective party. The letter was shown to Chamberlain before it was handed over. 'I think it is a healthy sign', Bright wrote to Helen on 25 May, 'when so many men will not bow to a Dictator, whose policy seems likely to ruin his party for years to come.' Gladstone seemed to have lost his wisdom and moderation, and it was only with difficulty that Bright refrained from speaking as strongly as he felt.

The Liberal factions now did their best to muster support, and the split deepened. Bright failed to attend a Gladstonian meeting on 27 May. The Prime Minister's speech on this occasion, however, did seem to rally Liberal opinion behind him. W. S. Caine, who was acting as Chamberlain's whip, reported to him that Bright's attitude would be crucial. The Chamberlainites met on 31 May. Bright was not present, but he did send Chamberlain a letter indicating that he had decided to vote against the Bill. According to Chamberlain, his reading of this letter had the effect of consolidating opinion in favour of outright opposition, as opposed to simple abstention. The letter, indeed, became a source of considerable subsequent argument. There were those who contended that Chamberlain distorted the message, indeed misquoted the words. It is unlikely, however, that Bright had serious grounds for complaint, although when he heard the result of the meeting, he tried to shift his ground a little, claiming that he would abstain if the House and country could be spared the catastrophe of a dissolution. He did not think, however, that a change in the position was likely.

> The chaos continues [he wrote to Helen on 4 June] & I see no way out of it. The Leader brought us into it & can only get us out — but I fear he is not magnanimous enough to make the sacrifice. He will throw the country into confusion & will break up his party in an effort to force them to accept what they in a vast majority of their hearts condemn & what he knows they condemn. If he dissolves the House, I think he will deserve to lose the confidence of the Liberals throughout the country . . . .

The full extent of the bitterness between the sections became apparent when, on 8 June, the Bill was defeated by 340 votes to 311. The ministers did decide not to resign but to dissolve and try their hand with the country.

The three most prominent Liberal Unionists, Bright, Chamberlain and Hartington, all opposed Gladstone's measures but did not precisely agree among themselves. As far as the election was concerned, they agreed not to sign a common statement, but to campaign as individuals. Bright hesitated only momentarily before accepting re-nomination for Birmingham Central, and he was returned unopposed. He used his influence to some effect during the campaign, writing many letters expressing surprise that purported Liberals should have the temerity to stand against sitting Liberal Unionist members.[22]

> To consider it a sin [he told one enquirer] to vote for a Tory candidate who represents your views on a vital question seems to me only a superstition. You cannot vote for a candidate who favors a dangerous proposition now before the country & perhaps soon to be again brought before Parliament.

On the other hand, in a letter to Arthur Chamberlain, he deprecated the formation of a Liberal Unionist Association. It would necessarily be 'a rival to the existing Liberal Association and Federation; and will it not add to the confusion into which Mr Gladstone has so unfortunately plunged us?'[23] When, the following year, Chamberlain asked Bright for an introduction to a volume of his brother's speeches on the Irish question, Bright declined. Although Bright confined his speaking to Birmingham, the campaign was enlivened by an exchange of recriminatory letters between Gladstone and himself.

The election of 1886 produced a majority of over a hundred for the Conservatives and Liberal Unionists over the Liberals and Irish. 'I have fled from London', wrote Bright in the aftermath, '& do not wish to return during the remainder of the session. I look upon the chaos with something like disgust & wonder that anyone should have placed the blame anywhere but on Mr Gladstone, at whose door lies the confusion which prevails.' He hoped the defeated Prime Minister would not return to office until purged of his errors. 'How are the mighty fallen', he wrote to Helen, 'the whole thing is a scandal.' Although Bright was anxious to stay resting in Scotland, Lord Hartington invited him to address a 'Unionist' banquet. He declined on the grounds that he could only condemn Gladstone and 'it would be impossible to avoid opening still more widely the breach which now exists between us.'[24] He had not changed his mind on the Irish question, praising A. V. Dicey's *England's Case against Home Rule*, and arguing that Gladstone had to change his mind.[25]

In his last year of significant political activity, 1887, and indeed until the end of his life, the Irish question dominated his thoughts and actions. In private and public letters, he denounced the course Gladstone had followed and the damage he had done to the Liberal party. He emerged as a fervent champion of Ulster's right to be heard against the ruffians and rebels of the south. 'We saved the country', he declared in his last political speech at a dinner to Hartington in August 1887, 'from the infliction of Bills — Bills the damage of which, not to Great Britain only, but I believe also to Ireland, it is impossible for any man to measure.'[26] Gladstone's Bills, he complained to Earl Grey in February 1888,[27]

> have been defeated in parliament & in the constituencies & he persists in adhering to a policy which, in my view, is full of peril. He has now allied himself with the men he put in prison as "suspected of treasonable purposes" & who have never disowned these purposes & who have made no change in the objects for which they have been & still are contending.

In one of his last political letters, he noted that the Gladstonians did not try to justify their own proposals, but preferred to attack the Tory government and denounce Balfour '& to spread abroad extravagant falsehoods as to the objects of the "Crimes Act" & as to the barbarous manner in which it is enforced'. They had great sympathy, he raged,

> for Mayors of Irish Cities, for Editors of disloyal newspapers, for Priests who forget that their own true

mission is one of peace & not of violence, & for Englishmen, country gentlemen & others, who show their patriotism by aiding the revolutionary movement in Ireland.

Yet the Gladstonians had almost nothing to say on behalf of the humbler class of men who were in prison for offences to which they had been excited by 'gentlemen disturbers of the peace'.[28] He accepted as genuine the letters printed in *The Times* implicating Parnell and other Irish leaders of crimes of violence and he did not live long enough to see them exposed as forgeries. In the last years of his life he had conditioned himself to believe that nothing good could come out of Ireland.

In May 1888, Bright was taken seriously ill at One Ash. In the late summer, he regained some strength, but fell away once more during the winter. He died, with his family around him, in March 1889. He was interred in the Friends' burial ground at Rochdale, amidst universal expressions of regret from mill and palace. Whatever life after death held for him, in his death John Bright had finally arrived. On the day of his funeral, all business in Rochdale was suspended for two hours. The letters and telegrams which poured into One Ash revealed that his generation had admitted him to the class of great Victorians, to be reverenced at their passing.

It had been a strange, paradoxical and inconclusive life. There was something immensely attractive about the brash and thrusting young man who burst into the alien aristocratic world of politics in the 1830s and 1840s. Such was his energy and enthusiasm that he could travel over one thousand miles in nine days, addressing seven great meetings. Opinions and conventions which did not accord with his own were treated with blistering scorn. His fame reached from Northumberland to Cornwall — in 1852, for example, Sir George Grey suffered electorally from a very remote association with this urban fire-brand.[29] Bright's part in the success of the Anti-Corn Law League cannot be denied, even if he was not the brain behind its organization. Only a little longer, it seemed, and Bright would make British politics bourgeois rather than aristocratic in predominant tone. He was disappointed to find that such a total change did not take place. The 'middle class', he found, was never as homogeneous and clear-cut as he had once liked to argue. John Bright, who had little contact with the expanding world of the professions, could not become the single voice of the 'middle class'. Many 'comfortable' men found that gradual modification of the political structure satisfied them, particularly if their own social elevation continued. Bright was not temperamentally the man to persuade such men to follow him. As a young man, his fame had rested on his capacity to attack men and institutions without fear or favour. His plain-speaking took him into parliament but he did not adapt swiftly to the methods of Westminster politics. The orator lacked Cobden's incessant, if fruitless, capacity to plan five steps ahead. His directness therefore became an indulgence rather than a means of promoting effective action. His years as a Manchester MP, far from being the occasion when the 'School' told England what to think, revealed the fragility of his position. There was something rather strange in advocating a middle-class order and simultaneously criticizing middle-class pretensions.

It is not surprising that such inconsistency did not seem odd to Bright himself, for he was also subject to the conflicting aspirations of the middle class; he was both 'radical' and 'conservative'.[30] The crisis of the Crimean War reinforced his 'radical' convictions, but it also exposed the dangerous possibility that, if he adhered rigidly to such views, any kind of political success would forever elude him. He could not hope to find, in mid-Victorian Britain, general acceptance for his views on war, disestablishment or capital punishment. He could not effectively counter Palmerston's appeal to confident nationalism. His ejection from Manchester therefore signalled the end of the middle-class movement on which he had placed his hopes hitherto. He emerged from his first breakdown white-haired and already contriving to appear wise and aged in his late forties. He did not, however, relapse immediately into conforming acquiescence. His campaign in the 1860s for parliamentary reform was a considerable agitation. 'It would fifty times have died away', wrote the *Birmingham Daily Post* in its obituary notice, 'had not Mr Bright raised once more the call to arms. Few reforms have been so much the work of one man as household suffrage was the work of John Bright.'

261

It was in this period that his oratory was at its height. Dr Dale was not alone in placing him above Gladstone, Disraeli or O'Connell amongst his contemporaries. In his opinion, he stood alone 'in that perfect blending of imagination, pathos, passion and the noblest ethical feeling'. His greatest asset was his facility in speaking — his notes (often only five half-sheets of paper for an hour's speech) were placed on the brim of his hat on the table before him. He talked 'as naturally when addressing six or seven thousand people as when talking to a friend at the fireside.'[31] His style had no specific model, but his command of language grew out of his sustained reading in Milton and Byron, Shakespeare and Spenser, not to mention Ebenezer Elliott, the Corn Law Rhymer.[32] Bright himself was well aware of the fact that the reputation of an orator was uniquely difficult for posterity to grasp and, sad though it may be, few now turn, as George Eliot once admiringly did, to Bright's speeches as a source of evening entertainment. Bright felt that, with the passage of time, speeches became flat and uninteresting and the fame of an orator should therefore rest simply on the comments of contemporaries. Judged by this yardstick, Bright's standing must be high. For a time, particularly in 1866, his speeches determined the boundaries of political allegiance in the country. Lincolnshire farmers, for example, who had once championed the Liberal cause, now hastened to dissociate themselves from the 'turbulent demagogue'.[33]

If they had known of his subsequent career, these worthy men who 'had a horror of Mr Bright' need not have been so alarmed. While, in a formal sense, he moved higher by accepting office in the Liberal government of 1868, he neither enjoyed executive responsibility nor excelled at it. He remained a man of the platform rather than the council chamber, and he never grouped men around him to challenge Gladstone's authority. His second breakdown meant that he could never be considered a serious contender for power. His return to the Cabinet was already noted by John Morley at the time as an event of little significance. It was 'only meant to lull the Dissenting storm' for the elections.[34] For the rest of the 1870s, Bright was generally content to lull the storm rather than direct it. Writing in 1876, Bagehot astutely detected 'The Conservative vein in Mr Bright', that is Conservative in the sense of character rather than of specific ideas. Bright, in his view, did not possess the 'Liberal turn of mind' by which he meant a willingness to admit new ideas and an impartiality in considering them. The traditions of his family, religious society, and early years, remained present in their essentials until the end. When the Queen was in question, despite earlier rebuffs, 'it would be impossible to name a more cordial Conservative'. The cry for women's suffrage revolted him far more than it did the bulk of the Conservative party. It had only to be proved that a particular proposal was not only new in detail, but new in principle, for it to lose all its charm for Bright. The specific election of labourers or artisans as members of parliament also seemed to him undesirable.[35] It was this attitude which the Positivist, Frederic Harrison, feared when he wrote in 1863: 'As a Mirabeau, as a destroyer of feudalism, follow Bright, but not to let him found a middle-class constitution.'[36] By the end of his life, if Bright had failed to establish such a constitution, 'feudalism' had been sufficiently emasculated to make the status quo preferable to any alternative.

It is, however, too simple to dismiss the Rochdale prophet as merely a passenger in the Liberal Party, living smugly on the reputation of his youth. His resignation over the Egyptian imbroglio in 1882 was an act of dissociation. His refusal to support Home Rule was also an individual protest against what he considered to be a surrender to the threat of violence. He seems to have been determined to end his career as an independent, whether 'radical' or 'conservative'; John Bright was his own man.

Notes

The numerical order of days and months follow modern British usage (26.11.1886 = 26 November 1886) instead of the Quaker usage which was to put the number of the month first. All references to Bright are to John Bright.

1 Family and education, 1811–27

1 G. Carter, 'The Early Life of John Bright's Father', *Journal of the Friends Historical Society*, 51, 1965, pp. 54–6.
2 Jacob Bright's report and suggestions regarding Ackworth School are in the Bright MS., Street, Somerset.
3 Bright to J. C. Collins, 26.11.1886, Bright MS., Street.

2 Local life and travel, 1827–37

1 Sir A. Pease (ed.), *The Diaries of Edward Pease*, p. 65.
2 J. R. Vincent, 'The Electoral Sociology of Rochdale', *Economic History Review*, 2nd series, 16, 1963–4, pp. 76–90.
3 W. R. Ward, *Religion and Society in England, 1790–1850*, pp. 183–5; E. R. Nightingale, 'The Church in Rochdale, 1820–1870', BA dissertation, University of Durham, 1969.
4 B. H. Harrison, *Drink and the Victorians*, and his 'Animals and the State in Ninteenth-Century England', *English Historical Review*, October 1973.
5 Bright's letters to his father, both from Europe and the Levant, are at Street. The diary of his travels appears in R. A. J. Walling (ed.), *Diaries*, pp. 16–51.
6 W. E. A. Axon, 'John Bright and the Temperance Movement', *Alliance News and Temperance Reformer*, 23.11.1911.
7 Priscilla Bright to Gwen Morgan, 29.9.1835, Bright MS., Street.
8 Bright to P. Bright, 27.7.1863, Bright MS., Street. Gwen married, it seems unhappily, and died young, being buried at Llwyngwril. In later years Bright kept in touch with her children. I owe information on this subject to Mr Gwyndaf Roberts.

3 Marriage and local politics, 1837–41

1 Bright's 'Appeal to the Radical Reformers of Rochdale' is at Street.
2 Bright's 'Observations' are at Street.
3 A. O. Boyce (ed.), *The Records of a Quaker Family*, pp. 209–10.
4 Bright's correspondence with his future wife is at Street.
5 Bright to P. Bright, 12.10.1838, Bright MS., Street.
6 T. Bright to J. Bancroft, 20.7.1839, Bright MS., Street.
7 Bright to J. Crosland, 30.9.1839, Bright MS., Street.
8 P. Bright to M. Lucas, 6.12.1839, Bright MS., Street.
9 Bright, *Address . . . on the late Church Rate Contests*.
10 Bright to J. Brotherton, 18.12.1839, Bright MS., Swarthmore.
11 Bright's letters to Rachel and Margaret Priestman are at Street.
12 Jacob Bright to Bright, 11.9.1841, Bright MS., Street.

4 The campaign in the country, 1841–3

1 Bright's letters to J. B. Smith are in the Manchester Central Public Library.
2 H. J. Hanham, 'The First Constituency Party?', *Political Studies*, 9, 1961, pp. 188–9.
3 The result is analysed in detail in J. R. Vincent, *Poll Books: How Victorians Voted*, p. 165.
4 Bright's letters to George Wilson are in the Manchester Central Public Library.
5 Bright's letters to Lord Brougham are at University College, London.
6 J. B. Mackie, *Life and Work of Duncan McLaren*, vol. 1, p. 231.
7 Bright to H. Renton, 23.1.1843, Bright MS., Swarthmore.
8 J. Morley, *Life of Cobden*, p. 264.
9 D. Large, 'The Election of John Bright as member for Durham City in 1843', *Durham University Journal*, 47, December 1954.
10 I am grateful to Mr David Darbishire for allowing me to see Bright's journal in which he noted this information.
11 Bright to J. T. Crook, 29.7.1843, Bright MS., Swarthmore. See also Vincent, *Poll Books*, p. 103, and T. J. Nossiter, *Influence, Opinion and Political Idioms in Reformed England*, pp. 118–23.

5 Parliament and repeal, 1843–7

1 J. T. Mills, *John Bright and the Quakers*, vol. 2, p. 97.
2 Bright to J. Livesey, 26.8.1843, Bright MS., Swarthmore.
3 Bright to P. Bright, 19 & 22.8.1843, Bright MS., Street.
4 Bright to J. Sturge, September 1843, Sturge MS., British Library, Ad.MS. 43845
5 F. Place to Bright, 12.9.1843, Bright MS., Street.
6 Bright to J. Bowring, 6.10.1843, Bright MS., Huntington Library.
7 Bright to E. Baines, 2.12.1843, Baines MS., Leeds Public Library.
8 Bright to G. T. Fox, 9.12.1843, Bright MS., Friends House Library.
9 R. Boyson, *The Ashworth Cotton Enterprise*, pp. 179–81.
10 Bright to N. S. Denison, 8.6.1844, Bright MS., Swarthmore.
11 Bright to J. S. Henslow, 30.12.1845, Princeton University Library.
12 Bright to J. Watson, 26.7.1845, Bright MS., Swarthmore.

13   Bright to J. Burton, 16.3.1845, Duke University Library.
14   Bright to J. Moss, 27.12.1845, Bright MS., Street.

6 War on the Whigs, 1847–52

1   Bright to Mrs Leatham and Miss Elizabeth Leatham; W. H. Leatham to Mrs Leatham, Bright MS., Street.
2   Bright to C. P. Villiers, 20.8.1846 and 9.9.1846, Bright MS., Street. Copies of Bright's letters to Villiers are in this collection.
3   Bright to C. Gilpin, 25.9.1845, Bright MS., Swarthmore.
4   Bright to J. E. Denison, 22.8.1848, Denison MS., University of Nottingham Library.
5   J. E. T. Rogers (ed.), *Speeches*, p. 175.
6   R. A. J. Walling (ed.), *Diaries*, pp. 95–107.
7   Bright's letters to his second wife are at University College, London.
8   Bright to J. Pim, 27.9.1849, Friends Library, Dublin.
9   Bright to Lord John Russell, 17.11.1849 (copy), Bright MS., Street.
10   The comment in J. M. Prest, *Lord John Russell*, p. 307, therefore seems erroneous.
11   J. L. Sturgis, *John Bright and the British Empire*, pp. 13–18.
12   Bright to A. Mackay, 16.12.1850, Bright MS., Street.
13   Bright to D. E. Ford, 14.2.1851, Bright MS., Haverford College Library.
14   Bright to E. Fry, 1.3.1849, Bright MS., Duke University Library; Bright to J. Sturge, 27.7.1850, Sturge MS.

7 Isolation and defeat, 1852–7

1   D. Fraser, *Urban Politics in Victorian England*, pp. 204–5.
2   H. J. Leech (ed.), *Public Letters*, pp. 99–111.
3   Bright to C. P. Villiers, 13.7.1852, Bright MS., Street.
4   R. A. J. Walling (ed.), *Diaries*, pp. 128–30.
5   Bright to Lord John Russell, 28.12.1852, Duke University Library.
6   Bright to Anon, 17.4.1853, Bright MS., National Liberal Club.
7   Walling, op. cit., p. 145. '
8   J. E. T. Rogers (ed.), *Speeches*, pp. 459–65.
9   Bright to Cobden, 28.11.1853, British Library.
10   Bright to Lord Aberdeen, 16.3.1854 (copy) Bright MS., Street.
11   Rogers, op. cit., pp. 224–39.
12   Walling, op. cit., p. 170.
13   As Mr A. J. P. Taylor suggests in 'John Bright and the Crimean War', in *Englishmen and Others*.
14   D. Read, *Cobden and Bright*, p. 127.
15   Taylor, op. cit.
16   T. Bright to J. Bancroft, 27.7.1855, Bright MS., Street.
17   W. Robertson, *The Life and Times of the Rt. Hon. John Bright*, pp. 265–7.
18   G. Bright to M. Lucas, 7.11.1851, Bright MS., Street.
19   Bright to J. Pease, 26.12.1851, Friends House Library.
20   R. Cobden to E. Ellice, 29.5.1856, Ellice MS., National Library of Scotland.
21   Bright's letters to his daughter, Helen are at Street.
22   Bright to J. E. Denison, 3.3.1856, Denison MS., Nottingham University Library.

23 Walling, op. cit., pp. 219–22.
24 Lady Login, *Recollections*, p. 198.
25 Bright to Sir James Hudson, 28.4.1857, W. L. Clements Library, Michigan University.
26 Bright to J. Bowring, 22.12.1848, Huntington Library.
27 T. Bright to J. Bancroft, 22.5.1857, Bright MS., Street.

8 The first Reform crusade: failure, 1858–61

1 E. P. Hennock, *Fit and Proper Persons*, p. 148.
2 J. R. Vincent, *The Formation of the Liberal Party*, p. 68; W. H. Mackintosh, *Disestablishment and Liberation*, p. 54.
3 Bright to J. Reed, 28.2.1860, British Library, Ad.MS. 44877.
4 Bright to W. E. Gladstone, 21.2.1858, British Library, Ad.MS. 44112.
5 J. E. T. Rogers (ed.), *Speeches*, p. 30.
6 Bright to J. M. Ludlow, 28.6.1858, India Office Library, MS. Eur. A 61.
7 Bright's Birmingham speeches on 27 and 29 October 1858 were published by the 'New Reform Movement'.
8 Bright to R. Congreve, 12.11.1858, MS.Eng.Lett.c.185, Bodleian Library, Oxford; F. Harrison to E. S. Beesly, 1858, quoted in R. Harrison, *Before the Socialists*, p. 258.
9 J. B. Mackie, *Life and Work of Duncan McLaren*, vol. 2, pp. 147–8.
10 Bright to Sharman Crawford, 9.1.1858, Public Record Office of Northern Ireland.
11 E. Pryce to J. Cowen, 16.12.1858, Cowen MS., Newcastle Central Public Library.
12 H. Cooper to R. B. Reed, 25.1.1859, Cowen MS. Bright himself wrote at this time that he did not think 'any considerable number of persons in Birmingham wish any other Bill than mine to be brought in'. Bright to W. Williams, MP, 19.1.1859, Yale University Library.
13 J. MacAdam to J. Cowen, 5.2.1859, Cowen MS.
14 R. A. J. Walling (ed.), *Diaries*, pp. 237–9.
15 Lord John Russell to Bright, 15.6.1859, Bright MS., Street.
16 *The Letters of Queen Victoria*, vol. 3, p. 349.
17 D.P.N. . .(?) to R. B. Reed, 7.3.1860, Newcastle Central Public Library, c.1290.
18 Lord Clarendon to the Duchess of Manchester, 27.2.1860, quoted in A. L. Kennedy, *My dear Duchess*, pp. 97–8.
19 H. Stacey to J. Cowen, 13.8.1860, Cowen MS.
20 Bright to J. Cowen, 13.8.1860, Cowen MS.
21 *The Times*, 13.11.1860.
22 B. and P. Russell (eds), *The Amberley Papers*, vol. 1, p. 110.
23 R. B. Reed to W. Hicks, 23.2.1861, Cowen MS.
24 Bright to J. B. Braithwaite, 10.12.1859, Friends House Library.

9 The American civil war, 1863–7

1 H. Maxwell, *Life and Letters of the Fourth Earl of Clarendon*, London, 1913, vol. 2, pp. 172–3.
2 Bright to F. Cousinery, 1.1.1845, Pierpont Morgan Library, New York.

3 He consented to become a Vice-President of the American Peace Society, Bright to G. C. Beckwith, 7.7.1855, Princeton University Library.
4 He wrote that he did not feel disposed to seek an opportunity for speaking upon the subject. Bright to T. Hodgkin, 14.5.1861, Yale University Library.
5 T. Bright to J. Bancroft, 22.3.1861, Bright MS., Street.
6 W. Robertson, *Bright*, p. 371.
7 Bright to J. Henderson, 4.9.1861, Bright MS., Street.
8 S. Lucas to H. Martineau, 13.11.1861, Birmingham University Library.
9 Bright to G. Bancroft, 29.3.1862, Cornell University Library.
10 Bright to B. Wood, 10.4.1862, Haverford College Library.
11 Bright to T. H. Dudley, 18.10.1862, Huntington Library.
12 F. M. Leventhal, *Respectable Radical*, pp. 47–8; Harrison, *Before the Socialists*, p. 259.
13 G. Howell to Bright, 7.10.1867, Howell MS., Bishopsgate Institute.
14 Bright to Mrs Harriet Beecher Stowe, 9.3.1862, Chicago Historical Society.
15 Bright to R. I. Walker, 27.7.1863, New-York Historical Society.
16 Bright to J. M. Forbes, 31.7.1863, Bright MS., Street.
17 Bright to T. H. Dudley, 2.9.1863, Huntington Library.
18 Bright to Lord Hartington, 17.12.1863, Devonshire MS., Chatsworth.
19 Bright to H. Greely, 1.10.1864, New-York Historical Society.

10 The second Reform crusade: success, 1863–7

1 Bright's correspondence with his son, John Albert, is at Street.
2 Bright to T. H. Green, 19.3.1861, Princeton University Library; M. Richter, *The Politics of Conscience*, pp. 259–76.
3 Bright to C. Gilpin, 27.4.1846, Swarthmore MS. Bright to Anon., 27.5.1847, (copy), Street MS.
4 Bright to C. P. Villiers, 2.9.1859, Street MS.
5 Bright to Lord Sydney Osborne, 22.2.1864, Swarthmore MS.
6 Bright to the Hon. J. P. Smith, 4.3.1864, Pierpont Morgan Library; J. E. T. Rogers (ed.), *Speeches*, pp. 503–10.
7 Bright to T. A. Woodnutt, 7.3.1872, Swarthmore MS.
8 Bright to T. Hankey, 25.3.1868, Trevelyan MS., Newcastle University Library.
9 Bright to J. E. T. Rogers, 29.7.1865, Rogers MS., by courtesy of Dr D. M. Rogers.
10 Bright to S. Fox, 24.10.1865, Bright MS., Street.
11 Bright to D. McLaren, 4.11.1865, Birmingham University Library.
12 B. and P. Russell (eds), *The Amberley Papers*, vol. 1, p. 468.
13 Ibid., pp. 471–2.
14 Lord Elcho to Ellice, 25.3.1866, Ellice MS., National Library of Scotland.
15 Bright to Anon., 19.5.1866, Friends House Library.
16 Bright to Howell, 27.6.1866, Howell MS.; Bright to Wilson, 27.6.1866, Wilson MS.
17 Bright to T. B. Potter, 30.6.1866, Potter MS. Bright's letters to Potter are in the Manchester Central Public Library.
18 F. M. Leventhal, *Respectable Radical*, pp. 73–9; Bright to Howell, 19 & 20.7.1866, Howell MS.
19 Bright to F. M. Edge, 9.9.1866, Bright MS., Swarthmore.
20 J. E. T. Rogers (ed.), *Speeches*, pp. 183–91; E. R. Norman, *The Catholic Church in Ireland in the Age of Rebellion, 1859–73*, pp. 172–3. J. S. Mill

regarded the honour being paid to Bright as 'an important step towards establishing . . . sympathetic co-operation between the English and the Irish Liberals. . . .' F. E. Mineka and D. N. Lindley (eds), *The Later Letters of John Stuart Mill, 1849–1873*, pp. 1207–8.

21 N. St John-Stevas (ed.), *The Collected Works of Walter Bagehot*, vol. 3, pp. 299–301.
22 Bright to S. Fox, 25.10.1866, Bright MS., Street.
23 J. Morley, *Life of Gladstone*, vol. 2, p.213 & pp. 222–3.
24 Bright to R. Congreve, 24.11.1866, Congreve MS., Bodleian Library.
25 Bright to J. E. T. Rogers, 12.12.1866, Rogers MS.; Bright to Howell, 22.12.1866, Howell MS.; Bright to W. H. Northy, 25.12.1866, Northy MS., British Library, Ad.MS 44877.
26 F. B. Smith, *The Making of the Second Reform Bill*; M. Cowling, *1867, Disraeli, Gladstone and Revolution*.
27 R. A. J. Walling (ed.), *Diaries*, pp. 296–7.
28 Bright to E. Beales, 5.3.1867, Friends House Library.
29 Bright to B. Disraeli, 9.3.1867 (copy), Bright MS., Street. Quoted in full in G. M. Trevelyan, *The Life of John Bright*, pp. 381–2.
30 E. Bouverie to E. Ellice, 10.3.1867, Ellice MS., National Library of Scotland.
31 J. S. Mill to J. E. Cairnes, 26.5.1867, *Later Letters*, p. 1272.
32 Bright to E. Beales, 26.7.1867, National Liberal Club.
33 Cowling, *1867 . . .*, p. 295.

11 The first Liberal government, 1868–74

1 Bright to J. McCarthy, 8.11.1867 and 18.12.1867, quoted in J. McCarthy, *Reminiscences*, vol. 1, pp. 100–1.
2 H. J. Leech (ed.), *Public Letters*, pp. 117–19; Bright to H. D. Hutton, 27.1.1868, Princeton University Library.
3 Bright to W. H. Northy, 26.12.1867, Northy MS.
4 J. E. T. Rogers (ed.), *Speeches*, pp. 700–13.
5 R. Blake, *Disraeli*, p. 502.
6 J. E. T. Rogers (ed.), *Public Addresses*, p. 85.
7 Ibid., p. 517.
8 Ibid., p. 104.
9 Ibid., p. 115.
10 Bright to Rev. J. Allen, 21.11.1868, Princeton University Library.
11 Rogers, op. cit., pp. 136–7.
12 Gladstone to Granville, 14.12.1868, in A. Ramm (ed.), *The Political Correspondence of Mr Gladstone and Lord Granville, 1868–1876*, p. 3.
13 Mill to W. T. Thornton, 16.1.1869, *Later Letters*, p. 1548n.
14 Granville to Overstone, 8.12.1868, in D. P. O'Brien, *The Correspondence of Lord Overstone*, vol. 3, p. 1164.
15 Sir J. Robinson to H. Martineau, 11.12.1868, Birmingham University Library.
16 E. Wallace, *Goldwin Smith: Victorian Liberal*, pp. 19–20.
17 Granville to Gladstone. 31.12.1868, in Ramm, op. cit., pp. 6–7.
18 Bright to Gladstone, 21.5.1869; Gladstone to Bright, 22.5.1869, British Library, Ad.MS 44112; Bright to Rogers, 25.5.1869, Rogers MS., Bright to H. B. S. Thompson, 9.6.1869 in Leech, op. cit., p. 223; Gladstone to Granville, 24 & 27.5.1869, in Ramm, op. cit., pp. 22–4.
19 R. D. Collinson Black, *Economic Thought and the Irish Question*, p. 62.

20 Bright to Kay-Shuttleworth, 18.10.1869, Kay-Shuttleworth MS., Manchester University Library.
21 Bright to Lord Clarendon, 14.10.1869, Clarendon MS., Bodleian Library.
22 Bright to W. D. Henderson, 23.10.1869, Duke University Library.
23 Bright to A. J. Mundella, 19.9.1869, Mundella MS., Sheffield University Library.
24 Bright to Lord Clarendon, 11.5.1869 & 14.10.1869, Clarendon MS.
25 Bright to Lord Clarendon, 4.12.1869, Clarendon MS.
26 Bright to Lord Granville, 25.9.1871, Granville MS., P.R.O., 30/29 52.
27 D. W. Bebbington, 'Gladstone and the Baptists', *Baptist Quarterly*, 26(5), 1976.
28 Rogers, op. cit., pp. 178–9.
29 A. Ramm (ed.), *The Political Correspondence of Mr Gladstone and Lord Granville, 1876–1886*, p. 288.
30 Bright to Rev. R. W. Dale, 7.1.1872, Dale MS., University of Birmingham Library.
31 Helen Clark to S. Bancroft. 8.4.1872, Bright MS., Street.
32 E. Drus (ed.), *A Journal of Events During the Gladstone Ministry, 1868–1874 by John, First Earl of Kimberley*, p. 41.
33 Bright to J. Chamberlain, 19.8.1873, Chamberlain MS., Birmingham University.
34 T. W. Reid, *Life of W. E. Forster*, vol. 1, pp. 559–74.
35 N. St John-Stevas (ed.), *The Collected Works of Walter Bagehot*, vol. 3, pp. 308–9.

12 Opposition, 1874–80

1 Bright to J. White, 14.2.1874, National Liberal Club; Bright to Anon., 3.2.1874, Friends House Library.
2 Bright to Hartington, 3.2.1875, Devonshire MS.
3 Bright to H. Broadhurst, 21.3.1875, Broadhurst MS. London School of Economics.
4 Bright to Mrs Rathbone, 3.3.1875, Rathbone MS., Liverpool University Library.
5 Bright to W. Escroyd, 23.6.1875, Bright MS., Street.
6 Bright to W. J. Parry, 12.2.1876, Bright MS., Street.
7 R. T. Shannon, *Gladstone and the Bulgarian Agitation, 1876*, pp. 78–9.
8 H. J. Leech (ed.), *Public Letters*, pp. 16–18.
9 J. E. T. Rogers (ed.), *Public Addresses*, p. 298.
10 Bright to Goldwin Smith, 19.11.1876, Cornell University Library.
11 Rogers, op. cit., p. 300 & p. 314.
12 Bright to Anon., 22.5.1877 and 30.5.1877, Birmingham Central Public Library.
13 Bright to Thompson, 26.9.1877, Duke University Library.
14 Rogers, op. cit., pp. 355–97.
15 Bright to Rev. T. Rippon, 4.12.1877, Liverpool University Library.
16 Wallace, *Goldwin Smith*, p. 82.
17 Bright to W. T. Snape, 26.9.1877, University of Chicago Library.
18 Rogers, op. cit., p. 459.
19 Bright to J. Bryce, 19.3.1878, Bryce MS., Bodleian Library.
20 Bright to A. J. Mundella, 18.5.1884, Mundella MS.
21 Letters to Isaac Sharp on Philip's education are at Friends House Library.

22 Bright to Goldwin Smith, 21.8.1879, Cornell University; Bright to J. Wilson, 8.7.1879, MS.Eng.Lett. e 86, Bodleian Library.

13 The last phase, 1880–9

1 L. Edel, *Henry James: The Conquest of London, 1870–1883*, pp. 363–4.
2 W. L. Arnstein, *The Bradlaugh Case*, pp. 56–7
3 Bright to T. Hankey, 15.7.1880, Trevelyan MS., Newcastle University.
4 Bright to S. M. Shannon, 13.5.1879, Public Record Office of Northern Ireland.
5 D. W. R. Bahlman (ed.), *The Diary of Sir Edward Walter Hamilton*, p. 87.
6 Memorandum on the Irish Land Bill, Ad.MS. 44625, British Library.
7 Bright to M. Wheeler, 14.5.1881, Bright MS., Street.
8 M. E. Chamberlain, 'Sir Charles Dilke and the British intervention in Egypt, 1882: decision making in a nineteenth-century Cabinet', *British Journal of International Studies*, 2(3), October 1976, pp. 231–45.
9 Bright to Lord Ripon, 2.10.1882, British Library, Ad.MS. 43632.
10 Bright to S. Beck, 24.1.1883, Duke University Library.
11 Bright to J. Chamberlain, 4.1.1883, cited in C. H. D. Howard (ed.), *Joseph Chamberlain: A Political Memoir*, pp. 79–80.
12 Bright, *The National Church and National Righteousness*, London, 1883.
13 Rev. S. Gladstone to Bright, 2.11.1885, Bright MS., Street.
14 Bright to W. Jack, 22.12.1884, National Library of Scotland.
15 Bright to J. G. Whittier, 18.3.1885, Bright MS., Street.
16 Bright to W. N. Molesworth, 15.4.1885, Duke University Library.
17 Bright to M. D. Conway, 15.4.1885, Bright MS., Street.
18 Birmingham Liberal Association, John Bright Celebration, Official Programme; Bahlman, op. cit., pp. 448–9.
19 Ibid., p. 604.
20 R. A. J. Walling (ed.), *Diaries*, p. 525.
21 Bright to B. Armitage, 6.5.1886, Manchester Central Public Library.
22 Bright to R. Annan, 24.6.1886, Duke University Library; Bright to P. Rylands, 24.6.1886, quoted in L. G. Rylands (ed.), *Correspondence and Speeches of Mr P. Rylands, MP*, vol. 1, pp. 364–5.
23 Bright to A. Chamberlain, 15.6.1886, Birmingham University Library; M. C. Hurst, *Joseph Chamberlain and Liberal Reunion*, pp. 268–9.
24 Bright to Hartington, 28.11.1886, Devonshire MS.
25 Bright to A. V. Dicey, 10.11.1886, Glasgow University Library.
26 Bright, *Last Political Speech*, 5.8.1887, London, 1887.
27 Bright to Earl Grey, 20/21.2.1888, Grey MS., Durham University.
28 Bright to C. Quilter, 4.3.1888, Duke University Library.
29 N. McCord and A. E. Carrick, 'The Northumberland Election of 1852', *Northern History*, 1, 1966, p. 97.
30 Nossiter, *Influence, Opinion and Political Idioms in Reformed England*, p. 134.
31 R. W. Dale, 'Mr Bright', *Contemporary Review*, May 1889.
32 J. T. Mills, 'An Orator's Library', *Journal of the Friends Historical Society*, Supplement 21, 1946.
33 R. J. Olney, *Lincolnshire Politics, 1832–1885*, p. 160.
34 Quoted in D. A. Hamer, *The Politics of Electoral Pressure*, p. 136.
35 N. St John-Stevas (ed.), *The Collected Works of Walter Bagehot*, vol. 3, pp. 317–20.
36 Harrison, *Before the Socialists*, p. 269.

Bibliography

John Bright's Speeches and Letters

Address to the Inhabitants of Rochdale on the late Church Rate Contests, Rochdale, 1840.
To the Working-Men of Rochdale, Rochdale, 1842.
Speech at the Corn Exchange, Wakefield, April 1843, Manchester, 1843.
Speech at the Nomination at Durham, July 1843, Manchester 1843.
Speech at the Proceedings of the Peace Conference at Edinburgh, Edinburgh, 1853.
Speech on International Arbitration, Manchester, 1853.
Speech at Birmingham, October 1858, Glasgow, 1858.
Speech on the struggle in America in relation to the working men of Britain, London, 27 March, 1863, Glasgow, 1863.
Speech at Birmingham, July 1865, Leeds, 1865.
Address in Manchester, October 1879, London, 1879.
Speech on the National Church and National Righteousness, May 1883, London, 1883.
Speech on the House of Lords, Birmingham, August 1884, London, 1884.
Speech in Somersetshire, October 1885, Ipswich, 1885.
The Last Political Speech, August 1887, London, 1887.
Letters on Home Rule, Birmingham, 1892.
Speeches on the American Question, ed. F. Moore, Boston, 1865.
Speeches on Questions of Public Policy, ed. J. E. T. Rogers (pop. edn.), London, 1869.
Public Addresses by John Bright, ed. J. E. T. Rogers, London, 1879.
Public Letters of the Rt. Hon. John Bright, ed. H. J. Leech, London, 1895.
Selected Speeches on Public Questions, introduced by J. Sturge, London, 1907.
The Diaries of John Bright, ed. R. A. J. Walling, London, 1930.
'Letters of John Bright to Charles Sumner', *Proceedings of the Massachusetts Historical Society*, 45–6, 1911–12.

Selected Biographies of John Bright

Ausubel, H., *John Bright, Victorian Reformer*, New York, 1966.
Mills, J. T., *John Bright and the Quakers*, London, 1935.

Bibliography

O'Brien, R. B., *John Bright*, London, 1910.

Read, D., *Cobden and Bright*, London, 1967.

Robertson, W., *Life and Times of the Rt. Hon. John Bright*, Rochdale, 1877.

Smith, G. B., *Life and Speeches of the Rt. Hon. John Bright*, London, 1881–2.

Trevelyan, G. M., *Life of Bright*, London, 1913.

Books

Adams, E. D., *Great Britain and the American Civil War*, London, 1925.

Anderson, O., *A Liberal State at War*, London, 1967.

Arnstein, W. L., *The Bradlaugh Case*, Oxford, 1965.

Bahlman, D. W. R. (ed.), *The Diary of Sir Edward Walter Hamilton, 1880–1885*, Oxford, 1972.

Baines, E., *Life of Edward Baines*, London, 1851.

Baines, E., *History of Lancashire*, 1888.

Bartlett, C. J. (ed.), *Britain Pre-Eminent*, London, 1969.

Bell, P. M. H., *Disestablishment in Ireland and Wales*, London, 1969.

Benson, A. C. and Esher, Viscount, *The Letters of Queen Victoria, 1837–1861*, 3 vols, London, 1908.

Best, G. F. A., *Mid-Victorian Britain, 1851–1875*, London, 1971.

Black, R. D. C., *Economic Thought and the Irish Question, 1817–70*, Cambridge, 1960.

Blake, R., *Disraeli*, London, 1966.

Bolt, C., *The Anti-Slavery Movement and Reconstruction*, London, 1969.

Boyce, A. O. (ed.), *The Records of a Quaker Family: The Richardsons of Cleveland*, London, 1899.

Boyson, R., *The Ashworth Cotton Enterprise: Rise and Fall of a Family Firm, 1818–1880*, Oxford, 1970.

Briggs, A., *Victorian People*, London, 1954.

Briggs, A. (ed.), *Chartist Studies*, London, 1959.

Brock, P., *Pacifism in Europe to 1914*, Princeton, 1972.

Brown, L. M., *The Board of Trade and the Free Trade Movement, 1830–42*, Oxford, 1958.

Burn, W. L., *The Age of Equipoise*, London, 1964.

Chaloner, W. H. (ed.), *The Autobiography of Samuel Bamford*, London, 1965.

Chamberlain, A., *Down the Years*, London, 1935.

Checkland, S. G., *The Gladstones; A Family Biography*, Cambridge, 1971.

Churchill, W. S., *Lord Randolph Churchill*, London, 1951 edition.

Cooke, A. B. and Vincent, J. R. (ed.), *Lord Carlingford's Journal*, London, 1971.

Cooke, A. B. and Vincent, J. R., *The Governing Passion*, Brighton, 1974.

Cowherd, R. G., *The Politics of English Dissent*, London, 1969.

Cowling, M., *1867: Disraeli, Gladstone and Revolution*, Cambridge, 1967.

Crook, D. P., *American Democracy in English Politics, 1815–1850*, Oxford, 1965.

Denison, J. E., *Notes from my Journal when Speaker of the House of Commons*, London, 1908.

Drus, E. (ed.), *A Journal of Events During the Gladstone Ministry, 1868–1874 by John, First Earl of Kimberley*, Camden Miscellany, 21, London, 1958.

Edel, L., *Henry James: The Conquest of London, 1870–1883*, London, 1962.

Ellison, M., *Support for Secession: Lancashire and the American Civil War*, Chicago, 1972.

Fay, C. R., *The Corn Laws and Social England*, Cambridge, 1932.

Fraser, D., *Urban Politics in Victorian England*, Leicester, 1976.

Fraser, P., *Joseph Camberlain*, London, 1966.

Bibliography

Gash, N., *Politics in the Age of Peel*, London, 1953.
Gash, N., *Reform and Reconstruction*, Oxford, 1965.
Gash, N., *Sir Robert Peel*, London, 1, 1961; 2, 1972.
Grampp, W. D., *The Manchester School of Economics*, Stamford, 1960.
Gwynn, S. and Tuckwell, G. M., *Life of Sir Charles Dilke*, London, 1917.
Hamer, D. A., *The Politics of Electoral Pressure*, Sussex, 1977.
Hanham, H. J., *Elections and Party Management: Politics in the Time of Disraeli and Gladstone*, London, 1959.
Harrison, B. H., *Drink and the Victorians*, London, 1971.
Harrison, R., *Before the Socialists*, London, 1965.
Hartwell, R. M. (ed.), *The Industrial Revolution*, Oxford, 1970.
Haultain, A. (ed.), *Goldwin Smith's Reminiscences*, London, 1910.
Haultain, A. (ed.), *Goldwin Smith's Correspondence*, London, n.d.
Heath, H. J. B., *Margaret Bright Lucas*, London, 1890.
Hennock, E. P., *Fit and Proper Persons*, London, 1973.
Howard, C. H. D. (ed.), *Joseph Chamberlain; A Political Memoir*, London, 1953.
Hurst, M. C., *Joseph Chamberlain and Liberal Reunion*, London, 1967.
Isichei, E., *Victorian Quakers*, London, 1970.
Jones, A., *The Politics of Reform, 1884*, Cambridge, 1972.
Kennedy, A. L., *My dear Duchess*, London, 1956.
Leader, R. E. (ed.), *Life and Letters of J. A. Roebuck*, London, 1897.
Leventhal, F. M., *Respectable Radical: George Howell and Victorian Working Class Politics*, London, 1971.
Login, Lady, *Recollections*, London, 1916.
Lyons, F. S. L., *Ireland Since the Famine*, London, 1973.
McCarthy, J., *Reminiscences*, London, 1899.
McCord, N., *The Anti-Corn Law League*, London, 1968.
Mackie, J. B., *Life and Work of Duncan McLaren*, London, 1888.
Mackintosh, W. H., *Disestablishment and Liberation*, London, 1972.
Maclagan, M., *'Clemency' Canning*, London, 1962.
Martin, A. P., *Life and Letters of Robert Lowe*, London, 1894.
Masterman, N., *J. M. Ludlow: The Builder of Christian Socialism*, Cambridge, 1963.
Maxwell, H., *Life and Letters of the Fourth Earl of Clarendon*, London, 1913.
Miall, A., *Life of Edward Miall*, London, 1884.
Mineka, F. E. and Lindley, D. N. (eds), *The Later Letters of John Stuart Mill, 1849–73*, London, 1972.
Molesworth, G. L., *Life of J. E. N. Molesworth*, London, 1915.
Moore, R. J., *Sir Charles Wood's Indian Policy, 1853–1866*, Manchester, 1966.
Morley, J., *Life of Cobden*, 1903 edition, London. *Life of Gladstone*, London, 1903.
Nightingale, B., *Lancashire Nonconformity . . . The Churches of Bolton, Bury, Rochdale, etc.*, Manchester, 1892.
Norman, E. R., *The Catholic Church in Ireland in the Age of Rebellion, 1859–73*, London, 1965.
Nossiter, T. J., *Influence, Opinion and Political Idioms in Reformed England*, Brighton, 1975.
O'Brien, D. P. (ed.), *The Correspondence of Lord Overstone*, 3 vols., Cambridge, 1971.
Olney, R. J., *Lincolnshire Politics, 1832–1885*, Oxford, 1973.
Pease, A. (ed.), *The Diaries of Edward Pease*, London, 1907.
Peel, A. (ed.), *Letters to a Victorian Editor*, London, 1929.
Pelling, H., *America and the British Left*, London, 1956.
Perkin, H., *The Origins of Modern English Society, 1780–1880*, London, 1969.
Petrie-Mills, I., *Life of John Mills*, Manchester, 1899.

Petty, J., *The History of the Primitive Methodist Connexion*, London, 1860.

Pollard, F. E., *Bootham School*, York, 1923.

Prest, J. M., *Lord John Russell*, London, 1972.

Ramm, A. (ed.), *The Political Correspondence of Mr Gladstone and Lord Granville, 1868–1876*, London, 1952.

Ramm, A. (ed.), *The Political Correspondence of Mr Gladstone and Lord Granville, 1876–1886*, Oxford, 1962.

Randall, J. G., *Lincoln, the Liberal Statesman*, London, 1947.

Richter, M., *The Politics of Conscience: T. H. Green and His Age*, London, 1964.

Ridley, J., *Lord Palmerston*, London, 1970.

Riethmuller, C. J., *Frederick Lucas*, London, 1862.

Robertson, W., *Old and New in Rochdale*, Rochdale, 1881.

Robson, R. (ed.), *Ideas and Institutions of Victorian Britain*, London, 1967.

Russell, G. W. E. (ed.), *Sir Wilfred Lawson, a Memoir*, London, 1909.

Russell, B. and P. (eds), *The Amberley Papers*, London, 1937.

Rylands, L. G. (ed.), *Correspondence and Speeches of Mr P. Rylands, MP*, Manchester, 1890.

St John-Stevas, N. (ed.), *The Collected Works of Walter Bagehot, The Historical Essays*, London, 1968.

Salter, F. R., *Dissenters and Public Affairs in Mid-Victorian England*, London, 1967.

Semmel, B., *The Governor Eyre Controversy*, London, 1962.

Shannon, R. T., *Gladstone and the Bulgarian Agitation, 1876*, London, 1963.

Silver, A. W., *Manchester Men and Indian Cotton, 1847–1872*, Manchester, 1966.

Smith, F. B., *The Making of the Second Reform Bill*, Cambridge, 1966.

Southgate, D., *The Passing of the Whigs, 1832–1866*, London, 1962.

Steel, J. W., *Historical Sketch of the Society of Friends in Newcastle and Gateshead, 1653–1898*, London, 1899.

Stewart, W. A. C., *Quakers and Education*, London, 1953.

Sturgis, J. L., *John Bright and the British Empire*, London, 1969.

Taylor, A. J. P., *Englishmen and Others*, London, 1956.

Taylor, A. J. P., *The Troublemakers*, London, 1957.

Thistlethwaite, F., *The Anglo-American Connexion in the Early Nineteenth Century*, Philadelphia, 1959.

Thompson, H., *History of Ackworth School*, London, 1879.

Vincent, J. R., *The Formation of the Liberal Party, 1857–1868*, London, 1966.

Vincent, J. R., *Poll Books: How Victorians Voted*, Cambridge, 1967.

Wallace, E., *Goldwin Smith: Victorian Liberal*, Toronto, 1957.

Ward, J. T., *The Factory Movement, 1830–1855*, London, 1962.

Ward, W. R., *Religion and Society in England, 1790–1850*, London, 1972.

Williams, W. E., *The Rise of Gladstone to the Leadership of the Liberal Party, 1859–1868*, Cambridge, 1934.

Articles

Anderson, O., 'The Reactions of Church and Dissent towards the Crimean War', *Journal of Ecclesiastical History*, 16, 1965, pp. 209–20.

Andrews, J. R., 'The Rationale of Nineteenth Century Pacifism: Religious and Political Arguments in the Early British Peace Movement', *Quaker History*, 57 (1), 1968, pp. 17–27.

Axon, W. E. A., 'John Bright and the Temperance Movement', *Alliance News and Temperance Reformer*, 23 November 1911.

Bebbington, D. W., 'Gladstone and the Baptists', *Baptist Quarterly*, 26 (5), 1976, pp. 224–239.

Beloff, M., 'Great Britain and the American Civil War', *History*, 37, 1952, pp. 40–8.

Burn, W. L., 'Free Trade in Land: An Aspect of the Irish Question', *Transactions of the Royal Historical Society*, 4th series, 31, 1949, pp. 69–74.

Calkins, W. N., 'A Victorian Free Trade Lobby', *Economic History Review*, 2nd series, 13, 1960–1, pp. 90–104.

Carter, G. W., 'The Early Life of John Bright's Father', *Journal of the Friends Historical Society*, 51, 1965, pp. 54–6.

Chamberlain, M. E., 'Sir Charles Dilke and the British intervention in Egypt 1882: decision making in a nineteenth-century Cabinet', *British Journal of International Studies*, 2 (3), October 1976, pp. 231–45.

Clark, G. S. R. Kitson, 'The Repeal of the Corn Laws and the Politics of the Forties', *Economic History Review*, 2nd series, 4, 1951, pp. 1–13.

Clark, G. S. R. Kitson, 'Hunger and Politics in 1842', *Journal of Modern History*, 25, 1953, pp. 355–74.

Cumpston, I. M., 'Some Early Indian Nationalists and their Allies in the British Parliament, 1851–1906', *English Historical Review*, 76, 1961, pp. 279–98.

Dale, R. W., 'Mr Bright', *Contemporary Review*, May 1889.

Fairlie, S., 'The Nineteenth-Century Corn Law Reconsidered', *Economic History Review*, 2nd series, 18, 1965, pp. 562–75.

Gowland, D. A., 'Rochdale Politics and Methodist Schism', *Wesley Historical Society, Lancashire and Cheshire Branch, Occasional Publication No. 1.*

Hanham. H. J., 'The First Constituency Party?', *Political Studies*, 9, 1961, pp. 188–9.

Henderson, W. O., 'Charles Pelham Villiers', *History*, 37, 1952, pp. 25–39.

Himmelfarb, G., 'The Politics of Democracy; the English Reform Act of 1867', *Journal of British Studies*, 6, 1966, pp. 97–138.

Kemp, B., 'The General Election of 1841', *History*, 37, 1952, pp. 146–57.

Kirby, D., 'The Attack of the English Game Laws in the Forties', *Journal of Modern History*, 4, 1932, pp. 18–37.

Large, D., 'The Election of John Bright as Member for Durham City in 1843', *Durham University Journal*, 47, December 1954, pp. 17–23.

McCord, N., 'Some difficulties of Parliamentary Reform', *Historical Journal*, 10, 1967, pp. 376–90.

McCord, N. and Carrick, A. E., 'The Northumberland Election of 1852', *Northern History*, 1, 1966, pp. 92–108.

McLaren, C., 'Reminiscences of John Bright', *North American Review*, September 1892.

Machin, G. I. T., 'The Maynooth Grant, the Dissenters and Disestablishment, 1845–1847', *English Historical Review*, 82, 1967, pp. 61–85.

Mills, J. T., 'An Orator's Library', *Journal of the Friends Historical Society*, supplement 21, 1946, pp. 3–24.

Moore, D. C., 'The Corn Laws and High Farming', *Economic History Review*, 2nd series, 18, 1965, pp. 544–61.

Moore, R. J., 'Imperialism and Free Trade Policy in India, 1853–4', *Economic History Review*, 2nd series, 17, 1964, pp. 135–45.

Rose, A. G., 'The Plug Plots of 1842 in Lancashire and Cheshire', *Transactions of the Lancashire and Cheshire Antiquarian Society*, 1957.

Rose, M. E., 'The Anti-Poor Law Movement in the North of England', *Northern History*, 1, 1966, pp. 70–91.

Sanderson, M., 'Education and the Factory in Industrial Lancashire, 1780–1840', *Economic History Review*, 2nd series, 20, 1967, pp. 266–79.

Bibliography

Stewart, R., 'The Ten Hours and Sugar Crisis of 1844', *Historical Journal*, 12, 1969, pp. 35–57.

Tholfsen, T. R., 'The Transition to Democracy in Victorian England', *International Review of Social History*, 1961, pp. 226–48.

Thompson, F. M. L., 'Whigs and Liberals in the West Riding, 1830–1860', *English Historical Review*, 74, 1959, pp. 214–39.

Vincent, J. R., 'The Electoral Sociology of Rochdale', *Economic History Review*, 2nd series, 16, 1963–4, pp. 76–90.

Ward, J. T. and Treble, J. H., 'Religion and Education in 1843: Reaction to the Factory Education Bill', *Journal of Ecclesiastical History*, 20, 1969, pp. 79–110.

Ward, W. R., 'The Tithe Question in England in the Early Nineteenth Century', *Journal of Ecclesiastical History*, 16, 1965, pp. 67–81.

Index